DISCARDED

Drought and Man

The 1972 Case History

Report on an IFIAS project

Volume 2:

**The Constant Catastrophe:
Malnutrition, Famines and Drought**

Other IFIAS Publications

GARCIA, R. V.
Drought and Man
Volume 1: Nature Pleads Not Guilty
Volume 3: Case Studies

KING, A.
The State of the Planet

KING, A. and HEDEN, C.-G.
Social Innovations for Development
A Symposium Report in the IFIAS Ulriksdals Seminar Series

NOTICE TO READERS

If your library is not already a standing/continuation order customer to this series, may
we recommend that you place a standing/continuation order to receive all new volumes
immediately on publication. Should you find that these volumes no longer serve your needs,
your order can be cancelled at any time without notice.

A Related Journal

WORLD DEVELOPMENT
The Multidisciplinary International Journal devoted to the Study and Promotion of World
Development

Free specimen copy available on request.

Drought and Man

The 1972 Case History

Report on an IFIAS project

Volume 2:

The Constant Catastrophe: Malnutrition, Famines and Drought

by

Rolando V. Garcia and José C. Escudero

HC
79
F3
D76
1981
vol. 2

and special contributions from

S. Ayalew
D. Banerji
M. Béhar
J. Gadano
A. Gillone
B. Inhelder
E. Lopez
B. Stavis

*Prepared at The Graduate Institute for
International Studies, Geneva, 1976–1979*

558576

PERGAMON PRESS

OXFORD · NEW YORK · TORONTO · SYDNEY · PARIS · FRANKFURT

LAMAR UNIVERSITY LIBRARY

U.K.	Pergamon Press Ltd., Headington Hill Hall, Oxford OX3 0BW, England
U.S.A.	Pergamon Press Inc., Maxwell House, Fairview Park, Elmsford, New York 10523, U.S.A.
CANADA	Pergamon Press Canada Ltd., Suite 104, 150 Con-sumers Road, Willowdale, Ontario M2J 1P9, Canada
AUSTRALIA	Pergamon Press (Aust.) Pty. Ltd., P.O. Box 544, Potts Point, N.S.W. 2011, Australia
FRANCE	Pergamon Press SARL, 24 rue des Ecoles, 75240 Paris, Cedex 05, France
FEDERAL REPUBLIC OF GERMANY	Pergamon Press GmbH, 6242 Kronberg-Taunus, Hammerweg 6, Federal Republic of Germany

Copyright © 1982 International Federation of Institutes for Advanced Study

All Rights Reserved. No part of this publication may be reproduced, stored in a retrieval system or transmitted in any form or by any means: electronic, electrostatic magnetic tape, mechanical, photocopying, recording or otherwise, without permission in writing from the copyright holders.

First edition 1982

British Library Cataloguing in Publication Data
Drought and man.
Vol. 2. The constant catastrophe famines
1. Droughts—Social aspects
2. Droughts—Economic aspects
I. Garcia, Rolando V.
II. Escudero, José C.
363.3'49   HC79.D/

ISBN 0-08-025824-7

Library of Congress Catalog Card No:
81-81228

Printed in Great Britain by A. Wheaton & Co., Ltd, Exeter

Contents

Introduction

WITHIN the long list of effects attributed to the 1972 drought, none of them has the dramatic connotations of the extended famines reported at that time. A recent study published by the U.S. Academy of Sciences* refers to it thus: "In 1972, a year when the climate was particularly unfavourable for food production, millions of people starved throughout the world."

There is a natural question to be asked when such a statement is made: How many people died because of the drought? The very serious difficulties the Project encountered in searching for an acceptable answer to this question led us to a type of study to which we devoted a great deal of efforts and which was not foreseen when the original plan was laid down. What were presented as clear, well-formulated, candid questions became the crossroads of a number of very diversified subjects putting formidable obstacles in our path.

The obvious answer to the above question appeared to be: "Just go to the statistics of the corresponding countries and periods and find out!" It seemed that, in the same way that we went to the FAO Year Books on production or to the UNCTAD Year Books on trade, it would suffice to ask for the relevant material from the responsible international health organization in order to find out what happened in the field of nutrition. But this was just the beginning of the troubles: what material? which statistics? The surprise of the non-specialist when he finds out that there are no world statistics of deaths produced by malnutrition changes into astonishment when he "discovers" that malnutrition, in actual medical practice, is virtually ignored as a disease. In fact, malnutrition is not given its proper rôle in statistics, that is as a cause of death or of morbidity, despite the vast bulk of empirical studies linking it with infectious and parasitic illnesses.

It was at this stage that one of the co-authors (Escudero) joined the Project and carried out or co-ordinated most of the case studies reported in the present volume.

The first health and nutritional studies on the Sahel, undertaken in mid 1976, came out with conclusions that were to be repeated elsewhere: the 1972 drought and subsequent famine were merely an aggravation of a previous situation which was very precarious in any case. The chronic, i.e. structural and permanent suffering of the Sahelian people—measured in terms of malnutrition, ill health and premature death—was so high already in any case, that the effects of drought *per se* had to be reduced to a much more modest level. Incidentally, it was shown that health data collection systems had proved to be completely unequal to the task of measuring either the health of the people before the drought or the effects of it; and that

* "Climate and Food", *A Report of the Committee on Weather Fluctuations and Agricultural Production*. The National Research Council, Washington D.C., 1976.

the rules of classification of causes of death in use in the Sahel and elsewhere in the world had a built-in bias against an acknowledgement of malnutrition as a cause of death.

This shifting of the emphasis of analysis from the "unfortunate conjecture"— drought—to the structural and chronic conditions of deprivation preceding and succeeding it was one of the very many indicators of the also shifting priorities of analysis of the Project: it was very clear that it was not only drought or other climatic misfortunes but the underlying social conditions that had to be studied, since it appeared that the effects of natural catastrophes are often transformed more through social structures and political processes, both within countries and in the world as a whole, than by the physical cause itself.

Hence, malnutrition was one of the focal problems of the Project, up to the point that some collaborators from other fields became puzzled by the prominence given to this subject. Why is it that we made an effort to carry out a sort of structural epidemiological analysis on a worldwide basis and, in particular, on some of the critical regions under study? The answer becomes a simple one, once we have grasped the overall perspective of the problems we are dealing with when we study the impact of a natural phenomenon on society.

With reference to the natural phenomenon itself, there is little doubt as to how it should be studied: we are specialists in the natural sciences! Thus nobody is surprised—not even the layman—that an "explanation" of the drought in the Sahel, or of the failure of the Indian monsoon, would involve a detailed reference to the General Circulation of the Atmosphere, a deep analysis of what are considered to be the "normal conditions" and serious consideration of whether there are signs of changing patterns in world climate. Climatologists have introduced in their jargon the expression "tele-connections" in the search for causal-chains trying to explain why a serious anomaly took place in such and such a region. This is clearly understood by everybody.

And yet, when a problem such as the famine in the early seventies is being studied, there is a tendency to consider that the reference to the "normal conditions" of malnutrition, its magnitude, its changing patterns and the causal links with other social conditions, is not quite relevant. Tele-connections are readily accepted in natural phenomena, but very reluctantly so in social phenomena.

Our view is that there exists a striking parallelism between the explanatory schemes for the drought as a meteorological event, and for the famine as a social event. To "explain" drought one needs a climatological analysis which automatically implies reference to large scale space and time processes. It is only within this long scale that the anomaly called "drought" can be given a meaning and can be provided with a meaningful explanation. Likewise, famines occur as anomalies within large-scale processes in society, regulating the changing patterns of nutritional levels. It is only with reference to this background that the famines have a clear meaning and that they can be given an acceptable explanation. The studies on malnutrition thus are the counterpart of the climatological studies.

The reluctance to accept tele-connections, and to go into deep waters when one is dealing with a *social* anomaly such as famine can be easily explained. No one would blame the Soviets for having a longer than usual snow cover over Siberia, or the Arabs for a heating on the Persian Sea, both of which may alter the Indian monsoon. Information about this natural phenomena is therefore not hidden. No country is, on the other hand, ready to expose its social diseases, and not very many people in the world feel comfortable when one tries to uncover the "tele-connections" of social anomalies.

Hence, the evaluation of the magnitude of malnutrition and, still worse, the assessment of the incidence of malnutrition on mortality is not an easy task.

After the first pilot study on the Sahelian famine, further health and nutrition studies were undertaken. In one, in which the investigation attempted to measure the chronic level of malnutrition in the Latin American countries—in order to evaluate the aggravating effects of drought upon it—it was ascertained firstly that this level was so high that the worst possible drought in that continent could only add a fraction to it—the high figure of 405,000 deaths "due to drought" in Northeast Brazil being only 10 percent of the annual figure estimated as caused by chronic malnutrition on the continent—and secondly that the quality of the data base was too limited to allow identification of a specific and short-term interference, such as one induced by a drought; the data base was so bad, in fact, that no trend analysis could be undertaken on chronic malnutrition in Latin America, to answer even the simple question of whether it is increasing or decreasing. It was apparent that only an obvious phenomenon such as massive famine could be able to penetrate the insensitiveness, in both senses of the word, of the data collection apparatus.

Further case studies were commissioned, in which different researchers studied the health and nutrition of countries which were held to be important to clarify debatable points. Two sets of control situations became apparent: one was the way in which drought in a country modified—or did not modify—a given health and nutritional situation after it returned to pre-drought levels. The other was whether countries where no drought had existed and their food-producing mechanisms had remained unimpaired were responding, in health and nutritional terms, to this "normality". For Latin America, two of its most populous countries were ideal: one (Argentina) had a great foodstuffs productive capacity and suffered no drought in 1972. Another (Brazil) was prey to recurrent regional droughts and was not spared the 1972 experience. Both countries showed extended ill health and a significant level of malnutrition.

A study on Ethiopia, the country with the greatest human loss in 1972–73, showed again the very precarious pre-drought situation and the impact of the drought. As elsewhere, an attempt was made to relate the structure of Ethiopian society to these effects.

China and India proved controls for each other: both countries experienced a drought in 1972. Yet the differences between them as far as health and nutrition are concerned were so great that it was quite clear that the explanation did not lie in any possible difference in the intensity of the meteorological anomaly, but again in deeper, more "stable" conditions.

Two studies were carried out on nutritional policies through food rationing in very dissimilar countries: one European, developed and one Asian, developing. They showed that egalitarian rationing was a useful tool for the allocation of food and as a "minimizer" of human suffering. These studies, based on national cases encompassing hundreds of millions of people, show what *can* be done to alleviate human suffering when food is in scarce supply, and also point out the fact that the traditional categories of "development–underdevelopment" had no predictive value as far as the nutritional situation of the people was concerned. Moreover, it became clear that "development", as conventionally known, may act as an aggravator of malnutrition, and an augmenter of vulnerability towards natural catastrophes. A "poor underdeveloped" country like China is eradicating malnutrition. A "developing" country, on the borderline to "development" like Argentina, has extensive malnutrition and has structural indicators that would point to an increase of it in the future.

The ultimate conclusion of this book is that countries have the level of malnutrition that the decision makers in the country wish them to have, or, put in other terms, the level that is consistent with their politico-economic situation.

Lack of food can be solved and malnutrition can be eradicated, provided the undertaking of the necessary measures is compatible with the maintenance of certain social structures, which immediately leads observers to a political analysis of what is ultimately a political decision on the part of those structures.

One final word. Every species, biologically unchecked, has the capacity to increase its numbers indefinitely. Death is a corrector, and an element in maintaining an equilibrium with other species and with the sheer capacity of the world to provide room. So death would be the answer, in individual terms, and mortality in collective terms, to the phenomenon of life.

Yet the modality of death is crucial. When reading what follows one must constantly bear in mind that the deaths from malnutrition of tens of thousands of emaciated children with bloated bellies has turned out to be the ultimate result that can be inferred of so many pages of analysis put forward and so many figures laid out neatly in rows and columns. The cause of death of those children—with or without drought—was lack of food and that cause, as this and other parts of the Project show, is one which need not exist in the present world. This adds an additional horror upon the original horror of those deaths.

No one can bring these children back to life, of course, but they keep on dying literally by the thousand every day and there is no "of course" about this latter situation. As the recommendations will state, the problem is ultimately political, and if the present political structures in the world continue to permit this happening, future generations will, with a mixture of disbelief and repulsion view the last decades of the twentieth century the same way as we now view the barbarianism of cave dwellers, which our civilization supposedly superseded.

Part One

The Background

CHAPTER 1

The Impact of Drought on Nutrition

A DECREASE in food production, due to any natural disaster of climatic origin, within a given area, may have a direct impact on the local population. The nature and the scope of the effects will depend on a number of factors, some of which are essentially local, while others are external and mainly conditioned by the insertion of the particular country in the world economy. If the natural disaster is widespread, affecting many areas in various continents, new factors may emerge and the combined effects may push the international system beyond some threshold of equilibrium. The regulation processes on the international markets, the world balance of power, world economic and political links of various types, international solidarity, and so on, will be called into play, to restore equilibrium or to aggravate the disequilibrium.

It is true that interdependency is a consequence of world development in modern times. No one may ignore it while analyzing problems such as those involved in our study. To identify the links between national and regional events, or between world structures and national events in particular countries, etc., is indeed one of the most basic tasks in research projects such as this one.

We must, however, be very careful in establishing links or in attributing interrelations among events which happen to be placed on a certain time-chain. Not every time-chain is a causal-chain. This is indeed a truism, but it seems necessary to repeat it time and time again when one is confronted with cause–effect associations of events that are not correctly deduced or inferred on the basis of available information.

The year of 1972, which has been chosen as the case study for the "Drought and Man" Project belongs to a complex period in the history of our contemporary world. A large number of events appear, at first hand, to be related to each other in such a way that one is tempted to explain some of them on the basis of the others. A deeper analysis shows, however, that these apparent relationships may not hold.

A survey of the literature related to the 1972 drought provides striking examples of this situation. These show that there has been a prevailing opinion blaming the climate for a number of disruptions in the world economy as well as in the social conditions of large areas in various continents. We do not deny that a serious drought *may*, and in certain cases *does*, *produce* some of the dramatic effects attributed to the 1972 case. In many countries there are vivid memories of famines following prolonged droughts. Food prices do oscillate in association with world production and pressures on the market. But the 1972 case provides clear evidence that they are, in many instances, just the superficial manifestations of much deeper mechanisms. In other words, although we may accept the existence of each one of the links that have been mentioned above, we question the validity of an explanation of the 1972 case based, most of the times implicitly, on a linear reaction process of the following type:

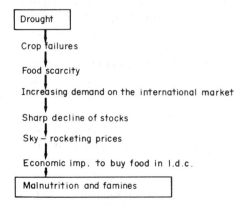

Most analyses will include another factor as a "cause" impinging on food scarcity: the population pressure, adding to the effect of crop failures. The incremental action of the demographic explosion would thus be felt every time the same "causal-chain" is repeated—when the next drought comes, the effect will be worse than the previous one.

The work carried out under the IFIAS Project "Drought and Man" in the 1972 case history has provided factual evidence to confirm the thesis that the chain of events illustrated above is not supported by the facts. There are two reasons for this. On the one hand, it includes events which were independent from each other or have had only weak interactions between them. On the other hand, it ignores some fundamental factors which play an essential role in any adequate "explanation" of the events involved in the case under study.

The studies carried out by the Project and reported in Volumes 1 and 3 provided conclusive evidence, in our view, to show that the statistics on the 1972 decrease in the production of food, the depletion of stocks and the sky-rocketing of prices of cereals on the international market cannot be taken as a basis to explain the assertion quoted in the Preface: "In 1972, a year when the climate was particularly unfavourable for food production, millions of people starved to death."

In this volume, the problem will be considered from another angle: the people who suffered and died, or those who suffered and kept on living in sub-human conditions. We have considered this theme as being the focus of the Project. The welfare of man—of *each* man—and of the society—insofar as it is an organization of *people*—is the main concern of our study.

We must, however, make a few remarks in order to avoid some common misunderstandings. The analysis of what happens to an individual or a community when a particular phenomenon hits a given society depends on both the type of input of the individuals of the society and the structure of the society as such (see Chapter 5). From this point of view, in searching for those factors which are at the root of a specific situation, and which are to be taken as the cause of this situation, our frame of reference is the whole structure of the society at that place and during a certain period of time. This is why we have directed so much effort in analyzing the socio-economic structures and their historical evolution in our inquiries on the Sahelian disasters and on similar situations in Brazil or India arising from, or attributed to, climatic events. However, our starting point is a concrete situation affecting *people*, not a low value of certain economic indexes.

It has been pointed out in the Introduction that the question "How many people actually died because of such and such a drought?" remains without an answer. The reason is that no one can ascertain how to separate the responsibility between the drought and the chronic malnutrition in the countries concerned.

As it is repeatedly emphasized in the following chapters, malnutrition is perhaps the most widespread disease in the world. It has seldom been recognized as such, although there are periods when world malnutrition attracts public attention. The 1972 situation marks the beginning of a period of rather intensive studies on this subject, culminating in the 1974 United Nations World Food Conference. There was a similar world interest in malnutrition and famines in the early 1960's, as well as in earlier periods. This "periodic awareness" of the malnutrition problems in the world is one of the most depressing facts in the history of food supplies and "food aid" at the international level. For it is not so much associated with an effective periodic increase of malnutrition in the developing countries, as with changes in agriculture and in international trade policies in the developed countries.

Thomas T. Poleman has shown this with impressive clarity in an article that puts the problem in the proper perspective. (1.1)* After an analysis of the first two FAO World Food Surveys (1946 and 1952), Poleman says:

> "The theme of deterioration was amplified 10 years later in the next major analysis of the food situation, the U.S. Department of Agriculture's (USDA) *World Food Budget, 1962 and 1966.* This study employed an analytical approach identical to that of FAO except that the USDA ventured into a few areas where even the FAO had feared to tread: included were most of the countries of Africa and Asia, among them, despite a total lack of evidence, China."

The USDA analysis referred to by Poleman concluded (quoted by Poleman):

> "For most of the 70 less-developed countries in the semitropical and tropical Southern Area, diets are nutritionally inadequate with shortages in proteins, fat and calories. These (diet-deficit) countries contain over 1.9 billion people. In most of them, population is expanding rapidly, malnutrition is widespread and persistent, and there is no likelihood that the food problem soon will be solved."

And Poleman proceeds:

> "Three years later the USDA repeated the exercise. The map on the cover of the second report (*World Food Budget,* 1970, 61.2) revealed few new diet-deficit countries. But it is difficult not to believe that an important political angle had been discovered. Exaggeration of the extent of hunger in the developing world was clearly good politics for the USDA (U.S. Department of

---

* Numbers in parentheses refer to notes at the end of the chapter.

Agriculture), faced as it was as that time with increasing and bothersome surpluses. Sales or gifts to the L.D.C.'s (Less Developed Countries) under Public Law 480 could postpone the day of more stringent controls or lower prices, or both, to American farmers." (1.1)

We do not entirely agree with Poleman's dictum about the "exaggeration of the extent of hunger". The situation seems to be rather different. There is as much malnutrition and hunger as indicated in the USDA reports referred to by Poleman. The only thing is that, the problem remains hidden until it is convenient to exhibit it for reasons such as those indicated by Poleman.

Ample evidence is provided in the following chapters to show that there is indeed no exaggeration in the figures provided by the USDA reports and other institutions when they do care to exhibit the problem. Tables giving the estimated number of people in developing countries for whom food intake is below the minimum critical level (cf. Chapter 3) show that, on average (for Africa, Latin America, Near East and Far East, excluding Asian centrally planned economies) 24 percent of the population, or over 400 million people, are below that level. The percentage does not change from the 1969–71 to the 1972–74 period (some increase in Africa is compensated by a decrease in Latin America and the Near East). When milder forms of malnutrition are included, the estimated population living below acceptable levels of food intake goes up to roughly 1000 million people. Some of them will die at a very early age; others will survive longer.

Drought or no drought, high prices of food or low prices of food, high levels of stocks of cereals in developed countries or low levels of stocks, the problems are always there, showing that they are not produced by contingent natural phenomena, nor by the elasticity properties of prices on the market.

From the point of view of our Project, the fact we want to emphasize is that although we have rough figures on the magnitude of malnutrition in the world, as yet no reliable information is available on the number of people dying because of malnutrition. The vital statistics systems of the world would record, in theory, all deaths which take place in certain defined geographical areas, as well as the causes of death. In practice, however, this does not happen, due to the three main reasons described in Chapter 4: (a) under-registration of deaths; (b) the unavailability of health services to much of the population (which prevents ascertaining the cause of death or of illness in many cases); (c) the existence of biases in the current system of determining "the basic cause of death", which significantly tends to underestimate the causal role of malnutrition. To these reasons, which alone would account for the fact that chronic malnutrition is permanently under-measured, one should add the incidence of the epistemic framework of the medical profession and of their underlying ideological biases. (cf. Chapter 4).

The fact that malnutrition as a cause of death is seldom properly registered has a double consequence which cannot be overemphasized. Firstly, the *magnitude* of the problem remains hidden. Although we do not mean to say that this is the reason for a systematic under-registration, it is clear that many governments do not worry very much when these facts are ignored. As already stated, no country likes to expose the depth of its social problems. Nor does the world at large like it. People who are always avid for sensational news—natural catastrophe or otherwise—

refuse to face a *permanent* situation of disaster affecting a large sector of mankind. Ignoring the problem is a well-known defense mechanism. Therefore one should not expect strong movements "in search of the truth".

Secondly, when there is a natural disaster such as the Sahelian drought, the deaths produced by malnutrition become too obvious. There is a tendency *to attribute all malnutrition-generated deaths*, and in fact malnutrition itself, *to the natural disaster*. The effects of natural disasters are thus greatly exaggerated. This goes well with the avidity for "sensationalism". Moreover, blaming the climate, or "nature" or some punishing God, leaves the conscience of the rest of the world with no other burden than piety and feelings of charity.

We simply do not know how many people were killed in the Sahel in the early seventies *by the drought*. First, because we do not know how many people died in the Sahel in that period. Second, because even if we knew how many deaths were produced during the famine, it would be unfair to attribute all of them to the drought or to food scarcities, whatever the reason for the latter.

This leads us to our main reason for insisting on this background scenario in our studies on the impact of drought. Deaths "produced" by a drought have, in general, a prerequisite, a background of low nutritional level in the sector of the society where the deaths occur. These pre-drought conditions are linked to structural problems which are socio-economic as well as—and very often more than—ecological. When drought occurs it simply transforms an already bad "normal" situation into a tragic one. But the relationship drought–famine is by no means a direct one and requires the kind of structural analysis propounded in Chapter 5. It may be argued that very severe, long and extended drought may lead to famines irrespective of the stability of the pre-drought socio-ecosystem. But even in such extreme conditions, the degree of vulnerability to the drought is a structural property of the socio-ecosystem (in the sense of Chapter 5) and the pre-drought levels of nutrition become a key element in determining the effects. The study on the Sahelian droughts taken in their historical perspective are conclusive in this respect (cf. Chapter 8 of Volume 1).

The most obvious effect of drought is found in the interference with food production. However, the impact is not proportional to the decrease in food production. It is, so to speak, *amplified* by the social structure. This is the reason for the occurrence, in well-documented cases, of vast famines which were started in connection with a climatic anomaly having only a moderate effect on food production. The natural phenomenon has, in these cases, the function of a "trigger" releasing a latent instability already present in the system. We shall deal with this problem more extensively in Chapter 5. From this perspective, the most important problem with which we should be concerned is therefore of pre-drought marginal conditions which render the society highly vulnerable when a drought situation arises. This problem involves, in fact, two different questions. First, what are the countries, regions, areas of the world where malnutrition prevails rendering their population highly fragile when drought strikes? Second, what are the characteristics of a given social structure which makes it either able to attenuate or likely to amplify the effects of a perturbation such as a drought?

The most accepted current explanation of the worldwide spread of malnutrition ignores the productive *process* and puts all the emphasis on food production: there are people who do not eat properly because their countries do not produce enough of the right food. And they do not produce enough, so it is held, for two main reasons: the lack of an adequate technology (backward, traditional agricultural practices) and a demographic expansion upsetting all achievements in increasing production.

Let us consider first the main argumental line contained in the assertion "people are undernourished in some countries because they do not produce enough food". Taken literally, it contains a gross oversimplification and in many cases it is plainly wrong. A simple example will illustrate our point. The amount of animal proteins contained in the average diet of a European is more than twice the average for Latin America. This does not mean, however, that Europe produces proportionally more meat than Latin America. In 1976, Western Europe imported (net!) 887 thousand tons of meat, whereas Latin America *exported* 582 thousand tons. This very simple arithmetic shows that the problem is certainly not *there*. In order to find out where the roots are, one must consider in some detail the production and trade structure of some representative countries. A few examples from Latin America will be given at the end of this chapter.

One last argument may still be advanced by those supporting such a view. After all—they may say—an adequate diet requires a minimum amount of animal proteins. The trend of transforming grains into meat is therefore a necessary one in countries not having enough pastures for cattle raising. The real problems are—they may continue—that the country does not produce enough animal proteins for everybody, that animal products are expensive and that only a small sector of the population can afford to buy them; the rest are exported because the country needs money for its development.

The above argumental line has two aspects to be considered independently. One is purely economic and it has been taken care of in Volume 1 by showing that the difference in the international prices of meat and cereal has evolved in such a way, particularly during the food crisis of the early seventies, that the terms of trade deteriorate progressively for the countries we are concerned with. (Sharp increases in grain prices vs only moderate increases in the price of meat.) Moreover, those who get the profit from this trade are certainly not "the country".

The second aspect of the argumental line referred to above, is concerned with the actual minimum requirements of animal proteins in the human diet. Chapter 2 will show that this subject has been overplayed and that the trend to increasing amounts of animal proteins in the diet has no nutritional justification.

The problem therefore boils down to a wrong structure of food production and trade, induced by foreign interest, with strong support from the affluent sector of the local population, and to the detriment of the nutritional levels of the larger sector of the population.

Food production in these countries as well as in a large number of developing countries is therefore roughly divided into two sectors: one, producing for export and for the local elite (only in a few cases for a more extended middle class); the second, producing food for the large masses of population. The first uses advanced technology, receives strong support from the government (usually in the form of credits, public irrigation developments, etc.) and employs, generally but not always, the labour force of salary earners; the second follows more traditional practices, does not have access to modern technology, nor to official support, and uses mainly family labour force. The first is oriented towards products having high market prices; the second is meant to produce cheap food for the country's labour forces. (On this important subject, see the paper by Portantiero in Volume 3.)

The relevance of these considerations to the subject matter of the Project becomes evident when we analyze the vulnerability of these countries to the impact of an external factor such as drought. It seems clear from the above consideration that one sector of the population will be much more vulnerable than the other *to the same drought*.

The above considerations show that in order to judge the nature and the scope of the "impact" of a drought one has to have a knowledge of the functioning of the society *prior* to the drought. Nutritional levels, their internal distribution within the country or region concerned, the characteristics of the productive system, and so on, are structural elements which carry considerable weight in defining its degree of vulnerability. They also determine the "normal" base line with reference to which the effects of anomaly have to be measured.

This leads us to a concluding remark to this chapter. The words "normal" and "normality" are generally used in a very ambiguous way. More often than not they only refer to long-term statistical averages. Nevertheless, when the expressions "back to normal" or "the conditions are now normal" are being used, people have a tendency to take them for synonyms of "the situation is now all right". The statistical meaning acquires, thus, a normative connotation. A proof of this could be provided by the fact that an expression such as "unfortunately, the situation returned to normal", somewhat does not sound right.

And yet, the two meanings of "normal", the *statistical* and the *normative*, refer to quite a different realm of ideas. The former means "as it happened to be, on the average, in the past", whereas the latter has associated with it the notion of "acceptable standards". We can only talk in a purely statistical sense of the "normal conditions" in the life of a deprived child in Haiti, Mauritania or India, for whom every year is a bad year. They belong to segments of human society living in a state of *permanent catastrophe*. They may go through a period of greater "stress" when droughts, floods or earthquakes hit their territories. Some of the children will die. Those who survive do not share the feeling of happy relief which the rest of the world experiences when the territory is officially declared "back to normal conditions".

A Latin American Example

The Central American countries are frequently mentioned as characteristic examples of a very high population growth and of deteriorating levels of nutrition. Let us consider the case of Honduras. The population growth is 3.6 percent, one of the highest in the world. Food production *per capita* decreased by 1.4 percent during the period 1970–76. The average intake of calories was 1987 in the period 1972–74 (to be compared with more than 3500 calories in countries like Belgium, Switzerland and the U.S.A.). About 38 percent of the population received an

TABLE 1.
Exports of Meat from Honduras
(millions of dollars)

1969	1970	1971	1972	1973	1974
8.9	9.7	12.5	15.9	21.7	16.7

Source (1.2).

amount of calories lower than the critical limit of 1.2 B.M.* Against this background, the structure of food production and trade is, to say the least, surprising. The exports of meat, for instance, show considerable growth, as given in Table 1.

This picture is by no means peculiar to Honduras. In 1973, the five Central American countries (Costa Rica, El Salvador, Guatemala, Honduras and Nicaragua) imported cereals from the U.S. amounting to 59 million dollars, but they exported meat amounting to 139 million dollars and fruit and vegetables amounting to 146 million dollars, not to mention sugar and coffee amounting to 270 million dollars.

The total figures of the food trade of these countries with the U.S. are as shown in Table 2.

TABLE 2.
Five Central American Countries: Food Trade with the U.S.
(millions of dollars)

	1960	1965	1968	1970	1971	1973	1974	1975
Exports to U.S.	162	259	305	373	349	598	649	668
Imports from U.S.	20	27	35	35	41	82	108	119

Source: (1.3).

The actual situation is, however, still more unfavourable to these countries, from the point of view of the drainage of food out of them. For the imports from U.S. are mainly grains and they are used to feed livestock for export.

This last remark deserves further consideration. The relationship between meat and cereals is at the core of the myth about the poor Latin American people being undernourished because they reproduce themselves too much and produce too little.

Let us take the example of Nicaragua. The panorama of beef production, consumption and trade has evolved as detailed in Table 3.

The Table is quite eloquent by itself and requires only a few comments. From 1959/63 to 1972, production increased by 146 percent, but domestic consumption only by 59 percent. Net exports went up 315 percent. Still more significant: by 1966 the consumption *per capita* had decreased 10 percent, with reference to 1959/63.

* See Chapters 2 and 3 for explanation.

TABLE 3.

Nicaragua: Beef Production, Net Exports and National Consumption
(carcass weight)

Years	Production Total	Production Index	Net export Total	Net export Index	Domestic consumption Total	Domestic consumption Index	Per capita consumption Total	Per capita consumption Index
1959/63	61.3	100	20.7	100	41.0	100	29	100
1964	79.1	129	32.4	157	46.7	114	29	100
1965	74.6	122	28.5	138	46.0	112	28	97
1966	83.8	137	38.7	187	45.1	110	26	90
1967	91.8	150	44.6	215	47.2	115	27	93
1968	105.5	172	52.0	251	53.5	130	29	100
1969	117.9	192	61.3	296	56.6	138	30	103
1970	131.8	215	74.1	358	57.7	141	30	103
1971	139.8	228	72.8	352	67.0	163	33	114
1972	151.1	246	86.0	415	65.1	159	32	110

Source: (1.4).

Demographic explosion? Failure of the production? No. Simply a sharp increase in the exports at the expense of domestic consumption.

And yet, it would be unfair to put all the blame on exporting and on the forces acting on the international markets. True, when we divide the world into "developed" and "developing" countries, the two categories reflect a clear-cut difference in food consumption patterns. However, to stop the analysis at this point would imply missing the core of the problem because countries cannot be considered as homogeneous units.

The *elite* of developing countries develop the same habits in their diets as those prevailing in developed countries. No wonder that countries like Mexico or Honduras put so much emphasis on the production of livestock. Part of this livestock is for export, but another part is consumed by local minority sectors of the population.

But this is only one side of the problem. Let us see what happens with the production and utilization of grains. A typical example is El Salvador, a country presenting the following general nutrition picture in Table 4, according to FAO's Food Survey.

It should be noted that the supply of proteins, which was already below accepted minimum requirements, actually decreased during the ten-year period reported in the Table. However, the utilization of grains in this country during the same period is shown in Table 5.

TABLE 4.

El Salvador: Per Caput *Daily Calorie and Protein Supplies*

Calories Supply 1961–63	Calories Supply 1972–74	Calories Requirement	Supply as % of requirements 1961–63	Supply as % of requirements 1972–74	Protein supply 1961–63	Protein supply 1972–74
1808	1885	2290	79	82	51.6	49.8

Source: (1.5).

TABLE 5.
El Salvador: Grain Production Consumption and Trade
(wheat and coarse grains, in 1000 tons)

Year	Production	Total imports	Total export	Domestic consumption	
				For feed	Human
1961–62	229	61	5	76	209
1972–73	383	112	5	148	372

Source: (1.6).

It is clear from this Table that the amount of grain used to feed animals is higher than the amount imported. The five Central American countries imported 346,000 tons of grain in 1971–72, and the domestic consumption for feed was 399,000 tons. The case of Mexico is much more flagrant and will be analyzed in Chapter 6. The general pattern is one of increasing difference between the amount of grain used to feed animals and the amount imported. Since the meat is either exported or goes to the table of the local elite, this increasing difference shows that the people of the country: those who produce and who are malnourished—get proportionally less cereal of their own production for their meals.

The current belief—that these people are undernourished because they do not produce enough food and that imports of cereals are forced by the demographic explosion is thus clearly refuted by known statistics accessible to everyone.

Notes to Chapter 1

1.1 Thomas T. Poleman, "World Food: A Perspective" in *Food: Politics, Economics, Nutrition and Research*, edited by Philip H. Abelson, AAAS, SCIENC, 1975.
1.2 FAO, Trade Yearbooks.
1.3 OECD, Trade by Commodities.
1.4 U.S. Department of Agriculture, "The Beef Cattle Industries of Central America and Panama", FAS M-208, 1973.
1.5 FAO, Fourth World Food Survey, 1977.
1.6 U.S. Department of Agriculture, Foreign Agriculture Circular, Grains, 1976.

CHAPTER 2

Human Needs of Food

Introduction

HUMAN NUTRITION is but a particular instance of the phenomenon of life on earth. The sun provides the energy from which, ultimately, all life on earth depends. This energy allows living things to fix certain elements (carbon, oxygen and hydrogen) and translate them into vegetable matter. Man, being an omnivorous animal, consumes for his own subsistence this matter, either in its original form or in the form of animal food after "processing" through one or a chain of animals. This choice implies a highly differential efficiency of the use of resources, as will be shown below.

Hydrogen is provided by water which may also help to provide some mineral nutrients. Hence, lack of water destroys a necessary pre-condition for the life process on earth. Thus, in many regions, drought hampers life.

Central to the argument of the amount of food that is needed to feed mankind is the structure of the diet that is to be considered desirable, in its amount of calories, non-animal proteins, animal proteins and other nutrients. By far the most important disagreement in this respect—insofar as it implies a great difference in allocation of resources—is the amount of animal proteins that should be put into a normal diet.

Recommendations on the number of calories (source of energy) needed daily are fairly well agreed upon and straightforward. (2.1) Basically, the energy requirements of individuals depend on four variables: (a) physical activity; (b) body size and composition; (c) age; (d) climate and other ecological factors. Overall, individuals of the same size, living in the same environment and with the same mode of life, have a similar energy requirement whatever their ethnic origin. Increased physical activity or body size, childhood, adolescence, pregnancy and lactation would increase energy needs, as would exposure to cold climate. Physical activity is the factor that most alters the total energy expenditure, sometimes more than doubling the "basal metabolic rate"—the energy expenditure needed to maintain bodily functions and temperature. The following tables give the average energy requirements of men and women according to occupation and body weight. (Tables 1 and 2).

Protein requirements represent a different situation altogether. The Report (2.1) states that "the application of energy requirement figures and suggested safe levels of protein intake must be on different theoretical bases". In the case of protein this being through the development of the concept of "safe level of intake"—one which is above the threshold of risk of needs not being met and which would result in

13

TABLE 1.

The Effects of Body Weight and Occupation on Energy Requirements of Men

Body weight (kg)	Light activity (kilo-calories)	Moderately active (kilo-calories)	Very active (kilo-calories)	Exceptionally active (kilo-calories)
50	2100	2300	2700	3100
55	2310	2530	2970	3410
60	2520	2760	3240	3720
65	2700	3000	3500	4000
70	2940	3220	3780	4340
75	3150	3450	4050	4650
80	3360	3680	4320	4960

Source: Modified from (2.1).

more conservative requirements than those that appeared in previously made requirements. The report comments that:

"A commonly held view is that an increase in protein food production will result in an increased average consumption and a reduction in the prevalence of 'protein deficiency' in a population. In a real population, however, this is most unlikely to be the case, owing to the inequitable nature of food distribution and consumption, which arises from a number of factors. Communities with low levels of malnutrition will be found to consume diets that provide on average more protein than the 'safe level' as defined in this report. However, 'the existence of such a surplus reveals little about the actual food consumption of households and individuals in that community. Such apparently satisfactory average intakes cannot be regarded as a target towards which planners, agronomists and public health administrators should direct their efforts. The proper basis for planning should not be from the national level downwards, for instance by the setting of national production targets for protein, but should proceed from the study of individual and household food consumption upwards. The nutritional status and the protein intakes of individuals in the different physiological groups of a population should be assessed

TABLE 2.

The Effects of Body Weight and Occupation on Energy Requirements of Women

Body weight (kg)	Light activity (kilo-calories)	Moderately active (kilo-calories)	Very active (kilo-calories)	Exceptionally active (kilo-calories)
40	1440	1600	1880	2200
45	1620	1800	2120	2480
50	1800	2000	2350	2750
55	2000	2200	2600	3000
60	2160	2400	2820	3300
65	2340	2600	3055	3575
70	2520	2800	3290	3850

Source: Modified from (2.1).

in relation to the 'safe level', first, as a means of analyzing the problem, which may not be in any way related to the overall availability of protein foods: secondly, for establishing priorities between programmes for action, which may include employment policies affecting purchasing power, the control of food prices, food distribution programmes for vulnerable groups, the education of consumers, etc.; and thirdly, to provide a continuous monitoring of the progress made by such programmes."

and that:

"When predictions are being made about food demands at a national level it should also be borne in mind that man seems to have a desire for protein foods, so that individuals' intakes are often considerably above those suggested as safe in the present report. Such demands on the part of the wealthier sections of a community may well influence the economic availability of preferred food, and hence the distribution of intakes between population groups. When man is not restricted by the availability of foodstuffs or by economic circumstances he tends to choose a diet that provides about 11 percent of its energy value from proteins."

It moves on to say that:

"Having considered these matters, the Committee realizes that while it can offer guidelines for the estimation of target *per caput* energy intakes, the data currently available to the Committee do not permit it to translate the prediction of individual protein requirements into meaningful guidelines for population feeding."

It then points out that the fact that populations tend to select protein intakes which contribute 10–12 percent of the dietary energy, would mean that an intake would not be higher than that required to meet physiological protein needs, which would be in the order of 0.55 g per kilo of weight per day for adults, 0.8 g per kilo of weight per day for children and 2 g per kilo of weight and per day for infants. In any case, these needs would be augmented in pregnancy and lactation, and—as is the case with proteins in general—will require an adequate balance of essential amino acids forming the diet.

A disagreement as to the amount of animal proteins needed in the diet could modify very significantly the amount of food needed to sustain a human population and also the required amount of land to grow it. A belief that a normal human diet should be composed of large amounts of animal proteins would indicate an increase in the amount of land destined for cattle raising, or a diversion of other land to produce food for them, for poultry and for pigs. The amount of capital needed, and the systems of commercialization chosen would change. As animals are less efficient producers of calories than plants, by a factor of 5 to 10, per unit of land,* and as the world currently spends one-third of its grain production in feeding animals, an amount that could feed approximately an additional 2000 million humans, (2.2) this decision on the amount of animal proteins to be required has momentous consequences in the world food picture.

---

* This observation is not linearly correct, as some land used for grazing cannot be used to raise crops.

As has been seen, nutrition experts are now more cautious on the need for high amounts of animal proteins in the diet and seem to place less emphasis on it. They stress the fact that a diet which is adequate in calories is also usually adequate in protein requirements. As a recent FAO document states: "in the light of the most recent recommendations to cover protein needs, it seems unlikely that a dietary intake that is sufficient to meet the energy requirements will be insufficient to meet the requirements for protein. This means that protein deficiency in the absence of energy deficiency is not likely to occur, a possible exception being in populations that subsist on cassava, plantains, yams or breadfruit, foods that are extremely low in protein content. In most of the developing countries, where cereals and pulses are the staples, the consumption of *more* food will simultaneously correct any insufficiency of energy and protein. This statement is valid for adults and older children whose ability to consume more food is limited and hence foods with a higher concentration of protein are needed". (2.3)

A field study in India would serve as an example for this. "In nutrition surveys based on 7000 households in four states of India, about 50 percent of those persons with calorie deficiencies also had inadequate protein intake. By contrast, only 5 percent of the households without calorie deficiencies had inadequate intake of protein." (2.4)

This chapter contains another section which is written by a well known nutritionist, and represents a reappraisal of traditional foods *vis-à-vis* "European" ones, and also a cry of alarm over the way in which "European" eating habits— which of course are not merely cultural traits, but also exemplify the dynamics of the Western mode of production—are encroaching upon many countries and produce results which are nutritionally harmful, quite apart from being a misuse of natural resources.

ANNEX 1

European Diets vs Traditional Foods

by *Moisés Béhar*

As an omnivorous animal, early man was able to survive and progress with a wide variety of different diets, determined predominantly by the ecology of the area in which he lived, and the food resources to be found there. Thus many Asian societies based their diet on rice, Meso-Americans on corn, and Eskimos on animals from the sea. In order to produce a balanced diet, they supplemented these staples with various products which could also be obtained locally. The different dietary patterns which emerged became a strong component of the cultures concerned, as food habits and beliefs were handed down from generation to generation and were sometimes even embodied in the people's religious practices. Large population groups developed on this basis, in harmony with their environment and enjoying adequate nutrition. In modern times, however, most nutritionists have not made sufficient effort to understand the value of traditional, non-European diets, the limitations these may have at present and, if so, how to overcome them by applying present knowledge to the socio-economic and ecological conditions in which these populations live.

For the population of Europe, wheat became the staple food, supplemented with animal products (meat, eggs, milk and milk products) and locally available vegetables and fruits. As the economy and technology of this population group developed and as it established relations, frequently of domination, with other populations of the world, its diet became increasingly varied with the introduction of many non-indigenous foods and a greater content of animal products and refined and processed foods: and so, with some local variations, a general pattern of what may be called the European type of diet evolved.

With the improvement of communications, particularly in the past few decades, the European type of diet came to be accepted as the model of an "ideal" diet, because most basic studies in human nutrition were carried out in countries with a European culture or by scientists of this culture in other areas. This tendency was further strengthened when professionals from developing countries with other cultures were trained in nutrition in countries with European culture and/or used books and other teaching materials produced in these countries. On their return home, these professionals advocated the European type of diet as the one recommended for health for populations which were neither culturally nor economically in a position to adopt it. In this way, programmes of so-called "nutrition education" were organized with these "scientific" principles as their basis, and without proper consideration of local conditions. In most cases they failed.

The elite groups, small but powerful minorities, in the developing countries have for the most part adopted European culture and way of life, including the dietary pattern. The rest of the population has thus frequently been influenced in its beliefs and practices, because foods have a prestige value which leads the lower social classes to try to imitate the higher ones. This situation has been compounded by commercial interests, with intense and often most effective advertizing, which again promotes changes in local diets towards a European dietary pattern, and may indeed modify the European dietary pattern itself in ways that make it even less applicable to many developing countries.

In spite of these influences and pressures, traditional diets have generally persisted, though some changes, frequently for the worse in terms of the health and economy of the population of developing countries, have been introduced and may have further repercussions if the problem is not recognized in time. These changes include:

—The rapid decline in breast-feeding, the traditional and most effective way to feed children during infancy, and its replacement by feeding with cow milk preparations which, at least under the living conditions of these populations, is unsafe and uneconomical, if not questionable under any conditions.

—Unrefined traditional products are being replaced by refined ones with dubious and frequently proven negative effects in terms of nutrition: refined instead of unrefined sugar; polished instead of unpolished rice; high extraction cereal flour and even pure starch instead of whole flour; canned instead of fresh fruits and juices.

—Traditional and locally-available cereal staples are being replaced by imported ones with little nutritional value but with serious negative effects on the economy of these populations and their countries; tortillas, chapatis and local "breads" made with corn, sorghum or other cereals or legumes are being replaced by European types of bread made with wheat.

—Bottled soft drinks, some of them with definite deleterious health effects and all of them uneconomical, are replacing more nutritious traditional drinks.

—Unproven assumptions and misguided beliefs—for example that animal products should be an important component of the diet—have been introduced, creating frustrations and encouraging dangerous misallocation of the meagre family budget.

—Some food fads, such as the regular taking of pharmaceutical vitamin preparations to complement over-refined food have also been introduced, again with serious repercussions for family and even national economies.

With this sad experience, and the present world situation with regard to food and nutrition in mind, we should ask ourselves the following questions: is the present European type of diet really ideal from the health point of view? Does it correspond to a rational use of natural resources, both for rich and for poor countries? Can nutritionally equivalent or even better diets be based on locally available and acceptable foods? Could they be socially and economically more desirable?

Is the European Diet Healthy?

I can perhaps best describe in general terms what I consider the European type of diet to be by taking what is recommended in a recent nutrition textbook (2.5) as a "moderate energy, well-balanced diet suitable for a patient in bed". This diet contains: bread and other cereal preparations, milk, eggs, meats (beef, fish or poultry), bacon or sausage, cheese, butter, vegetables, fruits, desserts. It provides 75 g of protein, the majority coming from 2000–2500 kcal per day, animal sources and more than 30 percent of the calories coming from fats. There are of course local variations, but this is probably a good example of the general pattern. There are also variations in total energy and composition of the diet between groups and between individuals within groups, but if we take average figures of available supplies, we find that for North America and Western Europe they represent (*per capita* per day) about 3000 kcal, 90 g of protein, of which some 50 g are of animal origin, and 130 g of fat (about 40 percent of the energy). (2.6)

Evidence has been accumulating in the past few decades to suggest that, strictly from the health point of view, and taking into consideration other living conditions of the population, particularly their energy expenditure, this type of diet may have some quite serious disadvantages: it is too high in total energy, unnecessarily high in animal protein, too high in fats (and the majority saturated), too high in refined sugars, too low in fibre and other residues, frequently too high in salt. Among the health problems which can be related to the dietary pattern, in association with other living conditions, are obesity, atherosclerosis and its consequences and complications (heart attacks and strokes), hypertension, gout, renal problems, diabetes, dental caries and constipation. Some questions remain to be answered with regard to the actual role that diet *per se* plays in the aetiology of some of the problems: there are still other problems in which the possible role of diet is suspected, and there may be others in which it has not yet even been suspected.

One thing, however, is clear, and that is that the type of diet outlined above cannot be described as the healthiest possible one. In populations with different diets, usually poor both in quantity and in quality, the prevalence of most of these health problems is much lower, but on the other hand they suffer from malnutrition. It can be argued that it is better to die of a heart attack than of hunger, or to die of anything but with a full stomach; but without going to such extremes, the question should rather be whether an intermediate, more rational, position exists. Should the efforts which are being made to improve the nutrition of populations at present living in poor conditions result in a repetition of the errors now recognized in the diets of affluent populations, if only from the health point of view? And let us now consider their economic implications.

European Diet—a Rational Use of Resources?

The chief natural resources of the earth, land, water and energy and their main product for human life—food—are now becoming scarce in relation to the earth's population, particularly when the problems of inadequate utilization and distribution are taken into account. We have witnessed the consequences of this imbalance in the exacerbation of hunger, acute or chronic, which has affected millions of the world's population in the past few years. It is recognized that there is still room for an increase in food production if some of the present constraints, mainly social and economic rather than technological, can be solved. It is also recognized that the current population growth rate cannot be maintained, but it is most unlikely that stabilization of population growth will come about in the near future. Even if policies and programmes of family planning are adopted, and carried out effectively, the generations already born and being born in the next few years have to be taken into account before the effects of these policies and programmes can make themselves felt. A more rational and efficient utilization of our natural resources is therefore a matter of serious concern.

From this point of view, the European type of diet is very wasteful because it contains a very high and, as will be discussed later, unnecessary proportion of foods of animal origin. To produce these foods, grains and other products are being used as animal feeds instead of being used directly as human foods, which would avoid the inefficient process of their conversion into animal products. In fact the conversion rate of energy of various animals varies, but it has been estimated that to produce a given amount of food of animal origin, it is necessary on average to use in the feeding of the animal seven times the energy that the product could provide if consumed directly. The significance and magnitude of this problem are readily appreciated if, as was recently done by Borgstrom (2.7) the energy provided by the diet as consumed is compared with that contained in the agricultural products used to produce it (primary kcal). It was found, for instance, that an average Indian diet, providing 1990 kcal per person per day, represents 2634 primary kcal when the conversion rate is applied to the animal products contained in it. In contrast, the average diet for the U.S.A., providing 3300 kcal represents the utilization of 11,886 primary kcal per person per day. It can be seen that there is enormous wastage not only of actual calories consumed per person but more especially of primary kcal. In direct food intake, a North American consumes an average of 1310 kcal more than an Indian, but in terms of calories produced by agriculture, he consumes 9252 kcal more per day than his Indian counterpart. This calculation does not, of course, take into consideration the extra costs of calories consumed in agricultural production (e.g. fuel, fertilizer, water distribution).

It is obvious that the European type of diet, and particularly with a level of consumption such as that of the U.S.A. could not possibly be applied to the whole population of the world. With the primary calories consumed by each North American, at least four people could be properly fed. The European type of diet, therefore, not only is not the best diet from the health point of view but is absolutely impractical in economic terms for the world population under the present circumstances. The next question is, therefore, can nutritionally equivalent or even better diets be based on locally available and acceptable foods?

Other Diets

Traditional diets for the great majority of the population in tropical and subtropical countries are based on cereals and legumes, with a very small amount of foods of animal origin—consumed only occasionally for the most part. When cassava or other starchy roots, tubers or fruits are the staple, these are usually supplemented with legumes or with animal foods such as fish. They have in general a lower concentration of proteins than does the European type of diet, most, if not all of which comes from vegetable foods; they also have a lower content of fats; often only the constituent fats contained in the foods, with no extra fats added.

The first practical question that arises therefore is how indispensable are foods of animal origin for humans. The special merit of these foods is their high content in proteins of high biological value. It was long thought that proteins of animal origin had a particular composition containing specific components which make them indispensable for human feeding. It is now well established that the biological value of proteins, that is the efficiency of their utilization as nutrients by the human body, is determined primarily by the concentration and proportion of the essential amino acids; in practice no other components are of value in this regard.

Proteins of animal origin generally contain a high concentration of all these essential amino acids in adequate proportions, hence their high nutritional value. Proteins of vegetable origin generally contain a lower concentration and frequently lack in essential amino acids such that the others cannot be utilized because they are not all in the requisite proportions. This is true for individual vegetable proteins considered in isolation; but when two or more such proteins are combined they frequently complement one another, each correcting the relative deficiency of the other. The resulting protein combination has a higher biological value than has each of its components, sometimes reaching values almost as high as those of animal proteins.

The complementary effect of these proteins occurs for instance when cereals and legumes are combined as in the traditional dietary patterns commonly based on corn with beans; rice with beans; or rice, wheat or sorghum with bengal gram, green peas or lentils. These protein combinations are of higher nutritional value than that of their components, and sufficiently high to satisfy the needs of humans when eaten in adequate proportions and sufficient amounts. We have therefore only now come to understand the scientific basis of what most populations have been doing for centuries as a fundamental part of their culture. Small amounts of animal foods can also have the effect of correcting the relative deficiencies of vegetable proteins and making them fully utilizable, but for this purpose they need not be the major protein source as they are in the European type of diet.

Protein Concentration

Another problem in connection with traditional diets in tropical and sub-tropical areas is protein concentration. In this regard, it must first be remembered that protein requirements are now generally agreed to be lower than was believed until recently. (2.8) Present indications are that for many populations suffering from malnutrition total calories and not proteins are the main limiting factor. If populations living on traditional diets, such as those based on cereals and legumes combined, ate enough to satisfy their needs for energy, they would also have enough proteins. There are observations and some experimental evidence that this is so, at least for adults and older children. For small children, however, during their first two or three years of life, it would seem that these diets may be too bulky, thus making it difficult for these children to eat enough: and, if not properly prepared, they may not be easily digested. In this case, small amounts of animal foods, or special preparations and combinations of traditional foods to increase protein concentration and quality, can be of great value. Traditionally this problem was solved by prolonged breast feeding; human milk, even in small amounts, completed the diet. However, if children are weaned early, as is unfortunately now very often the case, they may have problems with traditional diets unless special preparations are made for them.

Traditional diets in which the staple is cassava or other starchy foods present more of a problem because the protein concentration of these foods is far too low. They are frequently accompanied, however, by legumes or better still by animal foods such as fish, and in these cases, there should be no serious problem if the right proportions are consumed.

It should also be remembered that in these traditional diets, in addition to the staples, are included other vegetable foods (leaves, fruit) containing protein, which may not contribute very much quantitatively in this regard, but could be significant qualitatively in improving the biological value and hence the utilization of the total proteins.

In conclusion, I believe that adequate nutrition in regard to calories and proteins can be achieved with these traditional diets. With small amounts of food of animal origin (certainly much less than in the European type of diet) and with enough leaves, fruit and other vegetables, they can also provide adequate amounts of the other nutrients, vitamins and minerals required. Furthermore, they will be without most of the drawbacks of the European type of diet: excesses of protein and fats, refined sugar and low fibre content.

If, therefore, the populations in the tropics and sub-tropics, where malnutrition is now prevalent, were able to have adequate amounts and proportions of these traditional foods, their nutritional requirements could be met. Some minor changes or adjustments in composition or in methods of preparation, would perhaps be needed in some cases, particularly for small children, but these should always be made within the limits of available resources and respecting the cultural values of the people. Indeed, nutritional requirements would probably be met in a safer way than with the European type of diet which, as discussed, is not necessarily the most advisable nutritionally and is economically inefficient.

It must not be forgotten, either, that to ensure an adequate diet does not necessarily mean adequate nutrition. Unfortunately, other important contributing factors interfering with proper consumption and biological utilization of the diet are highly prevalent in the populations suffering from malnutrition, in particular infectious diseases, parasitism and diarrhoeas. They also need to be corrected and the approach must therefore be an integrated one. Further discussion of these related aspects of the problem is inappropriate at this time, since the present discussion is limited to dietary factors.

Social and Economic Desirability

There still remains the last question: Could these diets be socially and economically more desirable? This is assuming, of course, on the basis of the foregoing discussion, that they are nutritionally sound. The answer to this question does not need much elaboration. Food preferences are among the last things to change in any culture, and it is logical, therefore, to work towards the improved nutritional status of a society by respecting traditional food habits rather than by trying to impose new ones. This could also help in building up the interest and capacity of the populations concerned to solve their own problems rather than rely on others to solve them.

Economically, there are obvious advantages for a country or for areas within a country in relying on what can be produced locally to satisfy the food needs of the population. Among other things this could help rural families depending largely on agriculture to improve their income and food resources. Even if it is necessary to import certain foods into the country or area, it will be a more rational and economical use of the resources to import foods providing more nutritional value per unit cost. Indeed, taking into consideration the limitations in natural resources mentioned earlier, I believe that this is the only way to solve the serious nutritional problems that beset a large part of the world's population, particularly in poor countries in tropical and sub-tropical areas.

Conclusion

I believe that this discussion leads to the inevitable conclusion that the principles on which food and nutrition policies and programmes have been based are in need of fundamental change, in both developing and developed countries. Most countries have explicit or, more often, implicit food and nutrition policies and the population follows or tries to follow some general guidelines. These are influenced in the developed countries at least by technical and scientific groups of professional people such as nutritionists, pediatricians, food technologists, agriculturists; but even more by general social, cultural and economic factors such as agricultural and technological development, commerce and advertizing. Moreover, in the developing countries, through commerce and even through technical and material assistance, as well as through example, the economic and cultural influence of the developed countries is not negligible.

The rich countries now living with a luxurious European type of diet as part of their affluence must recognize that this has been possible until now only because of the very unevenly distributed use of the global natural resources, which cannot continue much longer. But they should also realize that for their own sakes, it is not wise, either for the health of their populations or for the creation of a more stable and prosperous social order among the nations of our planet to encourage the perpetuation of this system. Just as the dietary patterns of other populations are part of their culture, so a much more modest diet, within the existing pattern, would be healthier and more economical for the rich countries themselves as well as for world economy. Political leaders, scientists and technologists, industry, commerce, educators—all can contribute to bringing about this much needed change.

Perhaps it has indeed already started, at the level of the people themselves, as a result of the vastly increased opportunities for travel in recent years, which have enabled many, particularly among the young people from affluent societies to appreciate at first-hand at least something of the advantages of a simpler way of living in less prosperous societies.

The developing countries, therefore, should not feel frustrated by their inability to imitate the developed ones but should aim at contributing more positively to their own development, with their own efforts and resources, without counting so much on foreign assistance. In relation to food supplies and nutrition of the population, this process will of course be simplified if policies and programmes in this regard are oriented as suggested in this discussion.

I have ventured here to put forward concepts which may be challenged by food and nutrition scientists and by development economists and planners: I should welcome further analysis and discussion of these concepts, and particularly further observations and studies to prove or disprove them, as the subject is of such vital importance for the present and future of the world in regard to satisfying the food and nutrition needs of its peoples.

ANNEX 2

Early Cognitive Development and Malnutrition

by *Barbel Inhelder*

A team of researchers at the University of Geneva trained in Piaget's concepts and methods* investigated the intellectual development of African babies in three villages at the boundary between forest and savannah. A group of doctors and bio-chemists had just carried out an epidemiological inquiry into the nutritional state of young children in this region which had shown that one third of them suffered from moderate malnutrition or its effects. This led to the question, whether their malnutrition (or perhaps that of their parents) could influence the intellectual development during the first years of a child's life.

We were well aware of the complexity of such research, which we saw as being aimed ultimately at the improvement of the living conditions of the indigenous population. It gave us the privilege of working with doctors, dieticians and agro-nomists, both European and African, and was a unique opportunity for us to observe at close quarters the initial development of knowledge in children who move in a different cultural environment from ours.

Because the study we had envisaged led to problems of methodology and of theory of a general character, it was necessary first to establish the kind of criteria for comparison to determine the norms of intellectual development of African babies of precarious state of health living in traditional villages.

It was obviously not those which applied to young European children living in an urban environment and in good physical health. Comparison could only have a meaning if carried out with children of the same ethnic group, considered in good health and in similar material and cultural conditions.

There was thus a dual approach to our study. We first studied the longitudinal evolution of the sensory-motorial intelligence and of the symbolic function with a representative sample of Baoulé children, ranging from 6 to 33 months, and compared it with a similar Parisian sample (Lézine, I., Stambak, M., and Casati, I. 1969). We then compared the possible differences that occur in the rhythm and style of the development of two series of pairs of children, some considered to be in good health, the others showing signs of malnutrition. The children were paired according to age and could only be distinguished significantly by their anthropometric parameters and, to a lesser extent, by their biochemical parameters.

Any developmental psychologist aware of cultural relativity would of course hesitate to transpose from one environment to another experimental situations and

* P. Dasen, B. Inhelder, M. Lavallée, J. Retschitzki.

instruments of analysis which have allowed cognitive behaviour to be studied and evaluated against a European or American background. That is why the classic baby-tests, roughly based on Gesell's, proved quite inadequate, as was shown by a preliminary study we carried out. The tests derived from Piaget's genetic and episte-mological research, which he developed through the observation of his own chil-dren (the birth of intelligence (Piaget, 1936), the construction of the real (Piaget, 1937) and the formation of symbols (Piaget, 1946)), were found to be more suitable for throwing light on the constructive mechanisms of the elementary forms of knowledge. That is why, in our preliminary studies, we already made use of such tests which were standardized by Irène Lézine and her collaborators in Paris (Casati, I. and Lézine, I., 1968). Some slight modifications of the equipment used in the original work, although unusual for African babies, proved sufficient to arouse much interest in them; this seems to confirm the hypothesis that it is the patterns of action which bestow meanings to objects and, for this very reason, are common to children of various cultures.

It is worth noting that it is the problems set in epistemological terms and pertain-ing to the construction of the object, of space and of causality, that have brought to light the similarity of adapting behaviours to the real in children from the most diverse cultural backgrounds. Is this not because children need to introduce a certain coherence into their immediate universe in order to be able to adapt to the continuously varying situations they come up against?

We have found this same character of generality, and even of universality, during the study of the genesis of the symbolic function which is the basis of all represen-tation which in turn is the pre-requisite for all human thought. The results were identical both in induced situations and in cases of spontaneous behaviour. It is all the more astonishing if one takes into account the role imitation plays in the formation of games of fiction, and also how rich and varied the collective symboli-cal representations among the Baoulé ethnic group are. Yet, the small children from the Baoulé villages proceed in exactly the same fashion and go through the same successive stages as western urbanized children do. They do so for example in constructing what Piaget has called the pattern of the permanent object, or in discovering the "stick's behaviour" when they try to reach a wanted object that is too far from them. Of course, depending on the demands of the environment and of the type of activities, faster or slower rate of acquisition of knowledge can be seen.

The fact that we have so far stressed the generality of the processes which form intelligence independently from cultural context does not mean that we took no notice of differences in life-styles and behaviour. We were particularly struck by how slowly the Baoulé babies seemed to move. However, far from showing any deficiency, this slowness went with harmonious and graceful movements. We also noted that the baby often hesitates to take an initiative of which he is in fact perfectly capable. The mother's function as a mediator between him and his sur-roundings seems to us to be the consequence of a highly developed and extended symbiosis between mother and child (late weaning).

Through these differences in style and rate of development we were struck to find common structures again and again. These structures seem to us to be peculiar to human intelligence. We believe that without them there could be neither any convergence of linguistic activity, nor any convergence of the fundamental categories of knowledge that are common to varying cultures, nor would there be any understanding among men.

As for speed of intellectual development in the first years of life, Baoulé babies show a clear-cut advance in all respects on babies observed in Parisian day nurseries by I. Lézine and her collaborators. This advance is in fact more or less marked, according to the type of activity, and tends later to diminish. We believe that it can be related to motorial preconsciousness in the African baby. To be carried on his mother's back for most of the time till weaning, and to be constantly able to reach her breast creates a natural effective climate favouring his development and creating a great many stimulations and regulative adaptations. Besides, contrary to the widespread opinion according to which his surroundings are poor in objects (lack of toys) and that therefore there are hardly any stimulations, our observations of Baoulé everyday life have shown that small children have access to a great many objects and there seem to be no interdicts, not even in cases of some dangerous sharp objects.

The astonishing convergence we have seen in both the behaviour of small Baoulé children and young Europeans of the same age poses the central problem of relations between the innate and what results from constructive mechanisms peculiar to the subject's activities. By constructive mechanisms we mean the inventions of children which are not thought to be programmed by heredity. The most interesting problem in dealing with the relationship of what is innate and free construction on the part of the individual arises in the discovery of new conducts (to introduce a small chain into a narrow tube by gathering it in such a way that the operation becomes easy; to use a stick to bring nearer a distant object, etc.). Although creative imagination contains an element of imitation, it manifests itself in the very first symbolic conducts, in particular when the child comes across unknown objects such as a mirror or a doll. When the Baoulé baby first explores a doll, he establishes correspondences between his own eyes, mouth, etc., and those of the doll. After looking at himself in the mirror he turns the mirror to the doll so that she too can look at herself. He also symbolically imitates, without using any real objects, a series of actions by which his mother prepares foutou, for example.

While admitting that the preliminary conditions of the observed conducts are innate, does one not have the right to assume that the numerous new combinations cannot be reduced to a pre-programmed mechanism of the species, but that they result on the contrary from new constructions due to each subject's initiative in terms of the laws and mechanisms of cognitive development? To render an account of the convergence that has been noticed in young African and European subjects, it is not necessary to choose one or the other of the alternative terms: innateness or cultural origins of behaviour. Would it not be preferable to envisage a constructivist solution according to which the continuous overstepping and regulations of the subject's activity with regard to his environment would generate the general character of cognitive constructions? Psychological development would thus prolong the epigenetic regulating mechanisms characterizing embryogenesis.

The results of our comparative study, which was of a theoretical interest, enabled us to try and answer the problem of the possible impact of moderate malnutrition upon cognitive development in the first years of life.

A previous study carried out on 297 + 450 children between 0 and 5 years (Ravelli, G. P., 1972) has shown that although they did not present signs of serious malnutrition (kwashiorkor or marasmus), a great number of children showed signs of moderate malnutrition.

We know that to establish the rate of malnutrition McLaren, D. S. and Read, W. W. C. (1972) used anthropometric indices such as relationship between ideal and real weight for a given height and age, taking the sex of the child into account. Seasonal fluctuations can affect these measures; so we found it equally necessary to take into account the measurements around the arm and the head. These examinations were repeated five times during one and a half years and were completed by biochemical analyses.

We selected 23 couples of children, paired according to their age, whose anthropometric measures were situated between 75 and 85 percent for some and beyond 90 percent for the others, but were in all cases inferior to the 100 percent of the nutritional norms.

The Baoulé are above all an agricultural population living from its own produce, consisting of ignames, bananas, plantains, some rice, and, recently, winged beans (phosphocarpus) richer in proteins, to which comes game and occasional fish which is bought. Their only source of cash income comes from their sale of coffee and cocoa; the production of these crops is subject to great seasonal variations and the resulting income is thus subject to market fluctuations.

Analysis of the anthropometric measurements shows a statistically significant difference in the development of size and weight between the two groups studied. This difference however is not noticeable in the biochemical analyses (Reinhardt, M.). Although protein intake has been shown to be quite insufficient, protein metabolism on the other hand appeared quite normal. However, the whole population suffers from serious anaemia, and the hypergammaglobulinaemia that one can generally observe is probably due to chronic or repeated infections and to parasitic infestation in which cannot be excluded the important role of nutritional factors.

As far as anthropometric measurements are concerned, the two series of longitudinal examinations on sensory-motorial intelligence and on the beginnings of the symbolic function show a much less significant difference. These psychological examinations allowed us to compare the total progress accomplished by each of the children as well as the specific progress initiated by each of our tests composing our scale of intellectual development. We compared the levels of development—equal, inferior, or superior—in each experimental situation and for each pair of children. These comparisons show that moderate malnutrition, even though it does not have a severe effect, nevertheless has a marginal effect on psychological development. The effect varies according to age and to the level of development under consideration and is evidenced by a number of manifestations including a slight lateness in the rate of acquisition (in general, one or two months, never more than four months) while structures and succession of knowledge stay the same. The differences are not uniform during development; it seems that there are few of them in the first phases and that they appear mainly at the end of the first year or at the beginning of the second, which is a period when the child likes to experiment actively in order to discover and invent new means of adapting to new situations. And it is precisely these "to see" experiments requiring a higher degree of initiative on the child's part which seem to be the most affected by a precarious nutritional state at the beginning of life. Psychologists agree with Piaget in recognizing the importance of the first period of the birth of intelligence for the later construction of more elaborate forms of knowledge. So far, no experimental research has enabled us to determine either correlations between the rate of sensory–motorial development of intelligence and the rate of later development of the formation of operational thought, or, in particular, to establish the possible role in this respect in cases of prolonged malnutrition. Our own findings lead us to think that it is this "activity and exploration" aspect of cognitive development which would be the most affected by malnutrition in the long run.

In the Baoulé children whose evolution we could follow, none of our psychological examinations has shown in a repeated way the severe influence of a moderate state of malnutrition on cognitive development. The nutritional factor is of course not the only one in question. Although the economic, cultural and particularly the educational factors were practically identical for all the population we investigated in our study, the intellectual potential of the child during its first years of life nevertheless results from the interaction of numerous past and present factors (particularly the pre-, peri- and postnatal conditions, state of health of parents, chronic or repetitive infections, parasitic infections). These factors are fortunately compensated by the fact that the organism, and in particular the nervous system, seems to possess very powerful regulating mechanisms, even in precarious physical conditions, which can counterbalance cognitive development during the first years of childhood.

Bibliography

Casati, I. and Lézine, I. (1968) *Les étapes de l'intelligence sensori-motrice*, Manuel, Paris: Centre de Psychologie Appliquée.

Dasen, P., Inhelder, B., Lavallée M. and Retschitzki, J. (1978) *Naissance de l'intelligence chez l'enfant baoulé de Côte d'Ivoire*, Huber, Berne.

Inhelder, B., Lézine, I., Sinclair de Zwart, H. and Stambak, M. (1972) Les débuts de la fonction sémiotique. Colloques Internationaux du CNRS, no. 198; *Modèles animaux du comportement humain*, pp. 133–147.

Lézine, I., Stambak, M. and Casati, I. (1969) *Les étapes de l'intelligence sensori-motrice*, Monographie no. 1, Paris: Centre de Psychologie Appliquée.

Inhelder, B., Lézine, I., Sinclair, H. and Stambak, M. (1972) Les débuts de la fonction symbolique, *Archives de Psychologie*, **41**, 163, 187–243.

McLaren, D. S. and Read, W. W. C. (1972) Classification of nutritional status in early childhood, *Lancet*, **2**, 146–148, 1979.

Piaget, J. (1936) *La naissance de l'intelligence chez l'enfant*. Neuchâtel: Delachaux & Niestlé.

Piaget, J. (1937) *La construction du réel chez l'enfant*, Neuchâtel: Delachaux & Niestlé.

Ravelli, G. P. (1972) Enquête nutritionnelle en milieu rural africain. Thèse, Univ. Berne.

Notes to Chapter 2

2.1 *Energy and Protein Requirements*, Report of a Joint FAO/WHO *Ad Hoc* Expert Committee, World Health Organization, Technical Report Series No. 822, Geneva, 1973.

2.2 Diets in China are judged to be adequate on 450 pounds of grain per person per year: 350 pounds consumed directly as cereal or cereal produce and 100 pounds fed to domestic animals (See Jean Meyer, The dimensions of human hunger, *Scientific American*, Volume 235, No. 3, September 1976).

As the amount of grain fed to animals worldwide is over 400 million tons, this amount would approximately feed 2000 million people using Chinese nutritional standards.

2.3 1974 UN World Food Conference, p. 56.

2.4 P. V. Sukhatme, Incidence of protein deficiency in relation to different diets in India, *British Journal of Nutrition*, 24 (1970), quoted in R.G. p. 9.

2.5 S. Davidson, R. Passmore, J. F. Brock and A. S. Truswell, *Human Nutrition and Dietetics*, Sixth Edition, Churchill Livingstone, Edinburgh, London, New York, 1975.

2.6 From *Agricultural Commodity Projections, 1970–1980*, FAO, Rome, 1971.

2.7 D. Borgstrom, The price of a tractor, *Ceres*, Vol. 7, No. 6, November/December 1974.

2.8 *Energy and Protein Requirements*, Report of a Joint FAO/WHO *Ad Hoc* Expert Committee, World Health Organization, Technical Report Series No. 522, Geneva, 1973.

CHAPTER 3

The Magnitude and Distribution of Human Malnutrition

STUDIES on malnutrition as a human, economic and social problem have become much more frequent lately. This is probably not due to the fact that malnutrition is on the increase—although this is probably happening in many countries. "... the nutritional situation of the poorer groups of the population, particularly of children, has deteriorated in the last two years, due to the rapid rise in food prices". (3.1) Although this study shows that the problem is much more complex than one caused by rapidly rising food prices, it has to be stressed that the new interest in human malnutrition, which is however still smaller than the problem warrants, is spurred by the fact that it is being acknowledged among Public Health experts as a much more widespread phenomenon than was previously recognized.

Definitions as to what constituted a "disease" are to a large extent ideological, but it can be argued that malnutrition is perhaps the most widespread disease in the world. It has been estimated that this scourge causes half of the deaths of infants in the world, that 200 million children suffer from its effect, and that fully one-third of the population of "developing" countries (approximately 434 million persons) are malnourished. (3.2) Even in "developed" countries, about 30 million are severely malnourished. (3.3) In an average year, one thousand million people suffer from hunger or malnutrition; (3.4) on the whole, one quarter of the human population is malnourished, one-half suffers from hunger and two-thirds are undernourished. (3.5) It has been stated that "of the children less than five years of age in the developing countries 10 million are suffering from severe malnutrition, 80 million from moderate malnutrition and 120 million from less obvious and more difficult to define milder forms of malnutrition. Thus, something of the order of 50 percent of all young children in the developing world may be inadequately nourished." (3.6)

A calculation has been made to the effect that in the mid sixties, 56 percent of the population in the developing countries, or 840 million people, had a nutritional deficit of over 250 calories per day; and that another 19 percent of the population or 290 million, had a deficit of less than 250 calories a day. (3.7)

An FAO study (3.8) has produced estimates on the number of populations of the world who receive food in quantities smaller than a "minimum critical level"—defined as an amount of calories smaller than 1.2 Basal Metabolisms—One Basal Metabolism being the amount of energy needed to maintain bodily functions and temperature. The results are summarized in Table 1.

A brief comment on this Table is helpful. It is one of the few sources of data on human malnutrition which indicates a trend, and it happens that its second obser-

TABLE 1.

Estimated Number of People for Whom Food Intake is Below the "Minimum Critical Level", by Development Regions (excluding Asian centrally planned economy countries)

Region	Total population (millions)		Percentage below minimum critical level		Numbers below minimum critical level (millions)	
	1969–71	1972–74	1969–71	1972–74	1969–71	1972–74
Africa	278	301	25	28	70	83
Far East	968	1042	25	29	256	297
Latin America	279	302	16	15	44	46
Near East	167	182	18	16	31	20
Total	1692	1827	24	24	401	446

Source: modified from reference 3.8.

vation period (1972–74) coincides with the droughts whose existence originated this study. A study of the figures—despite their imprecision—would help us to arrive at a first impression on the sheer magnitude of the problem. It is a curious fact that the overall percentage of people suffering from malnutrition remains constant at 24 percent, increases in one area of the world being compensated by decreases elsewhere. As population has increased, so have the number of malnourished. Before a Malthusian conclusion is derived from this association, let it be remembered that the developing countries are net exporters of food, as shown in Chapter 1 (cf. also Chapter 6).

As regards mortality from malnutrition, and studying a continent where the 1972 drought was not extensive, it has been conservatively estimated that 400,000 people die annually in Latin America as a direct or indirect consequence of malnutrition, this representing approximately 17 percent of deaths from all causes in the continent (cf. Chapter 11).

Extrapolating these 400,000 Latin American dead from malnutrition from a population of 320 million in a very "quick and dirty" way to the continents of Asia and Africa (with a population, excluding Japan, of 2450 million), one would arrive at an annual figure of malnutrition deaths in them of about 3 million, and thus a total for the three continents of 3.4 million.

The limitations and roughness of this method are evident; but what it does is to highlight the sheer magnitude of the problem. A second conservative assumption is added to it: it is generally acknowledged that nutritional conditions are better in Latin America than in Asia and Africa, so that the world total would be higher. It is hoped that much more refined methods will permit the arrival at much more accurate assessments of deaths from malnutrition worldwide.

The figures presented until now are staggering. In Western terms, cancer would be perhaps considered the most important untamed disease, and one which raises a permanent image of fear, yet annual cancer deaths in 27 "developed" countries totalling 671 million inhabitants, or 18 percent of the world's population (3.9) adds up to 1.2 million.

Comparing cancer with malnutrition, it is evident that the former receives much more resources in the areas of training of physicians, allocations of health facilities, research funds, than the latter, while it has to be remembered that malnutrition is a disease which can be prevented or cured very easily. In macroeconomic terms, it can be stated that for the prevention of illness and death from caloric deficits in millions of people throughout the world—which add up to approximately 350 thousand million calories daily—it would suffice to redistribute about 3.8 percent of the current world availability of cereals. The cost of this caloric deficit amounts to 2.4 percent of the total GNP of developing countries, and 0.3 percent of the world's GNP. (3.10)

This very "cost effective" approach does not work with cancer. Using the simple criteria for health resource allocation expressed by the magnitude, importance and sensitivity (to modifying measures) of each disease, and comparing cancer with malnutrition, it is quite clear that the former is of less magnitude, less important in social terms (it largely strikes old people whose biological cycle is on its way to completion; said differently, its eradication would represent a much more meagre return in years of life expectancy added to a life table than the eradication of malnutrition), and tremendously less sensitive to action, being difficult and costly to diagnose and treat. By contrast malnutrition would be simplicity itself: a diagnosis that can largely be made by laymen (once they are made aware of it), and a disease that can be cured by the provision of a medicine—food—that is cheap to produce, is in abundant supply and can be prescribed and given out by a human health resource that requires virtually no training—in many cases the families of the sufferers.

The Distribution of Human Malnutrition

Where can one find malnutrition victims? As this and the next chapters will show, we do not know for sure. Figures of malnourished—in themselves estimates—are national or regional aggregates with little or no attempts to relate the prevalence of the disease with demographic, social or economic characteristics of the sufferers or with a more comprehensive explanatory frame. Little "epidemiology of malnutrition" exists, in sharp contrast with the rich and historically established epidemiology of infectious diseases first developed in the nineteenth century or with the sophisticated epidemiology of degenerative diseases being developed in this century. This lack of solid data and studies leaves the field free for guesses which researchers can fill with deductive reasonings from their ideology and Weltanscha-uung. If malnutrition is held to be caused by low education it will be found among the ill educated; if it is held to be caused by a death wish on the part of certain individuals it will be found among death wishers; if it is related to meteorological misfortune, to certain geographical areas of residence, or to certain occupations its prevalence will be correspondingly higher where these variables occur.

This is central, because malnutrition studies are not only few, but those which exist have an overwhelming unilateral intellectual framework. Not only is malnutrition not recognized in its magnitude, but also very little empirical data has been gathered on the way in which malnutrition victims are linked to the productive process, the latter being ignored entirely or treated in the most superficial way (as "occupation", "income" or "economic level"). As several recent empirical studies would indicate, malnutrition would increase as traditional patterns of agriculture, which provided the nutritional sufficiency of peasants, is replaced by "modern" agriculture which relies heavily on capital, technology, cash cropping and the existence of salaried agricultural labour. This would place "modernity" on the side of "ill health", and thus has momentous connotations for those who wish to study worldwide trends and their effects on health. (3.12)

Further verifications of this assertion by epidemiologists would be in order, but it would first require an acknowledgement by the "conventional wisdom" of the usefulness of this framework of analysis, which represents a clear alternative to the functionalist ones which are in vogue.

It is out of place here to review the numerous criticisms that have been addressed to the functionalist school in epidemiology, and to its inadequacy as a describer or predictor of events. The following quotation defines, as well as refutes, the underlying foundation of functionalist approaches to epidemiology.

> "The conception of disease as an individual biological phenomenon, which is the underlying one in the dominant medical thought, cannot explain it as a collective phenomenon, or understand what are its determinants. This conception cannot be the basis for a useful medical practice which could solve collective health problems, that is to affect the social phenomenon of health and disease."

> "Functionalist studies on medical subjects have no explanatory capacity. They limit themselves to describing certain phenomena and to proposing measures to achieve a greater functional adequacy of systems; or to account for the meaning of certain phenomena within a given social structure without a real possibility of generalizing beyond it, even though it frequently does so. Both the medical and the sociological conceptions are static and ahistorical. If the time dimension is included, it generally is so as an abstract historical mechanism, which pays no attention to the real historical process as presented in concrete socioeconomical formations. Either some element of the present is chosen as the truth, and historical development is seen as a successive approximation to it, or temporal relationships are verified, as, for example "the higher the economic development the fewer health problems there are". Neither of the two ways of stating the relationship are carried to a theoretical elaboration, as in the first case the central object is arbitrarily chosen and in the second a simply statistical fact is established." (3.13)

When it comes to the profuse mathematical treatments of functionalist frameworks of analysis, they would compound the problem, as they add statistical error upon conceptual limitation. Those who "prove" that malnutrition is "caused" by the low educational level of the mother, for example, because they have seen fit to measure this variable in their research to the exclusion of many others, and because this variable modifies a large amount of the overall variance, are the victims of a circular fallacy of reasoning: what they think *a priori* that explains the phenomenon is measured, and then it is seen statistically that in the course of the phenomenon .... What is called for is a more structural analysis of the society in which malnutrition occurs or the effects of drought are felt, and one which relates this illness or those effects to the way in which society is organized.

Notes to Chapter 3

3.1 The United Nations World Food Conference, 1974. Footnote to p. 57.

3.2 S. Almeida, *et al.*, Assessment of the world food situation—present and future, *International Journal of Health Services*, **5**(1), 95–120, 1975.

3.3 *The State of Food and Agriculture, 1975*, Food and Agriculture Organization of the United Nations (FAO), Rome, 1976.

3.4 Jean Mayer, The dimensions of human hunger, *Scientific American*, **235**, No. 3, September 1976.

3.5 J. M. Bengoa, Nutritional situation in the world, *Bulletin of the Swiss Academy of Medical Sciences*, **31**, 213–227 1975.

3.6 The United Nations World Food Conference, 1974, p. 64.

3.7 S. Reutinger and M. S. Selowski, *Malnutrition and Poverty, Magnitude and Policy Options*, World Bank Staff Occasional Papers, No. 23. The John Hopkins University Press, 1976.

3.8 *The Fourth World Food Survey*, Food and Agriculture Organization of the United Nations (FAO), Rome 1977.

3.9 The countries in question are Canada, U.S.A., Austria, Belgium, Bulgaria, Czechoslovakia, Denmark, Finland, France, G.D.R., F.R. of Germany, Greece, Hungary, Ireland, Netherlands, Norway, Poland, Roumania, Spain, Sweden, Switzerland, England and Wales, Northern Ireland, Scotland, Australia and New Zealand. Data are for 1971, except for U.S.A. and Belgium (1970). (Source: The ten leading causes of death for selected countries in North America, Europe and Oceania, 1969, 1970 and 1971, *World Health Statistics Report*, **27**, No. 3–4, 1974.)

3.10 Reutinger and Selowski, *op. cit.*

3.11 W. D. P. Logan, Cancer Survival Statistics: International data, *World Health Statistics Quarterly*, **31**, No. 1, 1978, pp. 62–73.

3.12 The role of "modern" and "traditional" agriculture coexisting in developing countries is analyzed by Portantiero in his contribution to Volume 3.

3.13 Asac. Lovrell, Investigación en Sociologic Médica: 1ᵉ parte, *Salud Problema*, No. 1, Mexico, January 1977.

CHAPTER 4

The Problem of Measuring Malnutrition

IT IS a sad paradox that the occurrence of certain tragedies is linked causally with an incapacity to record their existence of the damages that they produce. This is the case of the drought and famine which struck certain countries *circa* 1972, or with the phenomena of chronic human malnutrition which is the day-to-day lot of hundreds of millions of people.

This Project postulates that the fact that a famine or chronic malnourishment are allowed to exist points to a weakness in the organization, natural cohesiveness, political autonomy, capacity of response, economic independence and overall level of development of productive forces of the country suffering it, and usually also of the wealth of data—numerical and otherwise—available to record its effects or the chronic conditions surrounding it. The fact that the subject of the analysis—health levels—is to some extent an unquantifiable phenomenon, compounds the problem.

There is a basic problem about measuring health. The phenomenon of health is usually studied negatively, through such "non-health" developments as disease and death. The latter is unambiguous, but a very imperfect measure to use in order to measure health, the former is a better one but suffers from the handicap that a sick person is usually considered to be a deviant from "normality", either statistical or normative, and that this evaluation has in many cases a heavy ideological bias. Is a slightly compulsive bank clerk sick? A slightly hypertensive business executive? A slightly anaemic peasant? A textile worker with inactive TB? A slightly under-nourished child? Many of these cases would not deviate from the "norm" in the community or peer group where they would originate, but whether they are healthy or not is ultimately the result of a value judgement.

Despite these theoretical considerations, the developed countries have evolved over the years a series of complementary statistical systems to measure the health of their populations. Regular censuses, even with slight undercounting, produce reliable population figures; vital statistics with slight under-registration (explained below) produce data on birth, deaths and their causes.* The health services, whose coverage of the population is virtually complete, produce data on current disease and medical procedures undertaken; in parallel, a special network of reporting certain diseases of particular importance and a series of health surveys can be put together to present a picture of levels of health. A time series given by these statistical monitors of the health level can show variations, and the impact of a particular event on it. Nothing similar applies to the countries under study as victims of the 1972 famine where two underrated phenomena act as regards the measurements of chronic and acute malnutrition.

---

* Although in the case of deaths caused by malnutrition this is not always true.

One, and by far the most frequent, is that chronic malnutrition is permanently undermeasured, through mechanisms which this chapter will try to analyze. Malnutrition as a cause of the very high levels of permanent mortality and morbidity would always be there, but would be unacknowledged by the statistical system, which is a part of the encompassing social and political system. This leads to another phenomenon, which has been pointed out in Chapter 1, and will be developed further in Chapter 5, and which apparently is paradoxical: when a natural catastrophe such as drought strikes and a system in a precarious equilibrium becomes unbalanced, the catastrophe, which is only a trigger for the unleashing or exteriorization of effects which were always there in a hidden form, gets the whole blame for the scenes of human suffering that ensue, a suffering that had always been there in forms and numbers hardly less important before it, but which had remained ignored or obscured.

Researchers into the Sahel drought in 1972, confronted with massive malnutrition, premature deaths and susceptibility to disease could easily ascribe these circumstances to the drought but not necessarily realize that they were present before the drought and would be there after it. They could perhaps only see the drought as the cause of what they saw, being unacquainted with a chronic situation largely unrecorded, and this would reinforce their attitude to act on the situation as if it were a specific problem which requires an *ad hoc* short-term response thus susceptible to the emergency "Red Cross" solutions which this Project has repeatedly analyzed.

When it comes to measuring malnutrition, a reader of world health statistics, as recorded in such official publications as the Demographic Yearbook, the World Health Statistic Reports or the World Health Statistics Annual or Quarterly, would come across no figures comparable to those mentioned in the previous chapter on the magnitude of human malnutrition. Deaths caused by malnutrition in those reference books would only add up to a fraction of the millions mentioned in Chapter 3; morbidity by malnutrition would either not appear, or appear in such small numbers as to lead readers to believe that an entirely different disease is under consideration. The reasons why malnutrition is so badly recorded in the "official" world health statistics are interesting, insofar as they throw light on the epistemic framework of the medical profession and of Public Health Officials throughout most of the world, on their underlying ideology and on the uses to which information is put.

The following analysis will show that the magnitude of human malnutrition is much higher than reported in official health statistics systems. If it is agreed that data are valuable insofar as they lead to decisions to remedy bad situations then the lack of data about a health problem of high prevalence which is highly amenable to preventive measures is in striking contrast to the relative abundance of data on other diseases—again such as cancer—which are relatively much more impervious to health measures and also much less significant from a social viewpoint.

Mortality from Malnutrition

The most obvious measure of the impact of malnutrition in a country would be the recording of all malnutrition-caused deaths. The vital statistics systems of the world record, in theory, all deaths which take place in certain defined geographical areas as well as the causes of death. In practice, however, this does not happen, owing to the under-registration of deaths, to the unavailability of health services to much of the population (which prevents the ascertainment of causes of death in many cases), and to the existence of biases in the current system of determining the "basic cause of death", which significantly tends to underestimate the causal rôle of malnutrition.

THE PHENOMENON OF UNDER-REGISTRATION OF DEATHS

No system of vital statistics acknowledges itself to be absolutely accurate, and its degree of exactness is qualitative not quantitative. The amount of under-registration of the vital statistics systems of the countries of the world is sometimes considerable, in some countries the recording of a death is the exception rather than the rule; and in those countries which have never even undertaken a population census, a systematic attempt to record deaths, let alone their causes, would be an impractical undertaking. In many countries of the world, fertility, mortality, age, specific mortality rates and causes of death are obtained from a variety of estimation procedures, in which sample surveys and elaborations (where available) of census data play a prominent part. It must be stressed again that this handicap does not work randomly when it comes to recording malnutrition: those countries with the biggest problems of malnutrition are also those with the highest under-registration problems, and in these countries, it is usually those population groups with highest prevalences of malnutrition that are also those with a selective higher incidence of under-registration of malnutrition-induced mortality or of morbidity from malnutrition.

The African countries affected by the 1972 famine would provide a case in point. Of the eight countries: Mali, Mauritania, Niger, Senegal, Sudan, Ethiopia, Chad and Upper Volta, only Sudan has ever had population censuses. (4.1) For all the others, the population figures have been arrived at through extrapolations of Sample Surveys with various methodologies and undertaken in different years from 1960 to 1971. (4.2)–(4.4) If the universe of population suffering from a famine is not known with any accuracy, it is clear that any ulterior consideration of the effects of the famine is not likely to be known with any greater accuracy.

Vital statistics are so inaccurate in the Sahel countries, for example, as to be virtually useless. It has been stated that there are no statistics of causes of death in most of Africa. (4.5) Many examples of this situation can be cited. In 1963 in the Arrondissement Nakmar (Sine Saloum, Senegal), only 12 percent of births and 1 percent of deaths had been registered, and in the Arrondissement Paos Koto only 4 percent of births and no deaths. In Upper Volta, the mortality rate as registered by vital statistics was 5 per thousand, apparently one seventh of the actual rate. (4.6) In Ethiopia, "precise figures indicating the mortality rates are not available. Registration of vital rates is virtually unknown in the rural areas of the country and even in the urban areas registration is done only on a voluntary basis" (so that) "recorders failed to record more than half of the infants deceased". (4.7) There is practically no registration of deaths in the rural areas of the Sudan and the few deaths that are registered in the country, 6659 in 1970, are neither analyzed nor published. (4.8)

Few studies exist on the under-registration of deaths in those countries of the world such as the Latin American ones, where, on paper, registration would be the standard procedure for measuring mortality. A survey undertaken in 20 Latin American countries in 1975 (which drew a non-response from 10 of them) stated that 6 Latin American countries estimated their general mortality to be under-registered by at least 20 percent and that 5 countries estimated a similar under-registration in their infant mortality. (4.9)

Statements like the following can often be found: "It can be stated that, in general, those countries (of Central America and Panama) do not know the degree of integrity of their vital statistics recording system" and "the problem of omissions is greater for deaths than for births". (4.10) In Guatemala it was estimated that under-registration of infant deaths was 24 percent between 1945–1951 and that it had decreased to 12 percent *circa* 1964; (4.11) in Panama the omission of deaths was estimated as higher than 20 percent in the decade 1950–1951; (4.12) in Mexico infant mortality was underestimated by 16 percent in 1960–1965; (4.13) and in 1955–1960, the percentage of under-registration of deaths was 64 percent for Bolivia, 16 percent for Colombia, 13 percent for Costa Rica, 45 percent for Cuba, 17 percent for El Salvador, 40 percent for Honduras, 39 percent for Nicaragua, 17 percent for Panama, 22 percent for Peru, 49 percent for the Dominican Republic and 22 percent for Venezuela. (4.14)

In 1970–1972, a detailed study on childhood mortality in Latin America (4.15) analyzed approximately 35,000 deaths of children under 5 years of age in 15 study areas corresponding to 8 countries. Corrections were made for the usual misassignment of causes of death through the use of autopsies and hospital records. The initial finding was a significant under-registration of deaths in many areas. The areas under study were generally cities and their suburbs, and thus more developed than the remainder of the respective countries, so that the vital statistics from these areas could be expected to be better than national averages. Yet over 10 percent of the deaths had not been registered in the province of San Juan, Argentina; in La Paz–Viacha, Bolivia; in Santiago, Chile; and in Kingston, Jamaica; and over 22 percent of the deaths had not been registered in Cartagena, Colombia. (See Chapter 11 for details.) The investigating team of the study remarked that their own search had likewise been incomplete, indicating that the actual percentages of under-registration were even greater—and Latin America has a relatively privileged position in the Third World for the coverage and quality of its vital statistics.

MEDICAL SERVICES AVAILABLE IN THIRD
WORLD COUNTRIES

The great majority of the countries of the Third World have a common characteristic regarding physicians: there are very low physician-to-population ratios, so that a high percentage of people needing their services, i.e. sick people and people who are about to die, lack access to health care.

There are two main explanations for this shortage of physicians in Third World societies in which there is a great need of physician services. In market economy countries, entry into medical schools is usually severely restricted and far below any criterion of "need" of physicians on the part of the population. The emigration of physicians from "peripheral" to "central" market economy countries compounds this problem. Medical immigrants in the "central" countries are being used as "second level" medical manpower with much lower salaries and a much more restricted access to professional practice than their native-born colleagues. (4.16) (4.17)

It is only some Third World centrally planned economy countries that are successfully tackling the general problems of training physicians (or their equivalents) in massive numbers to even approach need criteria on the part of the populations, as the Cuban or Chinese experiences would indicate.

Physicians in market economy countries are very unevenly distributed, because, for lack of any other criterion, it is the "market" that allocates them. They thus drift toward those areas—mainly urban—and concentrate on those populations—mainly with chronic and degenerative illnesses—that can pay for their services. As shown in Table 1, the urban concentration of Latin American physicians is remarkable, but it is in the rural areas that malnutrition, parasitoses, and infections are most often found.

In Argentina, the difference in physician concentrations between the most favoured and least favoured province is approximately 12 to 1, (4.19) and a similar situation exists in Colombia, Nicaragua, Peru, and El Salvador, to cite but a few. (4.20)

In Ethiopia, a country struck very hard by the 1972–73 famine, two thirds of the hospitals, one third of health centres and four fifths of doctors and nurses are established in three provinces: Iboa, Eritrea and Harague, it being estimated that no more than 5 million of an estimated number of 22 million Ethiopians were provided with ordinary health services. (4.21) In Senegal, 75.2 percent of all physicians of the country are established in the Cap Vert region, with 18.55 percent of the country's population. (4.22) A similar situation of uneveness of distribution of

TABLE 1.

Rates of Physicians per 10,000 Inhabitants and Rural Zones in Some Latin American Countries, Various Years[a]

Country	Year	General rate	Urban rate	Rural rate
Bolivia	1974	4.7	17.7	0.6
Brazil	1969	5.0	8.8	0.5
Costa Rica	1973	6.4	14.6	0.7
Dominica	1974	1.6	4.1	0.6
Ecuador	1969	3.4	9.9	1.6
Guadeloupe	1973	6.5	18.7	1.7
Guatemala	1971	2.3	14.0[b]	—
Nicaragua	1971	4.6	13.1	1.4
Panama	1970	6.1	9.0	0.8
Paraguay	1970	3.8	15.9	0.5
Peru	1969	5.2	15.5	1.5

[a] Source, reference 4.18.
[b] Guatemala City only.

health resources occurs in the other Sahel countries, and for that matter, in the developing market economy countries of Asia and Africa.

As a consequence of this maldistribution, there is a high percentage of recorded deaths whose causes cannot be ascertained, as they are not certified by physicians, and most of these deaths from unknown causes occur in those geographical areas and social classes where malnutrition is the dominant pathology.

Thus, the concentration of physicians in highly-industrialized rich countries in urban areas, and in the service of wealthy sub-groups of the population, is an unsurmountable obstacle to any accurate measurement of malnutrition. Thus, lack of medical personnel to certify the cause of death is one of the major problems.

BIASES IN THE CERTIFICATION OF DEATHS

Moreover, the ironic fact is that medical professionals are ill-prepared to diagnose malnutrition; in fact, their professional training would bias them against seeing it.

Any description of medical education in the countries of the world is at the same time a description of the society in which that education takes place. Class-ridden societies would produce an equally class-ridden medical education and medical practice. The overwhelming majority of medical students in Third World market economy countries are recruited from among the upper or middle classes, and their training emphasizes individual pathologies, especially those where treatment can be paid for in the "market", over collective pathologies whose sufferers do not have the purchasing power which can generate an "economic demand" in the health market.

In general, physicians would receive an excessively detailed training in surgery, surgical specialities and in those pathologies which are considered important in the medical textbooks—mostly written in developed countries—which they read and which can be treated with the hospital equipment—mostly a product of the developed countries—to which they have access. They will usually not receive detailed training in those pathologies which correspond to the needs of those masses of population which either have no purchasing power, or whose sufferings are not part of the productive mechanism—drugs, technology, equipment—of what has come to be called "Western Medicine".

These factors are linked to the general ideological framework of the medical profession, which is specially strong in market economy countries. According to one observer, "The classical model of causality for professional medicine presents each and every disease as the result of the action of a specific pathogenic agent, usually of a biological nature. That is, every disease has its unique and individual cause. This conceptualization arose and had its golden age with the development of microbiology and is still the dominant model within medicine". (4.23)

On the other hand, malnutrition is a normal characteristic among the lower classes everywhere. As one of the basic conceptualizations of disease in dominant medical ideology is that of statistical normality, making "normal" that which is usual or common, "it is no wonder that in an isolated community...the witch doctor or "curandero"...will not cure TB or malnutrition, among other things, because he does not detect these conditions as abnormal, but conversely as inherent characteristics of the environment (this happens often with physicians, who hardly ever diagnose malnutrition, as this condition is very usual and in a certain sense then, not a disease)". (4.24)

In the country to which this quotation corresponds, and with regard to the teaching of nutrition to prospective physicians, it has been remarked of Colombia that "There are serious shortcomings in the systems of teaching and in the outlook given to nutritional problems. Regular courses are only being taught in three schools (of medicine), but with great differences in subjects, schedules and orientation. One school, of these three has a Department of Nutrition, and only two have resources for laboratory practices". (4.25)

A review of the information on the magnitude of malnutrition in Colombia reveals the basic medical and humanitarian incongruence and the economic-political logic of this situation: the malnourished Colombians do not enter into the national power equation which determines, among many other things, the structure of the country's medical curricula.

BIASES IN THE INTERNATIONAL CLASSIFICATION OF DISEASES

Every determination of causality implies ultimately an ideological framework. The death of an individual implies a series of "explanations" of varying complexity, from the most immediate and symptomatic (e.g. cardiac arrest), through the "disease" which apparently caused it (e.g. artherosclerosis), to more remote but perhaps no less causal explanations (e.g. hypertension provoked by "stress" or "by a condition of exploitation in a work situation"). It is astonishing, and a fundamental problem that malnutrition, *per se*, is not defined, nor even recognized, as a death-inducing disease.

In the case of mortality caused by malnutrition, we have seen how a combination of factors contribute to the underestimation of malnutrition as a cause of death. To these factors must be added another one: the International Classification of Diseases (ICD) tends to underestimate malnutrition as a cause of death by allocating to another disease—usually an infectious one—the rôle of "basic cause of death", even if both diseases are recorded in the death certificate.

The Eighth Revision of the ICD (4.26) presents a worldwide uniform method for determination of causes of death by choosing *one* "basic cause of death" for every death, a decision which greatly facilitates the processing of information. Most deaths clearly result from a long sequence of causes, and the determination of *one* cause among them is, logically, the result of a very definite decision. What the ICD attempts is to make that decision as standardized as possible so as to permit comparative studies.

MALNUTRITION AS A DEATH-INDUCING DISEASE

An infant death "caused" by a bronchopneumonia, which is in turn caused by a measles infection in a child weakened by malnutrition, will be assigned to "measles", and malnutrition will not even be mentioned as a causal agent, even though it is well known that fatality from measles is a function of nutritional status, thus making malnutrition as much a cause of death as the measles virus.* The following has been stated in this respect. (4.27) "Nutritional status seems to affect the epidemiological behaviour of the disease (measles). Protein deficiencies seem to be associated with a much higher incidence of complications, especially broncho-pneumonia and enteritis, and an attack of measles increases the effect of malnutrition in the child. .... Racial factors are unimportant. The severity of measles in Nigerian children is probably related to social, environmental and nutritional factors rather than to race, and the fact that measles was a much more severe disease in Europe a century ago supports this view."

While mortality from measles in some European countries has been among the lowest in the world, "in poor countries the situation is completely different, and measles maintains the same severity it had in Europe when it decimated even royal families. In the Indies, mortality is of the order of 0.3 percent. In Mexico it is 0.7 percent. In Black Africa, measles is a veritable social scourge. It is solely responsible for 25 percent of the mortality of children in their early years. Hospital mortality can reach 20 percent, in cities it is from 2 to 3 percent, and in rural environment, at least 10 percent. Measles kills one thousand times more in rural African environment than in the United States". (4.28)

Experimental research has confirmed that in a severely malnourished child, cellular immunity is depressed, which affects the evolution of viral processes and their bacterial complications (4.29) and that body loss of nitrogen during the illness is very high and greater than in other infections. (4.30)

Thus in a correct interpretation of causation, malnutrition should be considered as important a factor in causing deaths as the measles virus. Yet, according to the system permitting choice of the "basic cause of death" in use throughout the world, all of the deaths caused by both measles and malnutrition would have been attributed to measles and none to malnutrition.

The causal role of malnutrition in many deaths is found associated with many other infectious and parasitic diseases as well as in measles. The combination of malnutrition and infection has caused a re-evaluation of chronic and sub-clinical malnutrition as one of the diseases with highest prevalence in the world, and a cause of death of millions of people every year. (4.31) (4.32) This re-evaluation is not reflected, however, in the classification of causes of death in current use, and the 9th Revision of the ICD, which was supposed to come into general worldwide use on 1 January 1979 has done nothing to correct it.

AN ALTERNATIVE METHOD OF MEASURING MALNUTRITION-INDUCED MORTALITY

A possibility exists in undertaking mortality studies on malnutrition which would avoid the problems mentioned previously. Such studies would eliminate the under-registration of deaths through surveys which record every (or almost every) death that has taken place during a given period in an area, and would assess the causes

---

* The rules of classification of the ICD used to determine the "basic cause of death" state that in the case of a death certificate showing both an infectious disease and malnutrition, the "basic cause of death" will consist of the former and will exclude the latter. The classification lacks a code number for the concept "measles with malnutrition", which could be a compromise solution for the problem.

of those deaths using criteria which are less restrictive than the ones used by the International Classification of Diseases.

Such were the goals of the previously-mentioned study of childhood mortality in Latin America undertaken by Puffer and Serrano (4.15) in 1970–72 and which is treated more in detail in Chapter 11.

Researching approximately 35,000 deaths of children, under 5 years of age, the study team made use of a well-defined methodology for detecting the deaths and discovering their causes on the basis of data from autopsies and hospital records of the deceased children. Among the researchers' conclusions are the following:

> "Nutritional deficiency was the greatest problem that manifested itself through the study, as measured by its intervention in mortality. . . . Through the study of death by multiple causes it was discovered that 57 percent of the children under 5 years of age who had died showed evidence of immaturity or nutritional deficiency as a basic or associated cause of death. . . . It was observed that immaturity and nutritional deficiency were even higher in rural areas than in their neighbouring cities.
>
> "Mortality through nutritional deficiency reached its highest point in the first year, at an age as early as the first 3 or 4 months, but very different characteristics were observed in the 13 projects (study areas). . . . Mortality caused by protein malnutrition increased until it reached a maximum in children 12 to 17 months of age, while nutritional marasmus reached high rates in children of 2 to 6 months."

The Problem of Reporting Malnutrition-Induced Morbidity

Most of what are currently presented as morbidity statistics are, in effect, statistics of medical services rendered, and they thus give a very incomplete approximation of the extent of morbidity in a given population. On the one hand, the phenomena of "health" and "illness" are ultimately established by the ideology prevailing at a given place and historical moment and reflected in the structure of existing health services. On the other hand, population coverage by the health services and hence health services statistics are very incomplete in almost all of the developing countries, and it is reasonable to suppose that those groups that are most affected by malnutrition are, in effect, also those that have the least access to health facilities and whose sufferings are likely to go unrecorded. As a Brazilian researcher once said when asked about the incidence of snake bites in his country, "It is difficult to know, since where there are statistics there are no snakes, and where there are snakes there are no statistics."

This situation may also be observed with regards to malnutrition, as almost all health statistics in developing countries reflect morbidity which has been recorded in hospitals. The following considerations regarding Argentinian hospital statistics, but applying as well to other countries, may serve to summarize the situation:

> "Those patients who are looked after in hospitals are a fortunate minority which has been able to cross the economic, geographic and cultural barriers which block access to them. The medical specialities which are offered in

hospitals are not necessarily those which are needed, but those that the dominant medical system sees fit to provide. As there is no limit to potential demand for health care on the part of the population, any medical speciality, no matter how trivial or unnecessary, will immediately be swamped by patients seeking care. It will be a mistake to believe that morbidity as registered in hospitals with such a degree of distortion would correspond to any objective need for medical care on the part of the population, or should have any priority in the allocation of resources". (4.19)

Let us not forget that malnutrition is an "interesting" pathology neither for hospitals patterned on those of the developed countries, nor for physicians whose professional training focuses on the illnesses suffered by the upper social classes. Detailed figures on the numbers of those in the Latin American populations, for example, who are outside the medical care systems are lacking, but as a rough estimate, about 50 percent of the Latin American population may not have regular access to health care.

MORBIDITY AND NUTRITIONAL SURVEYS

Many of the problems of nutritional morbidity reporting stated above can be circumvented by means of nutrition surveys in selected geographical areas and population samples. Such surveys usually gather data on food consumption, dietary habits, food purchasing power, and clinical signs of protein–calorie malnutrition anaemia, or avitaminosis, and measure weight and height of individuals for comparison with data from standard tables.

It may seem arbitrary to use standards of normality which do not correspond to the country and social class of the population interviewed. However, it is noted that "the differences in bodily growth that have been observed between children in developed and developing countries are basically due to environmental factors, it being inferred that the genetic potential is probably very similar in both populations, and therefore the use of norms of developed countries is adequate". (4.33)

Among the numerous studies supporting this opinion, Perez Hidalgo and his co-workers (4.34) reported that 1067 children of higher-income groups in Mexico showed levels of growth similar to those in the U.S., while 505 children of middle-income and 425 of lower-income groups showed levels that were inferior, the latter remarkably inferior, to U.S. standards. In the Sudan, growth curves showed that Sudanese children with access to adequate diet and to medical care grew well in comparison with children from the developed countries. While under-privileged children started their lives equally well, their body weight became retarded between 1 and 2 years of age due to feeding problems which could follow weaning, which is a very common characteristic in developing countries. (4.35)

The magnitude of the problem, in contrast to the sparse information provided by official health statistics systems, is indicated by a review of health and nutrition surveys carried out in the last 10 years in Latin America and the Caribbean, (4.36) which reached the following conclusions:

"If it is true that the studies mentioned are incomplete, and do not represent the prevalent situation in all the countries of Latin America and the

Caribbean, or in all geographical areas of a country, they clearly indicate that in most of them there exist nutritional problems.

"The results of an analysis of vital indices and of nutritional survey point out that protein–calorie malnutrition, anaemias due to iron deficiency, vitamin B_{12} and folates (*sic*) deficiency, goitre, endemic cretinism, and vitamin A hypovitaminosis constitute grave public health problems in most of the countries of the region. At the same time, cardiovascular diseases, diabetes, and obesity, which are related to nutrition, are every day becoming more important as public health problems in Latin America and the Caribbean."

Food Consumption Statistics

Statistics on food consumption at the national level are a much-used indicator of nutritional levels. They lead to confusion, however, as they are merely averages, purportedly at the individual level, of national figures, and proceed on the fallacious premise that national food production gets evenly distributed. In practice, of course, this does not happen: arithmetical means mask the fact that a percentage of people eat more than they need and suffer from hypernutrition, and another percentage, which in the developing countries is overwhelmingly higher, eat less than they need and pay a price in sickness and death for this fact.

"Country averages, however, on food consumption, do not reflect within countries disparities discussed earlier. To make an estimate of the numbers undernourished, it may therefore be appropriate to use evidence regarding distribution of food intake as well as clinical and anthropometric data. For example, these data for children (although usually available only for small and often unrepresentative samples) indicate that up to 50 percent of all young children in the developing world may be inadequately nourished". (4.37)

According to one observer, "Availability of food *per capita* may lead to a misleading impression, as food distribution is not egalitarian, and the lower economic sectors are highly affected" (4.35) and another states, "It has been estimated that in many developing countries, the lower 20 percent of the population, in terms of income, has only half the caloric intake of the upper 10 percent of the population". (4.38) When the causes for this distribution have been studied, it has been determined, quite obviously, that "this maldistribution (of food) is mainly a function of income". (4.39)

Two additional elements have to be noted. One is that any food consumption table that attempts to relate consumption with "satisfaction of needs" according to physiological criteria enters the difficult ground of what those needs really are; a situation which is quite settled as regards calories but not so much as regards proteins. This has been discussed in Chapter 2. The other is that, given the protein requirements are held to very sharply by age, a country with a "young" age structure is likely to need many more proteins *per capita*, while the converse is also true.

Some of the current statistics on food availability for the Latin American countries illustrate the difficulties of matching the image of abundance of food *per capita* with the facts on malnutrition-induced morbidity and mortality in the same countries that will be reviewed later. For example, according to the Inter-American Investigation of Mortality in Childhood already mentioned, in 27 percent of all deaths of children under 5 years of age in the province of San Juan, Argentina, malnutrition was a basic or associated cause. (4.15) It may have been a consolation for these children to know that they died in a country where the average daily calorie supply covers 115 percent of needs; the same situation applies to the city of Sao Paulo, Brazil, where the corresponding percentage of deaths by malnutrition is 29 percent and the average national food supply covers 110 percent of national needs.

Notes to Chapter 4

4.1 Omar Ahmed El Tay "Mortality in the Sudan", *ESOB/WHO/EMR/MORT/C.P.* 9, 4 December, 1972.

4.2 *United Nations Demographic Yearbook*, New York, 1975.

4.3 Abdulah Hasan, The mortality situation in Ethiopia, Expert Group Meeting on Mortality *WHO/EMR/MORT/C.P.* 4, 30 November, 1972.

4.4 *I.N.E.D. France Bulletin de Liaison* Nr. 13, Juillet–Septembre, 1974.

4.5 Pierre Cantrelle, Mortalité-facteurs, in *Institut National de la Statistique et des Etudes Economiques, Afrique Noire, Madagascar, Comores: Démographie comparée*, Tome II, Paris, 1967.

4.6 Cantrelle, *op. cit.*

4.7 Hasan, *op. cit.*

4.8 El Tay, *op. cit.*

4.9 S. E. Natali, Analisis de los sistemas de información de estadisticas de natilidad y mortalidad que operan en America Latina, 1975, *Publication Series 3*, No. 4. Secretariat for Industry and Commerce, Mexico, 1976.

4.10 C. Arretx and G. Maccio, Evaluación de los datos demograficos-censales ye de registro disponibles en los paises de America Central y Panama, *Publications CELADE*, Series A, No. 75, 1967.

4.11 Z. C. Camisa, Las estadisticas demograficas y la mortalidad en Guatemala hacia 1950 y 1964, *CELADE*, San José, Costa Rica, 1969.

4.12 H. Araica, Informe sobre una encuesta experimental para medir la omision en los registros de nacimientos y defunctiones en la República de Panama, *Document ST/ECLA/CONF*, 19/L.L., October 20, 1964.

4.13 E. Cordero, La subestimación de la mortalidad infantil en Mexico, *Demografia y Economia*, Vol. II, No. 1, 1968. (Quoted in *Dinamica de la Población en México*, E. Colegio de México, México, 1970.)

4.14 Leiva, L. Alvarez, Algunos intentos de evaluación del grado de integridad de las estadisticas vitales en paises Latino-americanos, *Document ST/ECLA/CONF*, 19/L.16, 16 November, 1964.

4.15 R. R. Puffer and C. Serrano, *Characteristics of Mortality in Childhood*, Scientific Publication No. 262, Pan American Health Organization, Washington D. C., 1973.

4.16 Multinational Study of the International Migration of Physicians and Nurses, *Country Specific Migration Statistics*, Document HMD/764, World Health Organization, Geneva, 1976.

4.17 José Carlos Escudero, La Emigración de médicos latino-americanos, *Cuadernos del Tercer Mundo No. 15*, August 1977.

4.18 *World Health Statistics Annual*, 1974, Vol. III, World Health Organization, Geneva, 1976.

4.19 José Carlos Escudero, La Situación Sanitaria Nacional, *Cuadernos de Contramedicina*, Nr. 1, Buenos Aires, 1974.

4.20 V. Navarro, The underdevelopment of health or the health of underdevelopment: An analysis of the distribution of human health resources in Latin America, *Int. J. Health Serv.*, 4(1): 5–27, 1974.

4.21 R. Lutynski, "Advisory Services in Epidemiology and Health Statistics in Ethiopia" EMIEPID 13 *WHO*, February 1976.

4.22 République du Sénégal. Ministère de la Santé Publique et Affaires Sociales, Statistiques Sanitaires et Démographiques du Sénégal, Année 1973–Juillet 1974.

4.23 C. Laurell, Medicina y Capitalismo en México, *Cuadernos Politicos*, No. 5, Mexico, 1975.

4.24 A. V. Uribe, *Salud, Medicina y Clases Sociales*, Editorial La Pulga, Colombia, 1975.

4.25 R. R. Williamson, Quoted in A. Chavez, La Nutrición en la Practica Médica, *Revista Salud Publica de México*, Vol. VII, No. 1, February 1965.

4.26 *International Classification of Diseases*, Eighth Revision, World Health Organization, Geneva, 1965.

4.27 A. B. Christie, *Infectious Diseases-Epidemiology and Clinical Practice*, Second Edition, Churchill-Livingstone, London, 1974.

4.28 A. Fourrier, La Rougeole. In R. Bastin, *Maladies Infectieuses*, Flammarion, Paris, 1971.

4.29 L. J. Mata and W. P. Faulk, Respuesta inmune del desnutrido con especial referencia al sarampion, *Boletin de la Organización Panamericana de la Salud*, Vol. 77, No. 5.

4.30 F. E. Viteri and M. Béhar, Efectos de diversas infecciones sobre la nutrición del niño preescolar, especialmente al sarampión. *Boletin de la Organización Panamericana de la Salud*, Vol. 78, No. 3, March 1975.

4.31 M. C. Lathman, Nutrition and infection in national development, *Science*, May 9, 1975.

4.32 N. S. Scrimshaw, C. E. Taylor and J. F. Gordon, Interactions of nutrition and infection, *WHO Monographs*, Series 57, Geneva, 1968.

4.33 R. Martorell, *et al.*, Normas antropométricas de crecimiento físico para paises en desarrollo nacionales o internacionales, *Boletin de la Organización Panamericana de la Salud*, Vol. 79, No. 6, December 1975.

4.34 C. Perez Hidalgo, A. Chavez and L. J. Fajardo, Peso y Talla en un gruop de niños de diferente nivel económico, *Salud Publica de Mexico*, Vol. 7, No. 4, July–August 1965.

4.35 K. Bagchi, *Applied Nutrition in the Sudan*. EM/NUTR/65 SUDAN 5601, United Nations Development Programme, May 1974.

4.36 Situación Nutritional y Alimentaria en los paises de America Latina y el Caribe, *Boletin de la Organización Panamericana de la Salud*, June 1976.

4.37 *The Fourth World Food Survey*. United Nations Food and Agricultural Organization, Rome, 1977.

4.38 M. Béhar, Nutrition and the future of mankind, *International Journal of Health Services*, 6(2): 315–320, 1976.

4.39 *The State of Food and Agriculture, 1975* United Nations Food and Agricultural Organization, Rome, 1976.

CHAPTER 5

A Structural Approach for Diagnosing the Impact of Climatic Anomalies

"DROUGHT AND MAN" was intended as a study focused on the social, economic and political impact of a specific type of climatic fluctuation known as drought. This formulation, simple, direct and innocent in appearance may, however, lead to misunderstandings. One obvious interpretation is that drought is a purely natural phenomenon, independent of society, which is in turn the victim of its occurrence. Were this the case, we should have, on the one hand, a physical agent operating on a certain territory and, on the other hand, a society receiving its impact. This scheme has been questioned by many authors. We believe, however, that the criticism has very seldom been pushed sufficiently far to identify clearly the weakness in the argument, and to point the way to a more adequate methodology.

An increasing number of ecologists and economists are becoming aware of the role of socio-economic factors in some processes leading to a deterioration of the environment as, for instance, in the case of desertification. However, conflicts between man and nature, presented as an ecological problem on the one hand, and as a socio-economic problem on the other, have more often than not been approached as if both components were autonomous. Ecologists—even those using the most sophisticated models—as well as sociologists and economists, deal with the symmetrical problem (i.e. the socio-economic problem for the ecologists, and the ecological problem for the sociologists and the economists) as something injected from outside into their models. But the two problems are only two aspects of a complex situation which may be better described with reference to the internal interactions within an all embracing *system*. For here, we are evidently faced with a type of phenomenon where causes and effects, interactions and inversions, linear chains and feed-backs are mixed in an integrated, complex whole. The soil of a certain territory, the atmosphere above it, and the human settlements located and working on it, are not entities to be considered in isolation. They cannot be studied independently of each other, nor can the results be assembled in a unidirectional explicative scheme. They constitute a totality, a single system; they are only "parts" or "elements" or "components" interacting all the time within the system.

We may analyze the components of the system in quite different ways, each component being itself a sub-system which has, at a certain moment, a given structure and a varying number of constituant parts.

In a first approximation, we may consider the whole system as constituted by four components or sub-systems which for the purposes of this discussion we call:

(a) A *physical component*, which we shall refer to here as the "atmosphere".*

(b) A *physico-biological component*, briefly called the "soil" (including the basic physico-chemical structure and the recycling of nutrients by the natural fauna and flora).

(c) A *man-generated biological component*.

(d) A *socio-economic component*, which we shall designate as "human activities".

The four components are inter-related in the way shown in Fig. 1. The diagram represents the set of interactions which determine the state of the system at a given moment. Some of the interactions, represented by double arrows in the diagram, such as those between human activities and the biological sub-system, are rather obvious. The cycles (a) and (b) are perhaps less obvious.

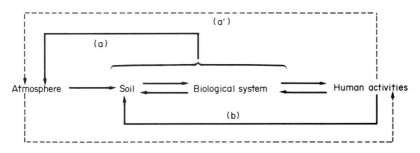

FIG. 1. Inter-relations and cycles among the components of an integrated ecological system

Cycle (a) represents the interdependence between the soil and its vegetation cover, considered to be a unit, and the atmosphere. The upper branch refers to feedback processes such as those originating in modifications of the albedo (Charney's theory, see discussion in Chapter 9 of Volume 1).

Cycle (b) takes into account the modification of the soil resulting from human activity. A typical example may be certain cases of salinization processes produced by irrigation.

As a result of this double cycle, the soil receives water from the atmosphere, but its accumulation and distribution capability is conditioned by the biological system as well as by the way humans use the soil. In turn, the soil surface may induce changes in the field of motion of the atmosphere above it which may either favour or oppose cloud formation and precipitation. The biological system, which emerges in equilibrium with certain conditions of water accumulation and distribution and certain soil properties, constitutes, together with the soil, a single entity interacting with the atmosphere, on the one hand, and establishing the production options open to human activities, on the other.

Cycle (a') represents the direct action of man on the atmosphere leading to changes in the composition (e.g. increase in CO_2), which modify the radiation

* A more complete discussion of the climate system, of which the atmosphere is just one part, is found in Chapter 9 of Volume 1.

balance and may lead to significant changes in the atmospheric circulation and thus alter climatic conditions.

A change in the system may therefore be generated in any sub-system, and lead to modifications in all the other components through the chain of interactions and positive or negative feedbacks.

Our specific problem can therefore be formulated as an analysis of the conditions under which a system of interactions and cycles remains unchanged or undergoes significant changes. But an adequate integration of physico-biological and socio-economic factors in a coherent system, with an internal dynamics determined by the actual interactions among its components, has proved to be a difficult task.

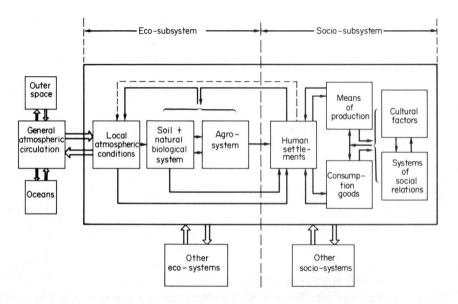

FIG. 2. A socio-ecosystem as an open system with in- and outflows

Current methods of system analysis do not carry us far enough. It also should be kept in mind that numerical models are not explanatory models. They are only research tools to investigate possible explanatory mechanisms of a given process, to make long and inter-related calculations too tedious to do by hand.

There is, however, another way of looking at the problem and we shall deal with it below.

A second approximation to a model of interactions in a complex system formed by a natural and a social environment, requires a higher degree of desegregation of the component units. The definition of the system itself also requires more detailed consideration. The following explanations refer to Fig. 2.

It should first be emphasized that the definition of a system is somewhat arbitrary. It may refer to a country, or to a region within a country, or to a continental region including more than one country. Sometimes it is useful to consider a system which coincides with a geographical area, having an identifiable ecological, economic or political unity. A more structural characterization of a system is however preferable, and will be given below.

The large rectangle in Fig. 2 represents the boundaries of a given system, however it may be defined. We shall call this system a *socio-ecosystem*. In an earlier version, we used the expression ecosystem, in an extended sense, to refer to the whole system. Although we would prefer to keep this terminology, we found it liable to lead to misunderstandings. Ecosystems are therefore considered, in this report, in the narrower sense, as sub-systems of the whole system.

The human activities of Fig. 1 have been spelled out in their various components, going down to the system* of social relations and to the cultural factors, which determine production relations, utilization of certain means of production, consumption habits, and so on, and in turn, are modified by them.

At the other end of the diagram, it is shown how the local atmospheric conditions (local climate) are the result of a quite complex set of inter-relations.

The double arrows indicate the interactions of the given system with other systems. The latter will be called, briefly, "the external world". These interactions are fluxes entering the system or coming out of it. It may be fluxes of matter such as air masses, running water, products, migrations of animals or people, etc. Or fluxes of energy in any of its forms. Variations of these fluxes will be called external fluctuations or external perturbations.

There are also sources and sinks inside the system: population changes (people die, children are born); political and economic power may be displaced, changing production patterns for instance; and so on. Variations of all these factors will be called internal fluctuations or internal perturbations.

The complexity of a given system depends quite obviously on the kind of its components. For instance, the ecological sub-system may be richer or poorer, in any sense of these words. But it also depends on the kind of inter-relations among the components. In fact, it is through the set of all inter-relations among the components that a system is defined as such. They determine the structure of the system. They provide the criterion to consider a set of elements as components of one entity having the "unity" referred to above which is necessary for identifying it as a single system.

A socio-ecosystem is therefore a single entity which is characterized by a number of components having among them a definite set of internal relations that define its structure, and which is in relation with other systems through exchanges (fluxes) of matter, energy, etc. The emphasis here is on the structure, rather than on the components themselves. As a structured entity, the system has properties which do not result from a simple addition of all component properties. In fact, the most significant aspects of the evolution of a system are the changes in its structural properties. This is an essential point to which we shall return.

In order to clarify the assertions made above, we now need to make a brief incursion into a theoretical approach to the dynamics of systems which, as

---

* The use of the word "system" to refer to this sub-sub-system does not present any ambiguity. We follow here the common practice in set theory where a sub-set is also called a set, so that one may talk without ambiguity about "the set of sets such that . . ." or "a set of sub-sets such that . . .".

indicated below,* departs from the current methods of system analysis. Recent advances in several fields dealing with the evolution of natural systems—covering a wide range of disciplines including biology, physicochemistry, fluid dynamics, populations dynamics—have led us to a much deeper understanding of their dynamic properties. The theories which have been developed in this connection now offer a new conceptual framework to approach the analysis of highly complex systems such as those we are dealing with.

We shall introduce a certain basic terminology, borrowed from thermodynamics, which will help to fix ideas. From a thermodynamic point of view, systems are classified in three broad categories: *isolated* systems, confined within boundaries that do not allow exchanges of either matter or energy with their environment; *closed* systems, exchanging only energy with their environment; and *open* systems, exchanging both matter and energy. Classical thermodynamic theory deals only with isolated or closed physical or physiochemical systems. The theory is mainly concerned with systems that, starting from a given initial state (defined by the values of the state variables) evolve towards steady state conditions, i.e. they go asymptotically towards a certain state, the properties of which do not change with time (equilibrium conditions). Perturbations introduced into the system, i.e. departures from equilibrium conditions may be such that the system returns to equilibrium by a succession of states which repeat in reverse order the changes produced by the perturbations. The system is said to have undergone a reversible process. Classical thermodynamics is by and large a thermodynamics of reversible processes. Strictly speaking this applies, conceptually, only to laboratory-controlled experiments. However, it is a remarkable fact that some natural systems, under carefully specified conditions behave as closed systems. Even the atmosphere may be treated as such for short periods of time.

When a system is open, i.e. exchanges matter and energy with its environment, the situation becomes much more complex. It is only in the last 20 years or so that important progress has been made in the study of such systems. Open systems may undergo processes which may be classified into two very characteristic types. One class of phenomena obtains when the variables defining the state of the system fluctuate in such a way that their values do not depart very much from the values they have under equilibrium conditions. The system under these conditions has a

---

* The fact that natural systems can have several levels of self-organization is not depicted by current theories of "systems analysis". In fact, classical thermodynamics also fails to provide understanding for this feature of complex, highly-interactive systems. Classical thermodynamics, for example, through the famous second law, leads to the prediction that, given enough time, systems degenerate into homogeneity. Energy is equally distributed throughout the system. Thus we would always expect evolution towards the lowest degree of organization of the system. The tendency of biological systems to evolve such as to continually increase the ledel of organization had been a paradox. In attempts to reconcile biology with basic physics, Prigogine was led to new insights and new concepts in thermodynamics, for which he was awarded the Nobel Prize in Chemistry in 1977. We may compare this extension of classical thermodynamics as analogous to the work of Einstein in extending the concepts of Newton. The Climate system, as discussed in Chapter 9 (Volume 1) shows similarities to the new thermodynamic structures discussed by Prigogine.

Newton's explanation failed to be applicable to known astronomical problems as well as to later discoveries: atomic forces and the behaviour of particles at speeds approaching the speed of light. Einstein introduced new ideas, which for the case of large masses at moderate speeds, reduced Newtonian mechanics, and also explained the newly discovered phenomena.

characteristic configuration, i.e. a distribution of its macroscopic properties, which is called an equilibrium structure.

A system in equilibrium has mechanisms of response to perturbations. The changes introduced by a perturbation generate forces opposing the changes. A well-known example is provided by the principle of Le Châtelier–Braun: "Any system in chemical equilibrium undergoes, as a result of a variation in one of the factors governing the equilibrium, a compensating change in a direction such that, had this change occurred alone, it would have produced a variation of the factor considered in the opposite direction." Internal responses of this type are usually called negative feedbacks. In biology they are called homeostatic mechanisms, a term which is now being used by ecologists. These mechanisms are responsible for the stability of the system, i.e. for its capacity to return to equilibrium after departing from it.

The second type of process obtains when an external perturbation or internal fluctuations of the state variables occur beyond a certain threshold, and take the system away from equilibrium. In such a case the internal responses arise which amplify the perturbation. The structure is no longer stable. The released instabilities lead the system to a new state of self-organization. The system may thus acquire a new structure which is then kept stable if the fluxes of matter and energy (i.e. the exchanges with the environment) are kept constant. The new structure of the system, which, we repeat, is kept stable by the flows of matter and energy into the system or out of the system, is called a dissipative structure.*

The self-organization of matter in open systems which are far from an equilibrium state is a subject which has led in recent years to very striking results. It has served to clarify the internal mechanisms of natural systems jumping from one state, with a characteristic structure, to another state, with a different structure, in a typical time sequence. The theory of dissipative structures has also provided an explanation for the spontaneous emergence of order in a previously structureless system. It has been shown, for instance, that a non-linear chemical system, not in thermodynamic equilibrium, can assume a very variegated spatial organization and pattern formation and that the introduction of diffusion leads to a spontaneous self-organization process in a previously homogeneous medium.

The analysis of the stability concepts we have just summarized when applied to the system described above (Fig. 2), conceived as an open system, lead to several relation notions. We identify three elemental characteristics of a system:

(i) *Endurance*: the power or capacity which a given system has of undergoing a perturbation without departing from near-equilibrium conditions.

(ii) *Resilience*: the capacity of resuming the original equilibrium conditions after a departure produced by a perturbation.

(iii) *Fragility*: the property of a system that makes it liable to structural changes under the action of perturbation. It results from the combined action of low endurance and low resilience.

---

* cf. Glansdorff, P. and Prigogine, I. (1971), *Thermodynamic Theory of Structure, Stability and Fluctuations.*

The fragility of a system is the manifestation of a property of its structure which we shall call *vulnerability*. In this precise sense, vulnerability is the property of a structure that makes it unstable under the action of perturbations.

A few comments may serve to clarify the above definitions:

—Systems of high resilience and high endurance are only altered under very strong perturbations, but they recover the initial state.

—Systems of high resilience and low endurance are easily altered, but they recover the initial state.

—Systems of low resilience and high endurance are resistant to perturbations, but once they are altered they may not return to the initial state when let alone after a perturbation. They have a vulnerable structure.

—Systems of low resilience and low endurance are fragile, hence they are easily altered, have a low capacity of recovery, and may not return to their initial state when they are let alone after a perturbation. These are systems with a highly vulnerable structure.

To sum up: a system may be more or less *fragile*; a *structure* is more or less *vulnerable*; a process may be reversible or irreversible; for a given *perturbation*; a system may be *stable* or *unstable*.

Let us apply these concepts to the analysis of some concrete situations. We shall first consider examples of processes which start as "natural phenomena".

Natural ecosystems are pre-adapted to climatic fluctuations. There are a number of well-known adaptation strategies which allow living organisms to survive, for instance, through drought pulses: deciduousness, hibernation mechanisms, high seed production in dry periods, etc. Agro-systems, i.e. systems of primary and secondary production created or managed by man, may have only very weak adaptation strategies for surviving drought. However, when an ecosystem is taken to a state of far-from-equilibrium conditions (for instance in the case of a prolonged drought) it may become unstable, i.e. there is no recovery to the original equilibrium conditions. The system may then undergo a complete change leading to the onset of new structures, i.e. new forms of organizations, under new equilibrium conditions. In the case of prolonged droughts, such an irreversible process may lead to desertification. In such cases, however, drought is one of the factors entering into the process, but not the only one.

Processes leading from drought to desertification can be seen in operation generally in territories with limited water resources and large seasonal variability, i.e. in semi-arid zones. Droughts operate in this case on natural ecosystems which are of low endurance and low resilience, i.e. highly fragile. But the vulnerability increases in agro-systems when the exploitation of ecological resources is extended beyond certain limits of risk which would thereby lead to disastrous conditions under a climatic stress. Since the agro-systems do not have in general homeostatic mechanisms to neutralize the drought pulse, they are the first to collapse.

Natural ecosystems, even though they possess adaptation strategies to live with drought, may however, retrograde when the drought brings an increase in the grazing pressure (either wild animals or domestic livestock) on a system which has naturally reduced its plant cover as a temporary adaptation mechanism to the drought.

Let us consider now an example where the "action" starts from the socio-sub-system.

A typical case is when foreign markets and capital investment set in motion certain processes which have a profound influence on the productive structure and "the way of life" in a given region. The starting point may be the introduction of highly technological agricultural activities, oriented to the export market, which take the place of native subsistence economies. The space available for the pastoral systems and subsistence agriculture is reduced. These native systems are pushed to areas of very high fragility where they play a destructive role in the natural environment and generate a desertification process. A dramatic example of this type of situation leading to drastic socio-economic changes in the local population (regression in the income distribution and the social stratification, in the levels of living, in health and nutrition) can be found in the studies made by G. Martins Dias and also by D. Gross on North-Eastern Brazil (cf. IFIAS Report on 'Drought and Man', Volume 1). The advancement of agriculture using high-level technology—both dry farming and irrigation agriculture—has been the origin, directly or indirectly, of desertification processes which have been well documented in the Caatinga of Brazil, in the Columbian Goajira, in the Argentinian Chaco (Formosa), in the Paraguayan Chaco, and in many areas of Africa (cf. J. Morello: "Enfoque Integrado y Niveles de Análisis en la Zona Semiárida de América Latina").

The examples given above are intended to illustrate in what way we refer to the structural properties of the system as a whole to explain the effect of a given perturbation acting on the system. In both examples the "action" starts in one of the sub-systems (the eco-system in the first case, and the socio-system in the second example), but the whole process can only be explained in terms of interactions between the sub-systems. In diagnosing a given situation with reference to a particular system, we have to make a careful distinction between:

(a) The factors that make the structure of a given system as it is;
(b) The properties that make the structure of a given system more vulnerable to certain perturbations.

With reference to (a), we should like to refer again to the theory of dissipative systems. Their essential characteristic is that they are open systems which adopt specific patterns of self-organization structure, as a response to the fluxes of matter, energy, etc. into and out of the system. At a given moment the structure is maintained by the fluxes. If the fluxes are cut off, the system becomes isolated and evolves towards a certain equilibrium structure. If the fluxes do not change beyond a certain threshold, some homeostatic mechanisms may provoke rearrangements in the internal components of the system, keeping the structure essentially constant. If the changes in the flux are large enough, the system will suffer more profound rearrangements leading to new patterns of self-organization, i.e. to new structures. The greater the stability of the system, the larger the perturbation needed to modify the structure of that system. An unstable system is therefore a fragile system which changes its structure under the action of small perturbations. Stable and unstable

conditions correspond therefore to what we called above, low and high vulnerability respectively, of a given structure.

For a given perturbation, the stability properties of the system will determine
whether or not the homeostatic mechanisms will function, keeping the structure
constant. Moreover, once a perturbation is large enough to destabilize the system,
the evolution of the process is no longer determined by the perturbation itself but
by the nature of the system and the properties of the structure. This is the reason
why relatively small perturbations may produce very large departures of a system
from its initial conditions.

*This is also the reason why the methodology of impact studies should be the analysis
of processes and not the description of states*, and these studies must go far beyond
examination of the initial perturbation.

We may now go a little further in applying the notions referred to above to
complex socio-ecosystems schematically represented in Figure 2. We shall consider
two typical examples of systems having quite different structures and undergoing
similar "perturbations" which for obvious reasons we take to be some serious
climatic anomalies.

Example 1 is a country with an agro-system which makes it self-sufficient for
food. It has, in addition, an advanced social organization and a high economic
level. A drought produces a failure of the crops. But the country either has enough
stocks or is in a good position to import all the food needed. Moreover, there are
social mechanisms to prevent side-effects such as unemployment or underemployment, to provide credits for farmers and social assistance to rural workers. The
country as a whole will feel some effects of the drought on the overall economy, but
no direct effects such as shortage of food will be felt in any sector of the community.
The social security schemes, on the one hand, and appropriate technologies, on the
other, will act as homeostatic mechanisms to reverse the changes produced by the
drought and to restore equilibrium when the "perturbation" ceases. The system is
stable. A good example was England in the 1976 drought.

Example 2, is a country with a food-producing system composed of large farms
where most of the labour is undertaken by rural workers on a wage basis and with
no social security schemes. The country has food stocks available on a commercial
basis. A drought or a flood partially ruins the crops. The price of food goes up and
speculation begins. Inflation sets in and salaries remain far behind price increases.
The rural agricultural workers become unemployed. The food, although available,
passes out of the reach of large sectors of the community. There are migrations of
rural workers, to towns or to industrial centres, searching for jobs and food. The
distribution of both the urban and rural population may undergo profound
changes. After the "perturbation" is over the system is not restored to the previous
equilibrium conditions: once the system passed beyond the point of instability, it
evolved to a new form of self-organization, i.e. a new structure.

It is clear that in this example the society did not have homeostatic mechanisms.
The perturbation did not need to go too far from the (precarious) equilibrium
conditions to become amplified by the internal response mechanisms. The society
had a *structural vulnerability*, which has nothing to do with the vulnerability of its
crops to droughts or floods. In a situation like this, if the nutritional level of the
population concerned was already low before the perturbation, the situation may
end up with starvation even though there is no actual scarcity of food.

CHAPTER 6

The Population–Resources Balance

STATISTICS concerning population growth, food production, and consumption *per capita* are well known. When *projections* are made for the next decades, the situation looks dark enough to excite the Malthusians: "While the gloomy predictions of the toll of wars, famines and pestilence associated with Malthus' principle have not come true under present conditions, in a sense we see even worse misery arising from his premise of population outrunning available food supplies, in the form of hunger and malnutrition on the increase." (6.1)

The alarm created by Malthusian-type arguments has been widespread and has produced a growing conviction that increased malnutrition in developing countries is being caused by population growth:

> "During the past 20 years or so, food production in the developing countries as a whole has, on the average, kept slightly ahead of the unprecedented growth in population. This is, of course, a tremendous achievement. But at the same time we must remember that in almost 40 percent of individual developing countries food production has failed to keep up with population growth and in almost two thirds of developing countries it has not kept up with the total increase in domestic demand. Again on the average, population growth accounts for about 70 percent of the increase in demand for food in the developing countries and 55 percent in the developed countries." (6.2)

The basic ideas expressed in the statements quoted above are widely accepted. Taken at their face value they lead however to misleading conclusions. Such is the case, for instance, with the authoritative analysis on "World Food Problems and Prospects", made by the well-known agricultural economist D. Gale Johnson. Under the sub-title "Reducing the Birth Rate" one finds the following statement:

> "The government of the developing countries must be encouraged to realize that there can be no significant improvements in *per capita* food supply without declines in birth rates and reductions in population growth rates. Unless their birth rates are reduced, most of the efforts they are making to maintain a rate of growth in food production of 3 percent annually will simply provide approximately the current level of food consumption for a lot more people." (6.3)

Johnson's position has far-reaching consequences. For instance, he explicitly *regrets* the final clause of Resolution IX adopted by the World Food Conference (Rome, 1974) which "calls on governments and on people everywhere ... to support, for a longer term solution, rational population policies ensuring to couples the right to determine the number and spacing of births, freely and responsibly, in accordance with the context of an overall development strategy".

Similar positions are even found at the highest levels of international organizations. Roy Jackson, in the address already quoted, concluded his remarks in the following way (it should not be forgotten that he spoke on behalf of the Director-General of FAO):

> "Let me re-state the two major points which I made. First, that action must be initiated now to reduce the rate of population growth if we are to have any chance at all of meeting the world's food needs 25 years from now. Second, while family planning and population policy are matters for individual governments, there is at the same time a clear need for international action."

It has already been said that these conclusions are, in our view, highly misleading and this requires some detailed explanation.

The above quotations, together with hundreds of other formulations of the population–resources problem in their multifarious presentations of neo-Malthusian analysis, contain implicit assumptions which are never brought into the open. Malthus himself, a very conscious and clever thinker; regardless of the historical fate of his theory, did start his assertions with some "ifs" often forgotten by those who invoke him.

So far, reference has been made to those who look at the population–resources equation focusing the attention on the population side and preaching population control in order to keep the balance. Other authors, more realistically, take for granted that there is no hope of drastic changes in population growth in the near future and they focus their recommendations on the resources side of the equation: all efforts should be concentrated on increasing food production in developing countries. Perhaps one of the more explicit thinkers in this group is Roger Revelle who was Director of the Center for Population Studies at Harvard University. In his contribution to the Symposium on "The Food–People Balance" at the National Academy of Engineering, (6.4) he maintains that

> "... overall, the poor countries need somehow to find the means to produce food to meet the future demands of their people, one reason for this being that at least for the time being they have very little to export to pay for food from the rich countries".

The widespread belief and hope, in the 1950s, was that the "Green Revolution" would lead to the solution. There is enough evidence today to prove that high technology agriculture was not a sufficient answer to the food production problems of developing countries. This is discussed below. Here we are concerned with bringing into the open the pre-suppositions we find in his quoted statement. They are shared by all those who believe that the food–population balance in developing countries can only be kept by decreasing the population growth or by increasing the capacity of these countries to produce more food. This seems to be very simple arithmetic. We question its logic. Scientists do not usually make mistakes in calculations, but they sometimes make mistakes in the logic leading to such calculations.

The Green Revolution philosophy amounts to the following: Developing countries do not produce enough food to nourish their population. They cannot import from the rich countries either, because they are poor. They have therefore to resort to extraordinary ways to produce more. High agricultural technology is the answer. These four basic postulates are unwarranted. As we have shown elsewhere (Volume 1, Chapter 1) developing countries are as a whole net exporters of food. To illustrate it we shall consider the case of two countries, India and Mexico whose food problems are frequently presented by neo-Malthusians as confirming the validity of their arguments.

India is perhaps the example most often referred to as a case of a country with food problems attributed to population growth. The counterpoint between India and China which is presented in Chapter 9 seems to be clear enough to demonstrate that the Indian problems are by no means the unescapable result of a process originated in an excess of population and which becomes irreversible unless the population growth is drastically reduced. This historical proof would not suffice, however, for the purpose of this report, insofar as our aim is to show that the population/production balance has been wrongly formulated. We shall present, therefore, some simple facts concerning India's production and trade structure which show the myth of India's incapacity to produce enough food for her growing population.

Everybody knows that India is the leading world exporter of tea and tobacco, not to speak of woven textiles. Much less known, and in fact rather shocking, is the fact that India's exports of animal food-stuff, fruits and vegetables, and fishery exceed the first two items. In 1967, India occupied the third place, after Peru and Argentina, in the list of developing countries exporting animal foodstuff (62.284 million dollars or 4.27 percent of world exports). By 1973, the export of animal foodstuff had more than tripled (210.9 million dollars) and was larger than tea exports (186.3 million dollars). The item of "fruit and vegetables" had gone up to 102.8 million dollars and the exports in the item of fishery reached the sum of 88.5 million dollars. Is this picture compatible with the idea of an India desperately in need of "food aid" because of her population growth?

Unquestionably India has a problem in her food trade. But the problem lies elsewhere. Her traditional hard-currency earning, agricultural exporting product was tea. Her traditional imports were, in addition to manufactured goods, food-grains. The progression of tea exports and cereal imports during the seventies is shown in Table 1.

A comparison of the years 1971 and 1974, just before and after the critical years 1972–73, is very revealing. In 1971, India's tea exports paid for 2.1 million tons of imported cereals. In 1974 her tea exports *increased* by 3 percent, but they could

TABLE 1.

		1970	1971	1972	1973	1974	1975	1976
Tea	(a)	205	199	203	188	205	219	237
exports	(b)	196	202	203	185	232	293	312
Cereal	(a)	4200	2500	660	3700	4458	7015	5832
imports	(b)	350	242	82	501	711	1208	979

(a) Thousand tons.
(b) Million dollars.

only pay for 1.5 million tons of the cereals she imported. This deterioration of the terms of trade of food products is a common feature of the trade structure of a large number of developing countries and appears to be the net result of the *new* food policy implemented by developed countries in the early seventies (Chapter 2 of Volume 1).

The analysis of the "Indian case" could not be complete without an account of the historical reasons of why and how India devoted so much effort and valuable land to grow tea and tobacco instead of more staples. This would take us beyond the scope of this chapter, but is an important matter. We shall only mention that such a study shows that colonial and neo-colonial policies, not population growth, are at the starting point of adverse agricultural production practices.

The Green Revolution was thought of as a panacea to cure Indian illness in agricultural production. In the paper already quoted, Revelle makes the following statement:

> "Just to give you some idea of the technical possibilities, at the present time in India, about 300 million acres are cultivated for a population of around 530 million people. The new varieties of wheat and rice which have nothing miraculous about them, but which are simply highly responsive to fertilizers, are so productive, about four to five times as productive as the varieties used in the past, that in India, at least, the total amount of cultivated land could be reduced to about 100 million acres from the present 300 million acres, in other words, reduced by two thirds. This would be sufficient to feed a population of 1.2 billion people, which is about the population expected in India by the turn of the century unless something drastic happens by way of fertility control. This would be sufficient to feed a population of 1.2 billion people at a level of diet twice as good as it is now, that is, with a diet of about 4500 calories per day as opposed to the 2200 that is now available per person in India."

History has shown, however, that this strong confidence in the new high-level agricultural technology was overoptimistic. The new varieties of rice, referred to in the quoted text, failed in India, like those of other crops except wheat, and yet the "Wheat Revolution" faced very serious limitations.

B. Dasgupta, in a detailed study of the Green Revolution in India between 1966 and 1976, considers three different phases during this period:

> "The first phase, from 1966 to 1971, was characterized by a rapid increase in the area under HYVs (high yields varieties), and in overall food production, and a decline in food imports. In 1971, the year the country's agriculture produced a record food production figure, production was large enough to accommodate the needs of the 10 million refugees who came from Bangladesh. Despite the impressive performance of the new varieties in some regions, there was no solid statistical foundation for the uncontrolled optimism of the government in the early seventies." (6.5)

Dasgupta finds here a misuse of the statistical information which, as we show repeatedly throughout the Project Report, distorts the facts and leads to attributing wrong causal relations among events. When the figures are more carefully looked at, the accepted explanations just dissolve. Dasgupta proceeds:

"In fact, the figures suggested that most of the eight million ton increase of 1971 came from states which were poorly endowed with irrigation water and which had not been subjected to the influence of the new technology: Rajasthan (four million tons), Bihar, Madhya Pradesh and Gujarat (another three million tons). In contrast, the production increase in Punjab, the heartland of the new technology, was no more than a hundred thousand tons in that year. The conclusion it drew from these figures was that the high figure of 1970–71 reflected the unusually favourable weather of that year, which showed the continued vulnerability of Indian agriculture to bad weather." (6.5, page 35)

What happened afterwards was a sad blow to overoptimistic views on the "Green Revolution":

"The second phase, from 1972 to 1975, was characterized by unfavourable weather, and vindicated the cautious stance of the Agricultural Prices Commission. While the overall acreage under HYVs increased substantially, yields declined. All the familiar problems of the pre-HYV era, dependence on food imports, harvest failure, and famine conditions in various parts of the country, were visible again."

To do justice to Revelle's position we should point out that he made it clear that technology alone cannot solve the problem. The sentence preceding the quotation above says just this: "The problem is not really a technical one, it is an economical and social and political one". We entirely agree with this statement. But then he continues:

"But if one looks into this a little more critically, one sees that what it really requires is a social revolution, because the new agriculture is primarily market agriculture and not subsistence agriculture. Farmers cannot grow large quantities of food unless they can purchase what the economists again call the factors of production, which are off-farm inputs such as fertilizer, irrigation water, the new seed varieties, pesticides, farm tools and farm machinery, and knowledge. In order to be able to purchase all these things, they have to be able to sell a considerable fraction of their crops, which means there must be customers available to buy these crops. The customers of course will be people who don't live on farms, but who live in cities or in towns and who do something besides farming." (6.6)

The social–political revolution envisaged by Revelle, however, may not be possible in the manner he foresees, owing to fundamental power structures in place and in control. For example, Dasgupta points out that:

"Industrialists in India are deeply interested in a food policy which would provide their workers with a regular food supply at a cheap price, and would reduce the cost of food imports so that more of the precious foreign exchange could be made available to import materials for industrial development."

The introduction of high agricultural technology was therefore supported by industrialists, but with an important proviso: that it would not upset the existing balance of forces in the rural sector. In fact, the Green Revolution brought about a convergence of interests of the two powerful economic groups in the country: "the rural elite which is powerful at the local level, and the industrial elite which is powerful at the national level". In this sense, it reinforced the power of the rural elite:

> "Whatever the influence of the industrial capital and the multinational firms on the formulation of the new agricultural strategy, there is no doubt that its adoption has strengthened the position of the ruling elite in the countryside. Firstly, it has increased the profits and assets, and consequently the economic power of this group (see Chapters III and IV). Secondly, through the new technology a new type of patron–client dependency relationship of the small farmers on the rich farmers has been created for the use of means of production which are owned by the latter, especially farm machinery. Thirdly, the rural elite has emerged as an intermediary through whose hands the inputs supplied by the government are delivered to the village. We have already noted the control of the rich farmers over co-operatives; in addition, in most villages retail shops for fertilizer, seed and other inputs are owned by the rich farmers."

It seems therefore that a "social revolution" is required, as Revelle indicates, but of a different nature, i.e. one which cannot be inspired by the past evolution of the countries which are *now* developed. The history of the relation between industrialization and rural development in developing countries does not follow such patterns.

A recipe which "worked" (regardless of social costs) in the period of industrialization of the leading industrial countries, does not work in today's world conditions. This is the root of our dislike of terms like "developed", "underdeveloped" and "developing". C. Hewitt de Alcantara puts the problem in eloquent terms:

> "A type of rural change which was inhumane, but in the long run efficacious, in Britain or in the United States a hundred years ago, is proving inhumane and inefficacious in industrializing peasant societies of the twentieth century." (6.7)

The relations between agrarian and industrial sectors in developing countries that have started their industrialization process is neither simple nor susceptible of being reduced to general formulas valid for all such countries. We refer to the contribution by J. C. Portantiero included in Volume 3 for an illuminating analysis of this problem in Latin America.

Let us now turn to the second example. Mexico is often mentioned as a paradigmatic case of a country which has reached self-sufficiency in food production, but which later on was forced to become a food importer because of the demographic explosion. The key data generally quoted to "prove" the case is the figure of 2.6 percent, the rate of increase of cereals production in the period 1970–75, as against a population growth of 3.5 percent, one of the highest in the world. This shows, so it is argued, why Mexico started to import cereals during that period.

TABLE 2.

1968	1969	1970	1971	1972	1973	1974	1975	1976
9.1	8.4	8.9	9.8	9.2	8.6	7.8	8.4	8.9

Source: *FAO Production Yearbook* 1975 and *Monthly Bulletin*, February 1978.

This conclusion is, however, just wrong mathematics: it amounts to mistaking the value of the derivative of a curve at a certain point (i.e. the rate of change) for the value of the function at that point. It is obviously true that if both curves continue with the same slope, in the long run the production will not be able to cope with the population growth. So far this has not happened. The figures are as follows: the production of cereals in 1975–76 was 119 percent higher than the production in 1960–61; the population in 1975 was only about 50 percent larger than in 1960; the production *per capita* in 1975 was therefore above the production *per capita* in 1960. These figures do not suffice though to provide the necessary insight to explicate what happened in Mexican agriculture.

By 1945 Mexico imported about 15–20 percent of the internal consumption of cereals (mainly corn and wheat). In the sixties the situation had changed. From 1964 to 1969 Mexico exported 1.8 million tons of wheat and 5.6 million tons of corn. The wheat yields had increased from 75 Kg/Ha in 1950 to 3200 Kg/Ha. The production of corn went up by 250 percent. The famous Green Revolution was in full force and the figures appeared to provide an irrefutable proof of its success. However, in the early seventies Mexico went back to importing cereals. Why? "Population explosion" became a ready-made answer to explain this "catastrophe". The facts are, however, somewhat different.

What happened in the seventies was in the first place an actual *decrease* of the *absolute* amount in the production of corn (in millions of tons) shown in Table 2.

Obviously, population growth has nothing to do with this decrease, since they are absolute figures. Nor is the climate responsible for the drop since 1971.

In the second place, the main argument used by the Malthusians is the changes in the pattern of food trade due to massive imports of cereals starting around 1972. The figures are shown in Table 3.

Are the jumps from 1972 to 1973 and from 1974 to 1975 due to population problems? Not at all. The first difference is 1.373 million tons. But the production in 1973 (10.185 million tons) was *lower* than the production in 1972 (11.549 million

TABLE 3.
Imports of Coarse Grains
(in millions of tons)

1971	1972	1973	1974	1975
0.173	0.140	1.513	1.571	3.065

Source: U.S. Department of Agriculture.

TABLE 4.

	Imports	Animal feeding
1974	1.513	2.436
1975	3.063	3.984
Difference	1.550	1.548

Source: U.S. Department of Agriculture.

tons) by precisely the same amount. The imports were just enough to compensate for the *decrease* in the absolute amount of production. What does the population growth have to do with it?

The second jump, from 1974 to 1975 was 1.550 million tons. But this difference corresponds exactly to the *increase* in the use of grains for animal feeding, the figures being shown in Table 4.

Finally, in 1976, the *production* of grains (wheat plus coarse grains) *increased* to 15.4 million tons. The Mexicans had therefore one million tons more than in 1975. Did the population have more grain to eat? Hardly so. The stocks of coarse grain increased by 300 thousand tons and animals ate 400 thousand tons more.

The use of grains for animal feeding is indeed one of the keys to explain Mexican grain imports. These are the facts:

(a) From 1966 to 1976 the increase in domestic consumption of wheat and coarse grains was about 7 million tons, distributed as follows:

Animal feeding: 3.2 million tons

Human and industrial consumption: 3.8 million tons

(b) The imports of grain were *every year* inferior to the amount used for animal feeding.

The story does not end here. So far, we have only talked about the production and trade of *cereals*. We have already considered at length (Chapter 1) the fallacy of taking what happens in the market of cereals as being representative of the food market.

The total figures for *food trade* shows that the picture of Mexico as a country which was forced to become a food importer (read: "cereal importer") as a result of the population explosion is totally wrong. The trade in the item "food and animals" (FAO's terminology) developed as given in Table 5.

In this table, FAO does not include the item of fishery. In 1973 Mexico *exported* 111.2 million dollars of this item (cf. UNCTAD Handbook Supplement 1977, p. 147). This amount was equivalent to 12 percent of all fish exports of developing countries and 3.4 percent of the world.

It is too easy to jump to conclusions on the basis of the preceding table and play with the idea that food exports have already reached a ceiling whereas food imports

TABLE 5.
Mexican Trade in Food and Animals
(in million dollars)

	1969	1970	1971	1972	1973	1974	1975
Imports	52.6	123.5	100.5	182.8	357.8	737.5	815.3
Exports	525.7	521.2	527.2	642.1	712.9	795.3	738.9

Source: FAO.

must continuously increase. This would again be wrong logic. The figures in the table represent *values* in dollars. We already saw in the case of India that the picture is different when we look at the quantities which are imported or exported. The changing structure of Mexico food production, where tomatoes, strawberries and vegetables for export became privileged with reference to the traditional staples which were corn and beans, explains the difference. But this subject is treated in Chapter 12 and in more detail in Volume 3.

Once this has been said, we are in a position to formulate the problem of the food-population race in more realistic terms. It would perhaps be wise to start by making clear what we *do not* mean to imply by our analysis. First, we do not deny that population growth is a problem which should be of serious concern for mankind as a whole and for some developing countries in particular. Second, we do accept the fact that population pressure is an important factor to be considered in the explanation of processes such as food scarcity, unemployment, desertification, insufficient educational coverage, and so on, in some places and some periods of time. Third, we do accept the fact that, should the present conditions continue, the apocalyptic predictions of neo-Malthusians may materialize in a not too distant future.

What we do specifically reject is the idea that population growth is the *cause*, or even *a* cause, of food scarcity for the developing countries, that malnutrition and famines are produced by it; that, in short, *any* of the social catastrophes originated by drought, floods desertification or what not, could be explained in terms of the problems posed by the demographic explosion. Our position is that, in *all* cases, demographic pressure is no more than an *aggravating factor*, an additional burden, and sometimes a trigger of internal instabilities already present in a social system (cf. Chapter 5). This parallels our argument for the role of drought.

Putting together what we accept with what we reject concerning the "population problem", the obvious conclusion is that by proclaiming the control of population as the most important recommendation to be made to developing countries (cf. Johnson's statement quoted above) the whole problem is taken out of focus. One may or may not agree with the view that affluence brings automatic self-control of birth rates. If it is true, the problem will be solved once the other problems affecting the developing countries are solved. If it is not true, some specific action will be required by the governments concerned. But in any case, so-called family planning could not be the starting-point of any serious attempt to solve the problems of the socially backward countries or regions of the world. They have to be considered afterwards or, hopefully, not at all.

ANNEX 1

The Neo-Malthusian Argument and Nutritional Policies

by *Elsa Lopez*

Introduction

The last years have witnessed a growing debate on population problems and on the availability of resources for them—especially food.

International agencies, development institutes, private foundations and institutions at national levels, plus national governments, have called notice to the problem of "the population explosion"—for the gloomiest ones "the population bomb", the "insufficiency of natural resources", the "shortage of food", "the lack of employment opportunities for a growing labour force", the "insufficient capacity of the State to provide health and education", etc. Blame on these situations would be laid on an excessive population growth, and its solution would lie in a reduction of birthrates, through measures that go from educational diffusion of family planning methods, all the way to more or less compulsive mass sterilizations.

The objective of this work is a discussion of some of the observations previously mentioned. For this purpose, the problem of population vs. resources will be placed in a framework which is closer to objective reality, by attempting to make implicit those sometimes *a priori* premises which form the foundation for the observations just mentioned.

It has been repeatedly stated that the underdeveloped countries have failed in their attempt to produce food in a sufficient quantity to feed their populations. This is a statement that cannot be sustained in the light of statistics of food production which have been analyzed in Volume 3 of this Project. The present work will attempt to prove that an increase in the production of food must be accompanied by a policy of equitable distribution. Without this condition, any improvements to be made in the production system will not translate themselves into an improvement of the nutritional level of the population. Other aspects to be dealt with will be the problem of lack of food in developing countries, by supporting the thesis that the deficit lies in an inequality of the distribution of income of the population and an agrarian policy oriented towards the "market", i.e. toward those who can purchase food. In many developing countries, a subsistence agriculture—which usually assured peasant families of an adequate nutrition—has been replaced by a commercial agriculture, whose objective is the export of the produce, or its commercialization in the national market for the benefit of small sectors of the local society. This agrarian policy also implies a separation of great peasant sectors from economic activities, in other words, it produces unemployment.

The Neo-Malthusian Argument

The neo-Malthusian outlook arose in the mid forties. It originally expressed an interest in the world's food problems, and then passed on to advocate a policy of population control. Its main line of reasoning was the food population balance.

A current analysis of the food–population relationships on the basis of Malthus' eighteenth-century outlook means mistaking the problem. Malthus' model did not contemplate the decrease in fertility which operated in the European countries from the nineteenth century onwards, or the technological improvements in agriculture. It is a model, therefore, that does not fit into the current situation, and is not useful for a present-day political economic or social analysis.

Between 1934–38 and 1969–71 the worldwide production of food doubled. During this period, the population of the world increased only by 71 percent. In the developing countries, food production increased by 112 percent while population increased by 97 percent. (6.8) These overall figures do not justify a description of a Malthusian situation as having taken shape in the world or in the developed countries.

Behind a neo-Malthusian line of argument, there lies an acceptance of the political, social and economic system that prevails in capitalist countries or, at the least, a non-critical attitude towards it, which is usually shrouded in a cloak of scientific objectivity. An analysis of demographic growth in an independent fashion from other problems affecting humanity means a limitation in both the observation and in the subsequent expression of recommendations to solve the problems involved.

A neo-Malthusian approach supposes two kinds of human beings. On the one hand, in the developed world, people have work, eat more than adequately, receive education during decades and live in comfortable houses. The underdeveloped world exhibits also, in small numbers, this kind of human being. But there are also those—the great majority—who possess nothing, because they cannot even have the product of their labour, as there is no room for them in the productive system of their countries. They are marginal to development, and they are also marginal to consumer markets, and to welfare. They suffer hunger and die in large numbers from preventable diseases.

Neo-Malthusian arguments point to a lack of land in relationship to population in the developing countries, and it is useful to recall that population density in the developed countries of Europe is much higher than in the developing countries of Latin America and Africa. (6.9) Landholding patterns would be more important. A FAO report on landholding (6.10) has estimated that the changes which took place during the First Development Decade had a limited scope, and were not oriented towards an improvement in the lot of rural populations. No efforts were made to integrate the rural masses to development, and most of the changes which took place in agrarian structures were the result of attempts to achieve economic development. This was largely implemented through a stimulation of large-scale modern enterprises, and also of multinational agricultural enterprises which reinforced the position of large entrepreneurs at the cost of rural labourers. According to Iftikhar Ahmedd, (6.11) the rural structures, which prevail in underdeveloped countries limit the access to technology to a privileged rural group, composed of large landholders.

Two researchers whom Ahmedd quotes, Berry and Clive, refer to a number of surveys carried out in India, Pakistan, the Philippines, Colombia and Brazil. They point out that yield per unit of land declines as the size of the holding increases. This was confirmed by Leith Griffin for Sri Lanka, Thailand and Indonesia. This is easily explained because in small parcels yield may become high because of a high concentration of human labour. Larger parcels must be worked by machines. Thus, it cannot be inferred that big agriculturalists, with a greater access to resources and technology, would necessarily increase yield. In fact it has been shown that new technology has brought almost no change in the relationship between unit size and productivity of the soil. Use of agrarian technology is closely related with the dominant agrarian structures in the developing countries, thus making agrarian reform a pre-requisite for a satisfactory level of efficiency, and to prevent unacceptable income differences. This is not, however, the only requisite or even the most important one. Control and commercialization of production also constitute key elements to be taken into account. A report from the U.S. CIA (6.12) maintains that, if population grows according to projections, two types of problem have to be solved: on one hand an additional production of food, on the other hand the physical, administrative and political problems of distribution. Apparently the CIA has not taken into account the most important element of the problem of distribution of food: namely who controls the national and international market.

Barraclough states (6.13) that by the end of the seventies it will no longer be possible to sustain the myth that poverty and malnutrition in the poor countries are the direct result of their vast population growth and of use of backward technology. This myth implies a belief that a reduction of demographic growth and the use of a sophisticated technology could permit the elimination of the problem.

In Chile, and quoting from the same source, (6.13) population rates of growth have shown a decrease in recent years. Chile also underwent a rapid urbanization and education levels are relatively high. After 1973 investments by multinational agroindustry have been encouraged. Any yet *per capita* agricultural production hardly exceeded population growth, and in fact the nutrition of sectors with less purchasing power deteriorated.

The case of Puerto Rico is also enlightening. Its population has not increased— mainly due to a massive emigration to the U.S. Education levels are among the highest in Latin America. The amount of investments by transnational agrobusinesses have been massive, responding to tax benefits and lower salaries than those paid elsewhere.

In spite of all these facts, agrarian productivity has been descending since the 1930s. Since 1967 the cultivated area decreased by 39 percent, and in 1976 more than half of the population was benefitting from the programme of U.S. subsidies, because their incomes were below the level of U.S. poverty. (6.13)

Nutritional Policies and Nutritional Levels

In general, any agricultural policy that emphasizes the consumption of animal instead of vegetable products implies an inefficient use of resources; the nearer to the end of the "food chain" that human consumption takes place, the greater the waste of energy of the overall system. This has already been presented in Chapter 2. "Consider the fact that the absorption of 10,000 pounds of radiolaria generate 1000 pounds of plankton, that 1000 pounds of plankton generate 100 pounds of small marine animals, that those in turn create 10 pounds of fish, and that 10 pounds of fish are required to "place" one pound of muscle tissue in a human being. The friction losses of the system are simply overwhelming". (6.14)

A similar example can be cited with respect to the consumption of animal proteins: the diet of a U.S. citizen, measured in direct calories is only about a third greater than that of an Indian. However, the fact that the U.S. diet is composed to a large extent of animal products—meat, milk, cream, etc.—compels every U.S. citizen to consume indirectly 11,886 calories per day, which have been utilized in the vital cycle of the animals involved. (Chapter 2) Annual consumption of beef in the U.S. increased from 55 pounds per person in 1940 to 117 pounds per person in 1972. (6.12)

There are no medical or nutritional reasons for this overconsumption of animal products: as Chapter 2 shows, the current tendencies among nutritionists is to play down the importance of animal proteins in the diet, to obtain the quantity and quality of the proteins needed through a combination of vegetables—such as the maize and beans pre-Spanish diet in Mexico—and to stress the risks which a diet excessive in animal fat brings with it: atherosclerosis, hypertension, vascular accidents and premature deaths.

No nutritional reasons can be brought forward for the trend that the U.S. diet exemplifies, which in agricultural terms means that an almost inelastic quantity of usable land is made to rear cattle instead of producing vegetables. The reasons have to be sought elsewhere.

It would be repetitive to mention here the fallacy of *per capita* statistics in the availability of food as an indicator of human nutrition. Arithmetical means are not appropriate measures to describe asymmetrical distributions, and in many Latin American countries the extremes of income and of consumption of food are very important. This means that "the rich have enough to eat, and can purchase better and cheaper food than the majority of the rich elsewhere. The poor, both rural and urban, must face chronic malnutrition, a periodic physical hunger and occasionally starvation". (6.13)

In spite of the fact that in Brazil the average diet is 10 percent over the caloric requirements needed according to FAO statistics, (6.15) in the Brazilian North-East there are about 30 million people who suffer the effects of hunger and malnutrition. (6.13) See also Chapter 11, below.

In Mexico, and according to studies carried out by the National Council of Science and Technology (CONACYT), it has been calculated that the 30 percent of the population which is the poorest has access to only 6 percent of agricultural production, while the richest 15 percent consumes almost half of it. (6.16) Cuba has a *per capita* availability of food similar to that of Brazil and Mexico. (6.13) Yet, an egalitarian distribution of income since the 1960s has resulted in the disappearance of hunger and malnutrition. Chapter 10 below will give more examples of egalitarian policies of food distribution and of their nutritional and health consequences.

Following this line of reasoning of an egalitarian distribution of resources, Sinha (6.8) says that "the importance of ensuring a minimal quantity of food and the elimination of deaths from starvation can easily be proved by the recent experiences of the People's Republic of China. Droughts and floods have continued, of course, to affect China more or less in the same way as India or other developing countries of the region, but these national calamities no longer lead to destruction or to a massive loss of life. If there is a decrease in grain yields, this decrease is equitably allocated, while in India the incidence of drought falls to a large extent upon dispossessed peasants, and the urban poor."

A further analysis of this comparison will be presented in Chapter 9.

The insistence with which certain sectors see in population control a remedy against shortages leads us to think that what is attempted to control is rather the social change that misery can bring forth. A decrease in fertility *per se* cannot improve nutrition and employment. It is the deeper changes of a social system which determine a new outlook on the priorities of a society and the best methods for arriving at them. A different way of looking at this problem can lead to genocide.

Notes to Chapter 6

6.1 P. V. Sukhatme, *The world's food supplies*, Malthus Bicentenary Discussion on Fertility, Mortality and World Food Supply, held before the Royal Statistical Society, London, 16 February 1966. Mr. Sukhatme was Director of FAO Statistics Division (1951–1971) and his paper published in *FAO Studies in Food and Population*, Rome, 1976.

6.2 *Ibid.*

6.3 D. Gale Johnson, *World Food Problems and Prospects* in Foreign Affairs Studies 20, American Enterprise Institute for Public Policy Research, Washington D.C. 1975 (Second Printing 1977).

6.4 Roger Revelle, *Aspects of the Food–People Balance*, Proceedings of the Symposium of Engineering at the Sixth Annual Meeting, Washington D.C., 1970.

6.5 Biplab Dasgupta, *Agrarian Change and the New Technology in India*, United Nations Research Institute for Social Development, Geneva, 1977.

6.6 R. Revelle, *op. cit.* p. 6.

6.7 Cynthia Hewitt de Alcantara, *Modernizing Mexican Agriculture: socio-economic implications of technological change 1940–1970, UNR/SD*, Geneva, 1976.

6.8 Radha Sinha, *Distribución equitativa: una precondición para asegurar una alimentación minima a una población siempre creciente*, Mimeo. XVIII General Conference of Population, Mexico, 1977. Also The determinants and consequences of population trends, United Nations, Volume I, Table XII, New York, 1973.

6.9 Population density in terms of inhabitants per square kilometer is 27 in Mexico, 12 in Venezuela, 8.6 in Argentina, 6.3 in Paraguay, 4.8 in Bolivia, 14.0 in Chile, 341 in Belgium, 329 in the Netherlands and 93 in France, *Brittanica Atlas*, 1974.

6.10 *The State of Food and Agriculture, 1975*, FAO, Rome, 1976.

6.11 Iftikhar Ahmedd *Cambios technológicos a la Agricultura y el empleo en los paises en desarrollo* (mimeo) XVIII, General Population Conference, Mexico, 1977.

6.12 Central Intelligence Agency, United States of America, *Potential Implications of Trends in World Population Food Production, and Climate*, OPR-401, August 1974.

6.13 Solon Barraclough, *Perspectivas de la producción agricola en América Latina*, Ciencia y Desarrollo, México, September–October, No. 16, 1977.

6.14 Victor Papanek, *Design for the Real World*, New York, Pantheon Books, 1971.

6.15 *Población, suministro de alimentos y desarrollo agricola*, FAO, Rome, 1975.

6.16 *Politica nacional de ciencia y tecnologia: estrategia, lineamientos y metas*, CONACYT, 1976.

CHAPTER 7

Responses to Drought-Induced
National Disasters

In Chapter 5 we put forward a theoretical frame as a proposal for a methodologi-
cally-adequate diagnostic tool to be used in trying to find out "what really happened" in past examples of national disasters attributed to climatic factors. In
Chapter 7 of Volume 1 and in Volume 3, attempts are made to use this tool in
understanding the specific situations exhibited by the anaiysis of case-studies. It
seems that the proposed methodology may also be a very useful scheme to be
applied in assessing characteristic responses, at both the international and the
national level, to food shortages originated by drought.

Any attempt at classifying the countries or regions of the world according to
their type of response to a drought situation ought to be started by drawing a line
that separates societies of high vulnerability, on one side, from societies of low
vulnerability, on the other side. The two examples given in Chapter 5 are, in broad
terms, representative cases of each type.

In a society of high vulnerability, such as in Example 2, drought triggers off an
instability which is latent in the system. The direct effects of the drought are
amplified by the release of these instabilities. Once the system is taken away from
its precarious equilibrium state, the pre-drought situation cannot be restored, even
if enough food is brought to the place, unless the "natural" evolution is interfered
with and structural changes are introduced in the proper places of the socio-
ecosystem.

Example 1 describes, on the other hand, a case of *a stable system*, in which the
social organization is such that it has ingrained response mechanisms to overcome
the effects of either short or prolonged droughts.

The line between the two types of country is not always well defined as there are
several kinds of intermediate stages. More important than that, the line itself, as
well as the position of each country or region relative to it, are functions of time.
The same country may be displaced in either direction at different periods in time.
The Sahelian countries are typical examples of an evolution in recent decades
towards more vulnerable conditions, as it is shown in Chapter 7 of Volume 1 and,
more in detail, in Volume 3. China provides an example of changes in the opposite
direction and, in fact, a remarkable case of a country crossing the line from high to
low vulnerability within an impressive short historical period, as shown by Stavis in
his paper included in this Volume.

The present critical situation of a large number of developing countries, in particular those belonging to the M.S.A. (Most Seriously Affected) group, becomes

clear when it is expressed in terms of *increasing fragility* due to the action of socio-economic factors which increase their *structural vulnerability*. International awareness of the semi-permanent crisis affecting these countries does not go beyond the recognition of certain symptoms, and very seldom is the real cause explored. The analysis remains, thus, at the level of "external" factors. When looking for the "culprit" among them, climate, population pressure and environmental problems come to the fore. The emphasis is placed on the production/population ratio or on the misuse of the soil, and the diagnosis misses the point, as the effects are taken for causes and vice versa. Even when the emphasis is shifted from production to *distribution* of food, the analysis remains superficial so long as the distribution problems are taken to be those associated with transport and storage, instead of those related to the *accessibility* of the food. The actual problem is the *distribution of means* which make the food accessible to people. This has much more to do with the structure of the property, the employment and the income, than with transport.

No wonder that the measures usually proposed to cope with some critical conditions, when the situation deteriorates beyond the limits that the sense of decency accepted by international standards may allow, are no more than palliatives. We have coined the expression "Red Cross Approach" (RCA, for short) to designate these types of measures. The expression is only descriptive and in no way derogatory. The RCA may provide a valuable set of instruments to help in getting out of serious emergencies, to aid people *in extremis*. Our criticism is twofold. In the first place, this approach only provides analgesics. Everyone suffering from toothache blesses the analgesics. But deep cavities in a tooth will get worse, not better, if only analgesics are applied. For instance, in Example 2, above, once the instability of the system is released, the RCA *can* help *some individuals*, but will not stop, nor even slow down, the deterioration of the social sector concerned. This is a structural reason why RCA can be, at the best, of only limited value.

In the second place, the RCA, insofar as it is applied internationally, is merely an expression of aid-programmes which do not have the proper mechanisms to act promptly and efficiently. They are not specifically tailored to help countries, although they do accomplish this task on some occasions. As it is argued elsewhere (cf. Siotis' paper in Volume 3) they are an integral part of the foreign policy of each country. As such, they are directed by political and economic considerations, the humanistic motivations being subordinated to them. In this respect, past history of drought-induced famines is unmistakably clear in showing how the purely humanistically motivated help arrives too late, or never, or in time but hardly in the required amounts, or it is wasted because of mismanagement. Sahel 1973 is a pathetic example of this. The situation differs when there are political reasons pushing the donors to proceed quickly and efficiently.

During the Sahelian famine in the early seventies, the roots of which are analyzed in Chapter 7 of Volume 1 and in more detail in Volume 3, the insufficiency of the aid provided at the international level was justified either on the basis of "late information", which prevented the help from arriving in time, or of a world "food crisis", which prevented the help from being large enough. The first justification has been repeatedly denied by several authors and we only need to quote, without comments, an authoritative statement on this point:

"To the AID and FAO bureaucracies from 1968 onward came significant and ever-increasing intelligence on the catastrophe overtaking the Sahel. The scope, depth and momentum of the drought year by year were methodically recorded in the annual public reports by AID on disaster relief. The 1969 report spoke of the 'prolonged drought across West Africa', of 'drought conditions . . . general' throughout the region, 'complete crop failure' in Senegal. By 1970, there were more than three million people requiring emergency food. 'This was not a new disaster', the document that year explained for Mali, 'but a continuation of that which was reported' in the previous report. Famine in Upper Volta, continued the report, 'was brought on by the same drought problem which was plaguing other countries across West Africa'. 'Hunger, if not starvation, has become increasingly frequent (and) emergency imports have become the rule rather than the exception', concluded the 1970 report. A year later, the description had become almost perfunctory. 'Many African countries are plagued by droughts *year after year*' (emphasis added), observed AID's 1971 disaster-relief report in describing emergency aid to over a half million victims in the Sahel." (7.1)

The second justification has also been disputed, but it deserves some further comments. It was eloquently expressed in the words of Lester Brown already commented on:

"... now, during the seventies, the depletion of world food stocks has weakened both the capacity and the will of the international community to respond to food shortages". (7.2)

We need only recall, to place this statement in its proper perspective, that the amount of grain requested as relief aid for the Sahel, in 1977–78, as in 1972–73, was only 700 thousand tons, i.e. little over one-tenth of one percent of the amount of grain used for animal feeding in developed countries; 2.7 percent of the grain bought by USSR in 1972–73; one-third of the "error" found in UNCTAD and FAO Annual Statistics on grain trade. We must look more deeply for the underlying problems, a point that is one of the main thesis of this Report.

This notwithstanding, the RCA may be applied with great success at the country level, where it may be locally organized and well planned. The Maharastra drought of 1970–73 in India provides a good example. The official response was quicker, more substantial and more opportune than in previous cases of Indian droughts (as compared, for instance, with the 1966–67 case). India did remarkably well in overcoming the drought effects of the 1972 period, which coincided with a year of minimum grain imports and no foreign help (except 1.8 million tons as a loan from USSR). However, she used up most of her stocks of cereals. One cannot help thinking that a more prolonged drought would have created unsurmountable difficulties of the Sahelian type. The low level of nutrition of large sectors of the population would not tolerate any reduction in the diet and, after the depletion of her stocks, the country would have been left at the mercy of international aid. . . . . There is little doubt that this would have been the case. Why is this so? The various answers one finds everywhere are merely variations on the same theme: overpopulation. The country, so it is held, can barely produce enough to keep up with the population increase; any crop failure would quickly eat up the meagre stocks. And yet, as we have pointed out in Chapter 6, India is a *net exporter* of food! The appalling low level of nutrition in large sectors of her population is not reflecting a lack of capacity of her agricultural system to produce enough food to cover her needs. What is here at stake is rather the *structure* of production, distribution and trade. Once again the vulnerability to drought is a property of the whole system and cannot be explained away by referring to the *direct* "impact" of a drought on the crops.

It is clear that as the world's productive forces increase—as exemplified by an increased production of foodstuff, by an improvement in the communication network, and by quicker facilities for transporting such a bulky commodity as food over long distances—it can be expected that the RCA will be increasingly efficient, and that its defenders will point out this fact to justify its conceptual usefulness. But we need to go a little further.

It has been said that drought was the best possible thing that could have happened to a Maharastra peasant in 1970: he started participating in a work programme, his village probably had a water tank built, his cattle were provided with fodder, he was provided with cheap food. The same peasant, after the drought was over, saw himself go back to pre-drought normal conditions which were bad and now probably worsening. The normal condition is endemic malnutrition, with or without a water tank.

The RCA, even at its best, could not prevent the spectacle of a world in which drought victims are looked after, but their fate before and after the drought continues to deteriorate, and in which, for example, the world's *stable* death toll from malnutrition is probably higher, by a factor of ten or twenty, than that caused by the sum of all droughts. No one would expect the RCA to solve this problem.

One would expect, however, that malnutrition, being the background situation where severe droughts get most of their victims, would bring at least as much world attention as the drought victims themselves. This is certainly not the case—except in some periods and for other reasons already referred to (cf. Chapter 3 above)—and this is not a minor subject within the context of our analysis. Any attempt to clarify this issue should enter deeply into the roots of problems such as "development" and "underdevelopment", should take the pieces of the so-called "international economic order" apart, should exhibit the myth and the real meaning of "interdependency". All this goes beyond the scope of our study. But the problems lie there. Without this frame of reference we cannot hope to draw near to our goal, which is to disentangle the social, economic and political reasons for the catastrophic effects of climatic anomalies (or, for that matter, any other "natural disaster") on certain countries or regions of the world. In this connection, the "case studies" presented in this Volume and in Volume 3 undertake the task of determining diagnostically the long causal-chains, the last link of which is a certain number of people, especially children dying of malnutrition.

The neglect of a permanent low level of nutrition as a precondition of the famines triggered by natural phenomena leads to typical distortions in the way any such a catastrophe is accounted for. In this respect Dr. Banerji, in his contribution to this Volume (Chapter 9) presents a very disturbing picture. He suggests that a new pattern is emerging in the treatment of victims of drought *vis-à-vis* victims of malnutrition: while the former would be dealt with in an increasingly efficient way, through RCA measures, the latter would be kept, without help, at a level of bare physical survival, and they ultimately may die of malnutrition-related diseases. The defenders of the RCA will have reasons to be highly satisfied: they may be able to show that no lives are lost in droughts. Though this may happen, the history of drought-induced famines will not end in this simple manner. Unless structural measures are taken, the social conditions of the countries concerned will keep deteriorating. The structure of the social system will become more unstable, and the instability triggered off by a drought will reach beyond the control of the RCA measures, which, at this point, will prove powerless. Evidence is supplied in Chapter 7 of Volume 1 to show that the Sahelian countries have reached this stage.

A typical Malthusian–RCA attitude considers that unless there is a drastic way of controlling population, nothing can be done, except helping *some* people in emergency situations. The extreme form of this position goes as far as suggesting a "triage" method. This method was invented by military health services under war conditions and it has found widespread application each time the amount of wounded people exceeded the capacity of the available medical infrastructure. In such circumstances the wounded were to be divided into three categories:

(a) those who were to succumb regardless of any amount of care;
(b) those who were to survive only if adequate care was provided; and
(c) those who were to manage to survive anyhow.

The *help* only goes to those of the second category.

Countries, and societies within certain countries, should be divided, according to this view, into three corresponding categories. Only the second should receive any "aid".

There is, however, an anti-Malthusian–RCA based on the growing conviction that human malnutrition and its aggravation under "climatic stress" are eminently preventable: current agricultural resources available in the world could eradicate them if they were equitably distributed. Some of the figures, already given in previous chapters, provide strong support for this line of argument. We shall mention only a few:

(a) The estimates made by FAO* of the total annual "caloric deficit" in the developing countries is based on the difference between the country's supply and the needs *per capita*. For the 1972–74 period, the figures are as follows (7.3) (72 developing countries, excluding centrally planned economies in Asia):

> *Deficit in calories* (daily):   320 thousand million
> *Equivalent in wheat*:   37 million tons
> (315 calories = 100 gr. of wheat)

(b) The figures given above represent about 3 percent of the total *grain* production in the world.

(c) During the same period the amount of cereals used for animal feeding in the developed countries, per year, was 416 million tons (one-third of the total production). The developing countries themselves utilized 41 million tons of cereals for animal feeding.

* FAO, The Fourth World Food Survey, 1977.

(d) On average, U.S. citizens, whose diet contains a high percentage of animal food, utilize daily 11,886 calories, out of which a considerable proportion has gone through the animal cycle; while the citizens of India have, on average, a daily consumption of 2636 calories, almost exclusively in the form of vegetables.

It is tempting but unsound to jump from these figures to some "easy" conclusions: the amount of food needed to eradicate malnutrition in the world is ridiculously small as compared with the global production; some countries are overeating; it is enough to distribute what developed countries are eating in excess; animals could go back to pasture fields in many areas of the world, since they are now eating what should rather be used to feed people; and so on.

One finds the above position clearly expressed by Barbara Ward in her foreword to *Hunger, Politics and Markets*. (7.4) After a masterly presentation of some of the basic facts concerning food distribution in the world, she points specifically to the problems we mention above, in the following terms:

> "It is also necessary to point out that they are overeating now. The increase in grain consumption in North America between 1945 and 1970 from about 1000 pounds of grain *per capita* to 1900 pounds of grain is due to a vast increase in meat and poultry consumption—in other words, grain eaten and digested by other animals to produce meat with something like a 70 percent loss of food value along the way. The Indians' 400 pounds—which is grossly inadequate—is largely eaten directly as grain. It is this increased pressure of the affluent stuffing themselves with high protein that has helped to push grain prices up to three times their 1971 level.
>
> "So before we put all the blame for world inflation on OPEC's pricing of its major and often single resource, the peoples of North America, Europe and Russia could usefully ask whether the stomach, too, may not become an unconscious monopolist. The question is specially relevant when we recall that Norway has, for medical reasons, reduced high protein imports, based on feed-lot meat production and that a hardly radical organization, the American Medical Association, has recommended a third less meat consumption for sedentary America. To have obesity a widespread disease in a starving world is itself a perversion of right order. 'Grain sheiks' we can all become, using our appetites to rig the market." (7.4, p. 14)

And she concludes:

> "If the human race cannot agree on food, on what can they agree? If those self-proclaimed 'Christian' countries of the West who pray 'Give us this day our daily bread', are not prepared to give it to anyone else, they deserve the mockery and collapse that follow upon too wide a breach between principle and practice. If those who worship Allah, the all-Merciful, the all-Compassionate, do not spontaneously help those whom their new wealth most depresses, they, too, weaken the ultimate moral cement of their own societies. 'The peoples of the Book' who have monopoly control of what the world most needs—bread and energy—are directly challenged to go beyond 'the idols of the market' and to create instead a moral community for all mankind." (7.4, p. 15)

No one can question the dramatic truthfulness of these statements. And, while we agree with much of Barbara Ward's diagnosis of the situation we do not think that her eloquent appeal to the consciousness of the people strikes at the root of the problem.

There is a profound immorality at the root of the problem we are considering in this Volume, but this immorality cannot be attributed to what powerless individuals do. The real immorality is to be found in the coercion, in the merciless exploitation, the sacking of certain countries by other countries, of certain sectors of the population by other sectors of the population gradually leading in the last centuries to the situation we have been describing. In modern times, there are much more subtle ways of taking advantage of initial differences in economic and political power. The power structure is the true immoral basis of the widespread malnutrition and famines in the era of scientific and technological wonders, and in the incontrovertible fact that there actually is in this present world enough food for all.

This situation is now deeply rooted in a socio-economic system acting at the international level, among countries, and at the national level, within countries. The final expression of such a system is inequality of possibilities *to have access* to commodities, in particular to food. Large masses of people are deprived of such an access, or have it limited to below-minimum levels. Not because the goods are not "available", but because they are out of their reach.

There is still another aspect of the problem which reveals both its complexity and the oversimplification involved in the purely "humanitarian" approached discussed above. The point in question is that confining the analysis to differences among countries the formulation of the problem becomes very misleading. People still talk about rich and poor countries; countries with high and low income; countries with a high level of nutrition and with a high level of malnutrition. It is however a commonplace that "averages" have little meaning. Everybody knows how rich the oil countries are; but malnutrition has not disappeared, either from the Middle-East or from Venezuela. Gabon has an income close to the GNP of France, and yet it has one of the lowest life expectancies in the world (about 30 years). Argentina has always been a major exporter of wheat and meat and yet at least 20,000 children die annually of malnutrition or malnutrition-related diseases.

In fact, the differences found *between* countries are also differences existing within countries. This means, in the first place, that the actual situation is worse than is indicated in the tables of "daily *per caput* calorie supply in developing countries".

The case studies included in this Report provide evidence that an adequate amount of food in a country will not guarantee an acceptable level of nutrition for the whole of the population of that country. The food availability *per caput* in Brazil and Cuba is about the same, and yet the latter has eradicated malnutrition, whereas in the former the number of undernourished people is estimated to be 40 million. (cf. Chapter 11)

The internal differences in developing countries add a new dimension—and a major one—to any rational approach to the ways of taking action which could be suggested as responses to drought effects. In order to focus the problem we shall consider the case of Latin American countries studied by J. C. Portantiero in his important contribution to the Project. (cf. Volume 3) The central hypothesis in Portantiero's paper is that: "Latin American agrarian problems are closely related

to the problems of social costs determined by the path leading to industrialization
(...) and the policies practiced by the State in order to follow this path. (...) This
means that, in Latin America, land and the corresponding State policies must take
charge of the costs of a dependent semi-industrialization process". Within this
general frame, the agrarian sector participates in two quite different ways into the
overall productive system of the country. On one hand, it is a source of high value
currency necessary to import raw materials, manufactured products and technology
for the industrial sector. On the other hand, it must produce cheap food for the
working class, in as much as high prices of food would have a direct and adverse
effect on the minimum level of salaries and thereby on the cost of production. This
double role of the agrarian sector implies that it must adapt itself to a double set of
requirements corresponding respectively to the external and the internal markets.
There is therefore a duality in the agrarian system which results in two quite
different sub-sectors: the "modern", oriented to exports (and production of more
sophisticated food for the urban élite), and the "traditional"—the "poor" one—
which, as Portantiero points out, carries the burden of the industrialization process.
More often than not, the support of the State, in the form of credits and investments goes only to the former. Thus the co-existence of the two sub-sectors and, in
particular, the permanence of the "traditional" one is not due to the "backward-
ness" of the population involved in it, but to the *effect* of State policies.

The relevance of this analysis for this Project becomes evident as soon as one
realizes that the impact of a "natural disaster" on each sub-sector of the agrarian
system produces entirely different effects. This poses a most serious problem for the
Project, because any recommendation intended to reach the roots of catastrophic
effects of droughts in the "backward" sub-sector of the agricultural system cannot
help dealing with the profound *structural* problems of the society, and, in particular,
with the system of internal relations within the trinity of agriculture–industry–state.
The whole problem of development is here at stake.

Notes to Chapter 7

7.1 H. Sheets and R. Morris, Disaster in the Desert: Failures of International Relief in the West African
     Drought, Special Report, the Carnegie Endowment for International Peace.
7.2 Worldwatch Paper 8, page 7.
7.3 "The Fourth World Food Survey", Food and Agriculture Organization of the United Nations
     (FAO), Rome, 1977.
7.4 *Hunger, Politics and Markets: The Real Issues in the Food Crisis,* edited by Sartaj Aziz, N.Y. United
     Press, 1975.

Part Two

Case Studies

CHAPTER 8

The Sahel and Ethiopia

Introduction

THE 1972–73 DROUGHT is still associated with the Sahel, but it was in Ethiopia that its human effects were felt most. Political effects were also salient in both cases; in Niger a change in government took place; in Ethiopia the alleged cover-up of the disaster by the Imperial Government and then its ineptness in carrying out relief measures had no small part in its overthrow.

The two following papers, on the Sahel countries and Ethiopia, place the 1972–73 drought in a perspective which goes beyond its actual incidence. They were commissioned at different times of the Study. The one of the Sahel was the earliest written for this Volume, and many of its findings have now been incorporated into other chapters. Its fundamental conclusion is that the structural conditions of human misery, as exemplified by premature death, high morbidity and malnutrition had existed preceding the drought and were likely to remain once it had passed; and that the data base in those countries was almost completely valueless to measure the extent of death, illness and malnutrition, both chronic and drought-induced.

An analysis of the Sahelian case is the framework within which this study has to be placed. The Sahelian situation proved however to be a very difficult one to analyze, and the structural roots of that situation are extensively discussed in Volume 3. The paper on Ethiopia centres on the "normal" living conditions in that country, against which the impact of a so-called external agent such as drought must be measured. With precarious housing, health and nutritional standards to begin with and with an overall economic-agricultural situation which the same author analyzes more extensively in Volume 3, drought appears as a clear aggravation of preceding conditions. Then, as has been said elsewhere, it seems that "unfortunately conditions went back to normal", unless the change of government which took place in Ethiopia soon after the drought can be seen as an element for decreasing the vulnerability of Ethiopia against natural calamities, as Dr. Ayalew suggests in his paper.

ANNEX 1

Health Levels in the Sahel and Incidence of the 1972 Drought

by *José Carlos Escudero*

Famines, which used to be a recurring fact in history, have been eliminated from Europe, certain other Western and Australasian countries and such Third World countries as China. Chronic human malnutrition, which exists in most countries of the world, is usually limited to varying percentages of the population, usually those marginal groups which are placed outside the economic productive process, and whose possibilities of finding employment, of participating politically and of receiving education are hampered one way or another. The spectacle of acute mass starvation of the type that took place in Africa from 1972 onwards, points towards a discrepancy between the theoretical possibilities of modern society and a concrete failure of that capacity, which ought to be analyzed along both technical and political lines.

Such analysis goes much beyond the scope of this Paper, which will limit itself to an evaluation of the health level of the Sahel countries, prior to the 1972 famine, and an attempt at measuring the effects of the famine on it.

Population Censuses and Vital Statistics in the Sahel

None of the six countries: Chad, Mali, Mauritania, Niger, Senegal and Upper Volta, have ever undertaken population censuses. Their population figures have been arrived at through extrapolations of Sample Surveys with various methodologies and undertaken in different years from 1960 to 1971 which, though accurate in an overall way, do not provide an exact basis for accounting for malnutrition deaths.

As said before (Chapter 4), vital statistics (the recording of births, deaths and their causes) are so inaccurate in the six countries concerned as to be virtually useless. Only a small percentage of deaths having occurred were even recorded, and those recorded deaths usually corresponded to people who had been relatively unaffected by the famine, due to the bias in the health statistics systems described in Chapter 4.

Health Services Statistics

As a theoretical consideration, it has to be stated that Health Services statistics do not reflect the morbidity status of the population, insofar as they only record the

TABLE 1.

Population Per Hospital Bed and Per Physician for the Sahel Countries and for Other Countries, Circa 1972

Country	Hospital beds			Physicians		
	Year	Number	Population per bed	Year	Number	Population per physician
Chad	1972	3551	1068	1972	60	63,167
Mali	1971	3718	1382	1972	135	38,883
Mauritania	1971	440	2727	1973	71	17,746
Niger	1971	2299	1796	1973	100	43,000
Senegal	1972	5453	750	1972	275	14,982
Upper Volta	1971	4875[a]	1174	1973	86	59,792
Cuba	1972	37,276	235	1968	7000	1153
India	1968	325,500[b]	1571	1970	112,000	4795
Italy	1970	568,520	94	1971	99,341[c]	544
Morocco	1971	22,727	870	1970	1163	13,345
Soviet Union	1972	2,793,000	89	1972	634,600	390
Sweden	1972	123,131	66	1972	11,920	681

Source: *United Nations Statistical Yearbook*, 1974.
[a] Government establishments only.
[b] Estimation.
[c] Including dentists.

demand for health services which has been satisfied by a health outlet, leaving aside the *need* for health care which may have been "filtered out" by various meshes (financial, geographical, cultural, etc). Yet, health services statistics are for many countries a useful indicator of health status. In the countries under study they could not be due to the incomplete and haphazard nature of the coverage of their health services.

The six countries have extremely high figures of population per bed and per physician, being among the highest in the world and suggesting that the health system is not accessible to much of the population.

Compounding this overall scarcity is an extreme unevenness of the coverage within the countries. In Senegal, 75.2 percent of all physicians in the country are established in the Cap Vert region, with 18.55 percent of the country's population. (8.1) A similar situation of unevenness of distribution of health resources occurs in the other Sahel countries, the incomplete and maldistributed coverage of population offered by health systems being demonstrated in Upper Volta by the mortality

TABLE 2.

Percentages of Deaths by Age. Upper Volta, 1957–58

Age	% of deaths in hospitals	% of deaths according to a demographic survey
0	26.6	29.1
1–4	20.9	25.1
5–14	15.8	9.6
Adults	36.7	35.8
Total	100.0	100.0

age structure within hospitals, which differed from that which appeared in a demo-graphic survey which showed that hospitals under-represent deaths of those under five years old—the age bracket that is most affected by malnutrition and that the overall hospital mortality rate for the country was apparently 1 out of 25 of the actual one for 1957–58 and 1 out of 40 for 1960. (8.2)

A General Picture of Health in the Sahel

As will be shown later, the real levels of mortality and morbidity in the Sahel countries, and the impact of malnutrition in them, both prior and during the 1972 drought can only be gathered by recourse to a multitude of partial sources, none of which can be remotely said to be categorical. The "mosaic" that appears, even though it is very much incomplete, gives a sobering picture of the state of health of a group of countries which, prior to the 1972 drought had one of the lowest standards of health in the world (Table 3).

As Table 4 shows, life expectancies for the six countries were very low, prior to the famine. For comparison purposes the life expectancies of other countries are also given.

The causes of death in the Sahel cannot be determined with any certainty. The partial studies that have been published on mortality and morbidity have only indicative value and the often mentioned biases against the recording of most deaths and of certain diseases prevent their findings from being used as indicators of what happens to the overall population. A listing of deaths from the twenty principal communicable and nutritional diseases for Mali in 1968 gave first place to

TABLE 3.
Life Expectancies at Birth (in years) for the Sahel Countries and for Other Countries

Country	Years	Source	Life expectancy Males		Females
Chad	1963–64	Sample survey	29.00		35.00
Mali	1965–70	U.N. estimate	—	37.20	—
Mauritania	1965–70	U.N. estimate	—	41.00	—
Niger	1965–70	U.N. estimate	—	41.00	—
Senegal	1965–70	U.N. estimate	—	41.00	—
Upper Volta	1960–61	Sample survey	32.10	—	31.10
China	1965–70	U.N. estimate	—	50.00	—
Cuba	1965–70	U.N. estimate	—	66.80	—
India	1951–60	Intercen. est.	41.89	—	40.55
Italy	1970–72	Country offic.	68.97	—	74.88
Morocco	1965–70	U.N. estimate	—	50.50	—
Soviet Union	1971–72	Country offic.	64.00	—	74.00
Sweden	1972	Country offic.	71.97	—	77.41
United States	1974	Country offic.	68.20	—	75.90

Source: *U.N. Demographic Yearbook* 1974, New York, 1975 (except for the U.S.: *U.N. Statistical Yearbook*, 1976, New York, 1977).
Infant mortality figures reinforce this picture of a high mortality.

TABLE 4.

*Infant Mortality Rates per 1000 Live Births for
the Sahel Countries–Various Years*

Country	Time period	Method of calculation	Rate %
Chad	1965–70	Survey	160
Mali	1960–61	Survey	120
Mauritania	1964–65	Survey	187
Niger	1960	Survey	200
Senegal	1960–61	Survey	92.9
Upper Volta	1960–61	Survey	182

Source: *U.N. Demographic Yearbook*, 1974.

measles with 1683 deaths and second to malaria with 1522 deaths, while the ranking of cases of disease gave the order malaria–dermatitis–inflammatory eye disease–diarrhea and bronchitis and pneumonia. (8.3)

Significantly enough, malnutrition is not mentioned in the list, either as a cause of illness or of death. A list of the principal causes of mortality in the same country in 1972 by age groups gave the ranking shown in Table 5.

In the case of Niger, a Public Health Report dated for 1972, while referring to the fact that 1969 and 1972 were measles epidemic years and mentioning several diseases affecting the country, does not refer to malnutrition in any way. (8.4) In Chad in 1974, a statistic on diseases at time of consultation is given. Of a total of 270,641, the number of malnutrition-included ones is 3330, or a bit over 1 percent. In the same report, mention is made of "a fight against great epidemic diseases", of which several are mentioned, but not malnutrition. (8.5) A report on Health in Senegal in 1973 does not mention malnutrition in the country as a health problem, (8.1) and produces the following morbidity statistics (collected in those Health Stations where the Chief is a physician) Table 6.

The studies presented previously are at odds with the ones that shall be described below on the impact of malnutrition as a cause of sickness or death in the Sahel, prior to and during the 1972 drought; and while a plausible cause of this discrepancy can be attributed to the extremely bad registration of deaths and the very low

TABLE 5.

Principal Causes of Mortality by Age Group in Mali, 1972

Infants less than 1 year	1–4 Years	5–14 Years	14 Years +
1. Malaria	1. Malaria	1. Malaria	1. Malaria
2. Measles	2. Measles	2. Dysentries	2. Tuberculosis
3. Gastroenteritis	3. Malnutrition	3. Trypanosomiasis	3. Dysentry
4. Bronchitis & Pneumonia	4. Gastroenteritis	4. Malnutrition	4. Trypanosomiasis

Source: Ministry of Public Health Archives, quoted in (8.3).

TABLE 6.
Morbidity due to Malnutrition and Related Causes in Health
Stations where the Chief is a Physician—Senegal, 1973
(1965 Revision of International Classification of Diseases)

Cause	In outpatient departments	In hospitals
A 65—Avitaminosis	18,988	1239
A 66—Other ill-defined endocrinous and metabolic	67	13
		648
A 67—anaemias	4282	
All other causes	2,441,159	150,410
Total	2,284,478	152,310

Source: Modified from (8.1).
As can be seen, malnutrition would only account for about 1 percent of the morbidity of Outpatient Departments, and only about 1.5 percent of that in hospitals.

coverage of Health Services in the countries mentioned, it has to be considered also that physicians and health workers in those countries are subject to a particular blindness towards malnutrition as a condition which causes death and illness and which interacts with various infection phenomena to produce more deaths. They are in good company, as so many of their colleagues in Latin America and Asia react in a similar way. This has been discussed in Chapter 4.

An Appraisal of the Health Impact of the Drought

The first figures that strike the eye are the number of deaths due to the famine. Where no censuses exist and deaths are in general unrecorded, it is clear that the absolute and relative impact of the drought in terms of human life will never be known. For the Sahel countries, the U.S. Public Health Service experts calculated at least 100,000 deaths from the drought during 1973 alone, most of the dead being children, while the way of life of two million pastoral people was destroyed. (8.6) It was acknowledged that Chad was the country hardest hit by famine. (8.7)

A World Health Organization Report (8.8) on the drought in the Sudano–Sahelian regions of Africa states that "several million human beings living in Africa south of the Sahara were threatened with famine and even dying of hunger as a result of an abnormally serious drought which depleted water supplies, jeopardized crops and decimated flocks. This famine is in reality the end result of 5 years of gradually increasing drought which has overwhelmed the slender resources of this particularly unfavoured part of Africa". In discussing the consequences of this phenomenon, the Report states that 80 percent of the communities studied in the countries through Sample Surveys showed serious forms of Protein Calorie Malnutrition (PCM) in the forms of marasmus; that the worsening of chronic malnutrition in the six States implied lowered resistance to endemo-epidemic infections and an apparent death rate of 200 or 500 per 1000 for children aged 6 months to 5 years. A comment was made that PCM was not always apparent by superficial examination because the age of children had not been realized. Before the drought, 20 percent of all children were below "normal" parameters of weight/height curves; during the drought 50–60 percent according to some estimations and as many as 80 percent were below them; all in all 40–80 percent of all children were to show nutritional disorders. (8.8)

Another report on nutritional illnesses in the Sudano–Sahel countries (8.9) referred to the existence of both marasmus among children below 5 years of age and of cachexia and nutritional oedemas among adults, and estimated that 1–10 percent of the children mentioned previously had a serious form of PCM.

When the drought struck, a number of special surveys were carried out in the countries affected, to compensate in some way for the lack of a more systematic way of data collection, and they were summarized in a World Health Organization publication. (8.10) These surveys were also compared to surveys that had been undertaken prior to the drought. After stating that "the data available are categorically insufficient to be able to evaluate in depth the nutritional situation in the countries, but they permit to discern tendencies", the report shows Table 7, drawn together from various sources.

Almost all of these studies were done before the drought, and it appears to be quite evident that the nutritional state of children was quite precarious then.

The results of other surveys became gradually known. In Mauritania, a CDC/USAID study in September 1973 among children of 6 months to 7 years used as criterion for malnutrition a weight/height relationship below the 80 percent Harvard Norm. It reported PCM of a moderate type among 13.9 percent of children and marasmus among 4.9 percent of them. In Senegal, a survey among 4849 children of 0–4 years in a Demonstration Area (Fatriek) showed first-degree PCM among 21.2 percent of them; a second-degree PCM among 9.8 percent and third-degree among 1.9 percent. In the Department de Motam 39.5 percent of children of 4–14 years had a weight below 80 percent of normal and 0.2 percent of boys and 1.1 percent of girls had weights below 80 percent of normal. No oedema was observed in children, on the other hand, 3.5 percent of males and 5.9 percent of females in the

TABLE 7.
Percentages of Young Children Affected by Protein Calorie Malnu-
trition (PCM) Before the Worst Effects of Drought Struck

	Serious PCM	Less serious PCM
Mauritania (Modm)	5%	—
Senegal (Niayes)	7.2%	25%
Mali 1965 (Bamako)	3.5%	—
(Mopti)	5.4%	—
(Gao)	4.5%	—
(Jagon)	1.5%	—
(Sikasso)	5.4%	—
1968 (Sanonkoroba)	—	34%
Upper Volta 1971	10 to 15%	30 to 40%
Niger 1970–71 (Health Centres)	—	13 to 38%
1973 (Bamako)	—	38%

Source: Modification of (8.10).

15–59 age group showed oedema, and 12.5 percent of males and 18.7 percent of females above age 60 showed it. Four percent of pregnant or nursing women showed oedema. In the camp at Tombouctou (Mali), in August 1973, out of 38 children, 17 percent had oedema, 14 percent had moderate malnutrition, 27 percent had severe malnutrition and 44 percent had extreme cachexia. A CDC/USAID study in July–August 1973, using the same criteria as that in Mauritania, reported PCM of a moderate, acute type in 17 percent of the sedentary population and 19 percent in the camps. A survey in May–June 1974 reports 19 percent of moderate PCM in the camps and 12 percent in the sedentary population. This study and others noted a steady improvement in the conditions in the camps. In Upper Volta, a survey on the nutritional status and Vitamin A deficiencies among low-age children was undertaken in November 1973. Moderate PCM was noted in 48 percent of cases and grave PCM in 13 percent. Higher rates were observed among shepherds (68.5 percent) than among cultivators (41.0 percent) and in the semi-urban population (43.0 percent) and an incidence of night blindness. This higher incidence of malnutrition among shepherds runs as a consistent line in all studies undertaken. In Niger a CDC/USAID study for August 1973 arrived at the conclusions shown in Table 8.

TABLE 8.
Percentages Below Malnutrition Threshold, Niger—August 1973

	Nomads	Sedentary pop.	Total
North ($N = 251$)	14	3	9
South ($N = 187$)	8	5	6
Total ($N = 438$)	12	4	8

Source: (27).

According to the local population, measles and famine were responsible for 73 percent of deaths among the nomads, and 32 percent among the sedentaries.

In Chad, a CDC/USAID survey in three Prefectures, came up with the following percentage of undernourished population: 22 percent at Manem, 17 percent at Lac and 13 percent at Chari Baguirmi. The publication referred to mentioned that acute malnutrition had been frequent in 1973, becoming less so in 1974, and that diarrhoeal and respiratory diseases, especially measles, played an important role in the appearance of PCM and Vitamin A deficiency, and that lethality during epidemics was high.

Conclusions

It appears that the 1972 drought aggravated what was already a very precarious health and nutritional situation in the Sahel countries. What the drought did—in countries where the margins for survival were narrow—was to push many people beyond that margin; a quantitative difference which may be very small, in physical or economic conditions becoming a qualitative change in the possibilities of survival, leading to migration or death. Many people died and many more were uprooted either temporarily or permanently.

None of these phenomena can be documented with any accuracy, the statistical systems of the countries having proved completely unequal to the task of measuring the human cost of the drought and famine, as they had also been unable to describe the "normality" that preceded them. (All this irrespective of the conceptual and operational problems in measuring health levels.)

From isolated demographic health and nutritional indicators, none of which is completely reliable, it was possible to reconstruct a health situation prior to the famine which has been abolished for the past hundred years in the most affluent countries of the world, and about which there exist technologies and resources in the present day world to improve drastically in a few years. An extremely low life expectancy, extremely high mortality rates, especially infant mortality, a high prevalence of malnutrition, a high incidence of infectious and parasitic diseases which interact with it—and which are usually considered to be the sole causal factors of disease and death, forgetting the existence of a malnourished background which is causal to the disease or the death—an extremely low and uneven density of health resources and facilities, form a picture which is typical—even if in some cases it may be extreme—of what have come to be called the Third and Fourth Worlds.

From a study of various National Health publications during the years corresponding to the famine, it would appear that malnutrition was not considered a significant health problem in many countries—this despite a wealth of evidence from drought-induced surveys which pointed to the existence of massive malnutrition.

ANNEX 2

The Ethiopian Famines of the 1970s: Living Conditions in Ethiopia

by *Solomon Ayalew*

The manifestation of the underdevelopment of Ethiopia is the extremely low living conditions of the people. In what follows we will use certain indicators like *per capita* income, unemployment, health conditions, health and education facilities, nutrition, housing and sanitation to show the level of life of people of this country.

Per capita Income

It was estimated that an Ethiopian peasant farmer tilling 1 to $1\frac{1}{2}$ hectares and maintaining a few head of cattle produces an annual output of about U.S. $100 to U.S. $150 at farm level prices. (8.11) From this miserably low level of income he fed, clothed and sheltered his family, paid taxes to the government and if he was a tenant, paid rent to the landlord. (8.12) In other words, well over 50 percent of the produce of peasantry goes to a very small group in the ruling class and the bureaucracy (to a population not exceeding 2 percent of the total), to enable this class to live a life as comfortable as that of the rich in the West and at the expense of the peasantry living a life of misery and degradation. (8.13)

While the extremely low income of the peasants (which is discussed above) can also be observed from the housing and sanitary conditions of the people (which will be discussed below), the declining income of peasants in the seventies was reflected in the mounting unemployment in the cities and widespread famines in the country-side (which will be discussed later).

Housing and Sanitation

Many of the problems of housing conditions and sanitation are well known. Here it should be sufficient to resume some of the main problems so as to show that they are related to the overall problem of underdevelopment.

The majority of the rural population live in a highly dispersed and scattered setting with individual farms, each individual farm being composed of a cluster of some ten or less huts.

The round hut which usually has a single entrance and no windows provides the kitchen and the sleeping facilities for the whole family. Recently, however, with the availability of corrugated iron, some rectangular structures have started appearing in towns, cities and in larger villages along highways. They too seldom have more than one room. The other houses are those belonging to nomadic tribes which are very small in size but collapsible and transportable.

In almost all houses in rural areas and many houses in villages, towns and cities, latrines are not commonly used. Since defecation is carried out in the open fields, this practice is a source of serious public health problems.

The provision of water for domestic use is also a formidable problem. People in rural areas mostly reside far away from rivers—perhaps to avoid diseases like malaria or for reasons of security. In the absence of traction techniques, the hauling of water is performed by women and children by way of earthenware containers carried on their backs or heads from distant places. Thus enough water is not available for cooking and basic hygiene purposes. A further problem is that since the source of water might be a river, a stream, a lake, a spring or a pool in which rain has collected and which is mostly polluted it is hazardous to health.

There are, however, millions of other people who are in worse positions than the working peasants and labourers. These are namely the unemployed men and women of this country whose members are continuously increasing. Unemployment conditions will be briefly explained below.

Employment

INDUSTRIAL EMPLOYMENT–URBAN UNEMPLOYMENT

In the 1950's it was assumed that in the Third World countries the existence of rural underemployment formed a potential reservoir for economic growth of the modern urban sector by outward migration from the agricultural sector without loss of agricultural output. (8.14) It was further assumed that the modern sector would absorb the excess labour released from agriculture.

The policy of import substitution based on the modern manufacturing sector was welcome and was put into practice. This policy did not take much time before it was revealed to be a failure. Firstly, it proved to be capital intensive and labour displacing; secondly, the rate of growth of industry was unsatisfactory as it was confined to the production of luxury goods for the upper class and the bureaucracies. Thirdly, it was mainly dependent on foreign capital and technology, and imported inputs which caused a loss of surplus resulting from international monopoly price dictations.

These general remarks apply as much to Ethiopia as to most other underdeveloped countries of Africa. Ethiopia has pursued an import substitution strategy ever since the First Five Years Plan (a little over twenty years ago) with all its implications with regard to cheapening of capital but with no appreciable increase of employment in industries. (8.15)

In the 1970's urban unemployment has increased, while rural urban migration increased at a fast speed, due to the growing failure of agriculture to hold the increase in population, industry did not grow as fast as in the early periods because the rapid growth of import substituting industries whose temporary success was artificially achieved (protection, exchange rate policy, interest depressing measures) left a series of distortions in the economy and made it difficult for the modern sector to grow as fast as in the early periods.

In 1973 urban unemployment was in the magnitude of 300,000 or over 3 percent of the total labour force. Between 1967 and 1973 unemployment had grown by about 300 percent. This may not still be considered serious when compared with other underdeveloping countries whose unemployment rates are over 15 percent.

Yet such a comparison will be misleading, particularly due to the low level of urbanization in Ethiopia, and the preponderance of a high level of disguised unemployment in the rural sector. Thus when the 1973 unemployment is compared to the size of the urban labour force it comes to 22 percent unemployment rate in the cities.

The estimate of unemployment shown in Table 1 relies heavily on data that have serious shortcomings: The Employment Office as such does not include as unemployed those who have given up hope and do not bother to register, nor does it have estimates of those who are ignorant of its existence. This latter point was particularly significant right after the drought of 1972, where thousands of people migrated into the cities looking for food. Estimates of urban unemployment which corrected the above showed a total urban unemployment of about 500,000 or over 35 percent of the urban labour force. Two-thirds of the unemployed were under 25 years of age and over 50 percent were illiterate. (8.16)

Rural Unemployment

Unlike the urban areas open unemployment is a rarity in the rural areas. The reason is simple: "An economy consisting of self-supporting families each working

TABLE 1.

Occupation Distribution of the Labour Force
(in '000)

	1971		1973	
Economic sector	Employment	Percentage of total labour force	Employment	Percentage of total labour force
Agriculture	6330.0	84.4	7040.0	80.9
Industrial sector*	516.5	6.9	680.0	7.8
Service sector**	554.6	7.4	702.0	8.1
Total employment	7401.1	98.7	8422.0	96.8
Size of labour force	7500.0	100.0	8700.0	100.0
Unemployed	98.9	1.3	278.0	3.2

* Included in the industrial sector are Mining and Quarrying, Manufacturing, Building and Construction, Electricity and Water.
** Included in the services sector are Transport and Communication, Trade and Commerce.
Source: The employment data for 1960 is compiled from two sources. The figure on employment in agriculture is taken from CSO. *Results* of National Sample Survey Second Round—vol 1, p. 31, while those on the industrial and service sectors are taken from MNCD and SA's publication, *An Assessment of Ethiopia's Manpower Requirement, 1961–70*, p. 7.

their own land must always enjoy full employment, since each individual is free to work as long as he considers the real reward he obtains a sufficient inducement for his efforts." (8.17) As a consequence most of the labour in agriculture is idle part of the time. But even when members of the labour force are at work their productivity is usually very low. (8.18) In this respect what exists in rural areas is not open unemployment. (8.19) It is what is known as disguised unemployment which has a far-reaching consequence on living standards as it encompasses far more population than that of the overt unemployment in the cities.

In order to know the magnitude of the problem, we shall attempt to make some estimates. However, estimates of disguised unemployment will face difficulties because of the problem of identifying the underemployed (who despite their low productivity are engaged in some kind of work).

With full admittance of the weakness of such a venture it was estimated that as much as 16 percent of the labour force in agriculture is disguisedly unemployed in 1970. (8.20) Between 1972 and 1974 overt unemployment was no more the exclusive story of the urban areas. As a result of the drought some villages were abandoned, cattle died, people moved out of their homes looking for food. By 1973 unemployment (open and disguised) could not have been less than 30 percent. Even in the present state of inadequate knowledge, it is possible to reach important conclusions about the nature and malaise afflicting the region's indigenous agriculture and the obstacles that are likely to hinder improvement. The theory that underdevelopment (disguised or open unemployment) can be overcome by a stream of investment expenditures (8.21) has been disproved, it being demonstrated that the institutional framework in which agriculture is cast and the international economic order into which the economy is integrated is highly inimical to improvements in productivity and employment. The landlords' command over agricultural resources did not only deprive means for increasing productivity but it also eroded the initiative of the tenants who performed the actual farm work. To this, when the economic surplus (for productive investment in industries) that is lost in international trade is added, the possiblity of development becomes remote.

Health Conditions

As much as unemployment is the failure of the economy to absorb all able-bodied people willing to work, the low health conditions are similarly the failure of the system to afford better health conditions. Owing to the great burden of ill health caused by communicable diseases (like malaria, intestinal infections, parasites, eye and skin infections, venereal diseases, measles, tuberculosis, leprosy and smallpox) and nutritional deficiency which are the ills of underdevelopment (mostly unknown in developed economies), morbidity and mortality rates are high. Infant mortality was estimated at about 200 per 1000 (for developed economies it is less than 20) and life expectancy is about 36 (for developed economies it is over 60 years). (8.22) (8.23)

Although reliable morbidity statistics are also difficult to come by, it is known that many serious infectious diseases are widespread and along with other pressing problems like malnutrition and lack of sanitary control, they result in epidemics. (8.24) These health statistics represent the situation of ordinary times of the general poverty conditions of the 1970's. For example in 1973 it was estimated that some 200,000 people of all ages died from famine and 15 times more people were starved (Table 2) and dislodged permanently from their way of life. (8.25) Therefore, during famine conditions infant mortality will be higher and life expectancy lower than what is shown during an unaggravated situation of the "normal" times.

TABLE 2.
Population Affected by the Drought

Province	Total population (CSO 1975)	Nov. '73	Jan. '74	March '74	Aug. '74 (ENI)	July '75
Wollo	2,216,500	900,000	900,000	750,000	600,000	400,000
Tigrie	1,897,500	322,000	322,000	250,000	400,000	400,000
Harrarghe	2,740,900	220,000	220,000	325,000	300,000	500,000
Shoa	4,587,100	120,000	120,000	125,000	100,000	200,000
Gemu Gofa	878,500	7000	150,000	100,000	100,000	200,000
Sidamo	2,459,800	—	87,500	200,000	200,000	200,000
Bale	767,000	—	87,500	175,000	300,000	213,000
Kafa	1,416,400	—	25,000	95,000	10,000	11,000
Eritrea	2,127,300	—	—	—	80,000	500,000
Illubabor	1,686,600	—	—	—	—	200,000
Wellega	1,770,800	—	—	—	30,000	10,000
Begemdir	1,800,500	—	—	—	30,000	—
Arussi	954,200	—	—	—	—	10,000
Total	*	1,569,000	1,912,000	1,950,000	2,150,000	2,614,000

* Addis Ababa and Gojam not included.
Source: Relief and Rehabilitation Commission, September 1975.

Inasmuch as mortality conditions in general are related to standards of diet and housing (economic growth in general) they are also known to have strong relationships with the state of medical technology and the organization of medical practice, public health services and environmental sanitation. (8.26)

A recent study showed that with expansion and improvements in the efficiency of the health services (including health education and environmental hygiene) infant mortality in Ethiopia could be brought to 61 per 1000, which needs a change in socio-economic set-up of the country, will take a much longer period of time before the economic growth achieved trickles into an improved living condition of the people. (8.27)

More on Health Conditions—Nutrition

The only comprehensive nutritional status survey was conducted in 1958 by the American Interdepartmental Committee on Nutrition for National Defense. (8.28)

The results of this survey showed that the over-all nutritional status of the Ethiopians was somewhat lower than what is required for their level of activity. Using "the Medico–Actuarial Standard for height and weight relations widely employed in the United States", the survey showed that 12 percent of the population was below 70 percent of the "standard weight". The height and weight growth for boys and girls is 2–4 years behind that of comparably aged European and American children.

The average daily dietary *per capita* of approximately 2500 calories faces a caloric deficit of up to 400 calories per person per day. Protein malnutrition was present as evidenced by cases of kwashiorkor and growth retardation of children. Levels of total plasma proteins were high but when fractionated revealed inversion of the albumin/globulin ratio, with elevated beta and gamma globulins. In the infants and pre-school children there were low albumin levels.

Endemic goitre was identified in several areas. Mild rickets was present in up to 30 percent of the pre-school children.

The dietary, biochemical and clinical studies indicate that the intakes of thiamine, riboflavin, niacin, calcium and iron are adequate. Fantastically high levels of iron, from 100 to 500 milligrams per day, are present in the diet.

The dietary data reveal sub-optimal intakes of Vitamin A. Physical lesions attributable to lack of Vitamin A were present in a significant number of subjects. The blood levels of Vitamin A and carotene, however, did not indicate seriously depleted stores.

Biochemical evidence indicates low intakes of ascorbic acid in four regions of the country. Rather extensive gingival lesions were present. Results of therapeutic Vitamin C supplementation indicate that the gum conditions were not entirely ascorbic acid-dependent.

Parasitologic studies revealed widespread infestation among all age groups throughout Ethiopia.

The incidence of dental caries in the Ethiopian population was very low but when present usually progressed to the destruction of the tooth involved. Periodontal diseases were prevalent and major destruction of the gingival tissues was common.

The survey which was conducted at the end of the rainy season as cereals and vegetables were becoming more generally available overlooks the dietary situation in non-harvest seasons (the hungry season). (8.29) This may be part of the reason why the survey showed a somewhat high nutritional status. Should the result be reliable and represent the nutritional status of the population of that time, then current studies which show a lower nutritional status are a deterioration of conditions of life over a span of 20 years.

A dietary survey (somewhat limited in scope) of Arsi people (province of Arsi) in the Rift Valley, in 1971, focusing especially on young children, covering two seasons (the harvest season and the non-harvest season (or the hungry season) showed a very low nutritional status in general and also a great variation between the two seasons. Using FAO/WHO recommended standards for intakes of calories, the conclusion is reached that major deficiencies existed, especially with respect to intake of calories, Vitamin A and ascorbic acid. This was marked during the "hungry season" but also noticeable during the harvest season. (8.30) A similar study conducted in the city of Addis Ababa with a population of over a million gave illuminating information of the underprivileged population in the urban areas.

The dietary intake was recorded during the third trimestre of pregnancy "among twenty non-privileged and 10 privileged primigravidae" in a two-day weighing inventory survey. With the exception of iron and thiamin, the "non-privileged group" had a diet that was deficient in all nutrients (which was their regular diet) with an average daily protein and energy intake below 60 percent of the FAO/WHO recommendations. The result of the survey showed infants born to the non-privileged women having a significantly lower mean birth weight when compared with the infants of the privileged women. (8.31)

Another study, more comprehensive than the other two, and whose results are not yet published (covering 8 of the 14 provinces) showed that diets in general are balanced but are short in quantity. The average intakes (using FAO/WHO standards) are below by 40 percent for protein, by 50 percent for carbohydrates, by 80 percent for Vitamin A, by 60 percent for Vitamin C and by 90 percent for calcium. (8.32)

So far the surveys conducted are fragmentary and small in scope, but they all show the seriousness of malnutrition and undernutrition (8.33) in the population in general and the pre-school age, school age and pregnant and lactating women in particular. These generalities apart, there seems to be a great need to study in regard to the peculiarities of regions and different segments of the population (i.e. cash crop farmers, subsistence farmers, pastoral farmers, industrial labourers, etc.). Such studies are important because there are strong evidences showing that subsistence farmers have better nutrition than city workers although during drought periods subsistence farmers suffer more because emergency food supplies are difficult to send.

Cash crop farmers, industrial workers, low paid office employees, and the nomadic population (8.34) all appear to be affected by a food price inflation that has been sky-rocketing particularly in the last 5–6 years. (Tables 3A and 3B).

TABLE 3A.
Retail Price Index for Addis Ababa
(excluding rent)

Year	General index	Total food
1966	126.8	135.6
1967	127.8	133.2
1968	128.0	132.3
1969	129.8	135.0
1970	143.0	155.6
1971	143.7	155.4
1972	135.0	136.8
1973	147.0	154.3
1974	159.7	163.6

Source: CSO, Information p. 88 (January 3, 1975).

TABLE 3B.
Retail Price Index for Addis Ababa (excluding rent)
Base 1963 = 100

| Major groups | 1975 | 1976 | | | | 1977 |
		1st Q.	2nd Q.	3rd Q.	4th Q.	1st Q.
General index	170.1	193.4	219.5	225.0	236.8	233.2
Food	175.1	207.5	251.7	261.0	273.4	262.2
Household items	179.8	194.5	197.6	201.1	227.5	236.1
Clothing	190.6	207.8	207.0	202.2	202.5	214.3
Medical care	179.1	197.1	194.6	192.9	195.5	202.0

Source: Central Statistical Office.

Health Services

In the discussion of health conditions we have neglected a basic fact: namely that Ethiopia is a class society where each class has its own specific health conditions. Although due to the absence of separate statistics for each category of population, separate statistics were unable to be provided, various limited studies showed that the health conditions of the high class is markedly different from that of the other classes. (8.35)

The health service expenditures, besides being one of the lowest in the world tends to replicate the different levels of health conditions just described. Although, rural–urban population for 1970 was about 8:1, most of the health institutions are concentrated in urban areas serving mostly the relatively well-off population. For example Addis Ababa (the capital city) with 4.2 percent of the total population has 51 percent of the country's physicians and 45 percent of the country's nurses (Table 4). Since over 50 percent of the services are subsidized, it is the well-to-do population, the middle and the higher social classes who are rich enough to pay the nominal fees that take advantage of the subsidies. (8.36)

Education Services

The modernization of the State in Ethiopia was required so that it could efficiently carry its role as a client state as well as for co-opting or oppressing the

TABLE 4.

Percentage Distribution of Population, Health Facilities and Personnel by Administrative Regions

Administrative regions	Estimated population	Hospital beds	Health centers	Health stations	Medical doctors	Health officers	Sanitarians	Nurses (all type)	Pharmacists	Druggists & hosp. pharmacy attendants	Medical techn. (all type)	Health assistants (all type)	Non-medical personnel
Arsi	3.5	1.4	3.8	4.4	1.5	5.0	4.4	2.0	4.8	4.3	2.2	3.5	2.7
Bale	2.8	1.1	3.8	3.4	0.6	3.3	1.6	1.1	—	2.1	1.3	1.7	1.4
Begemdir & Semien	6.6	2.2	11.3	5.0	2.5	7.2	6.0	3.1	9.5	2.1	5.8	4.1	2.9
Eritrea	7.9	27.0	2.8	12.1	9.9	3.9	3.3	11.7	9.5	8.5	7.7	12.4	11.8
Gemo Gofa	3.2	1.6	3.8	4.8	1.2	3.9	3.3	1.5	—	2.1	1.6	2.6	3.0
Gojjam	6.6	2.8	6.6	4.6	3.1	5.6	6.6	3.2	—	4.3	3.9	4.1	4.6
Harrarghe	10.1	9.6	9.4	11.0	7.7	7.2	9.3	5.4	9.5	8.5	7.7	7.4	9.5
Illubabor	2.5	1.9	4.7	5.0	1.8	4.4	3.8	1.9	4.8	2.1	2.2	2.4	2.6
Keffa	5.2	2.7	5.7	6.0	5.2	5.6	6.6	2.6	4.8	2.1	2.9	2.8	3.1
Shewa	16.1	6.8	14.2	12.1	6.2	16.1	12.1	8.1	9.5	19.1	10.6	13.2	9.1
Sidamo	9.1	4.9	7.5	8.8	2.8	5.6	6.0	4.0	—	2.1	1.3	5.8	5.9
Tigraie	7.0	3.4	8.5	6.3	2.2	5.0	7.7	3.6	4.8	4.3	4.8	5.0	4.6
Wellega	6.5	3.4	6.6	7.7	3.1	5.6	4.4	4.6	—	2.1	3.9	5.1	6.1
Wollo	8.5	2.2	11.3	6.9	1.5	6.7	6.6	2.6	4.8	4.3	3.5	4.4	3.8
Addis Ababa	4.2	29.0	—	1.6	50.6	15.0	18.1	44.5	38.1	31.9	40.5	25.4	28.7
All administrative regions	100.0	100.0	100.0	100.0	100.0	100.0	100.0	100.0	100.0	100.0	100.0	100.0	100.0

Source: Comprehensive Health Service Directory (Addis Ababa: Ministry of Health) Table XII, p. 23.

opposing forces. Some of the most vivid illustrations of the growing strength of repressive and reactionary ideology came in the field of education and educational policy. This, which will be shown in an outline form, demonstrates that schools function to perpetuate inequality and to foster a culture of domination of the ruling class and of international capital.

The domination of literary and academic training rather than a vocational training is in line with the failure to create an adequately developed indigenous manufacturing industry. It is rather in line with the objective to modernize the bureaucracy by recruiting civil servants from graduates in the humanities or law.

For this purpose the school curriculums are complete transplantations from the West. This was reinforced by a strict control through the system of licensing of text books to ensure the elimination of any dangerous thoughts and to foster the virtues of emperor worship, tribalism and religious bigotry.

The schools (like the health services) are unevenly developed favouring the urban areas. The capital city alone accounts for 15 percent of the total enrolment, while also three of the fourteen provinces (Shoa, Wollega and Britheria) account for 40 percent of the total enrolment in 1977. To this must be added the fact that as a large proportion of the schools are private institutions, and that many of these are run as commercial enterprises, the majority of the population is thus excluded from the school system. In 1971–72 only 18 percent of the relevant age group was enrolled in primary schools and 3 percent in secondary schools (Table 5). The two universities had a full-time student population of 5200.

In addition, there is wastage at all levels and this denies the optimum use of the system (8.37): of 100 students entering Grade I, 40 enter Grade VII, 30 enter Grade IX and only 6 go to the universities. (Only 18 percent of 12 grades sitting for the university entrance examination received the passing grade.)

With the bureaucracy which is the traditional source of employment now exhausted and with almost no employment opportunities in the stagnant agricultural sector and with limited opportunities in the industries, the school drop-outs join the ranks of the unemployed in the cities.

The records of employment exchange offices for any of the years in the 1970's show that about 50 percent of the registrants are illiterate, some 30 percent with primary school education, about 14 percent with second level education, about 3 percent with technical education and less than 3 percent have university education. (8.38) That is why in the Ethiopian context, expanded educational opportunities meant the conversion of illiterate unemployed to educated unemployed which is more dangerous to the system than the former, and the ruling class aptly decided against a fast expansion of schools, bringing out what it called an educational reform. As it turned out the intention became obvious among students and teachers that the so-called sector review was not just a reform, it was a reactionary attempt to block the rising consciousness of the masses. (8.39)

It must therefore be noted that the educational establishments are part of the overall system that strengthens social stratification; a stratification that is supported by attitudes which themselves have been moulded by the prevailing institutions.

TABLE 5.

Trends in Education 1971–72 to 1975–76

	1971–72	1972–73	1973–74	1974–75	1975–76
Primary government	525,921	556,954	644,998	742,888	774,129
Non-government	191,034	205,732	214,733	216,384	328,002
Total	716,955	762,686	859,731	959,279	1102,131
Participation rate	18.0	18.1	20.4	22.2	25.0
Lower Secondary government	67,747	76,160	84,601	106,338	125,902
Non-government	11,591	14,199	17,138	18,246	14,915
Total	79,338	20,379	101,739	124,584	140,819
Participation rate	7.0	7.4	8.1	10.0	11.0
Higher Secondary government	56,267	66,326	74,662	61,062	87,947
Non-government	5086	4456	6634	3151	2144
Total	61,353	70,782	81,296	64,213	90,091
Participation rate	3.0	3.2	3.5	3.0	4.0

Source: *Basic Information on Education in Ethiopia* (Ministry of Education, July 1977) p. 69, Table 2.

Conclusion

By February 1974 all the possible indicators of living conditions vividly showed that the system had failed to meet the minimal requirements of life. Ethiopia's ailing economy and deteriorating living conditions had deservedly placed her among the 25 least-developed nations of the world.

In the 1970's the economic situation deteriorated so much so that life became unbearable to peasants, workers and to all low-paid employees in government and in business.

—*Per capita* income declined largely because agricultural production failed to match the increasing population; inacceptable for two reasons: (a) no relation between income and population and (b) population increase was *not* the problem.

—With declining nutritional status and a deterioration of life in general, epidemics were common features of the already low level of health conditions.

—Unemployment in the cities and in the countryside continued to mount up.

By February, dissatisfaction against the ruling class became open and nationwide. The agitation that started on 18 February 1974 with taxi-drivers protesting against an increase in fuel oil prices the day before, gave the initial spark that expanded to encompass the city and rural people alike, which demanded major political and economic changes. The decade-old slogan "land to the tiller" came on with increasing pressure and force. This consequently led to the nationalization of all rural land (4 March 1975) and urban land (7 August 1975), thereby ending the centuries-old feudal system of land tenure in the country. (Also ending the political control of the feudal lords in the rural areas.)

This victory, however, is not enough to bring forth a healthy, educated and eventually rich society. So long as the economy continues to be an appendage of international capital it is futile to think of settling social questions affecting the peasants and the workers. The country must also win economic independence in the sense of establishing a control over its own economic surplus for productive capital investment in a planned way. Short of this, the people of Ethiopia will continue to remain poor, hungry, sick and illiterate.

Notes to Chapter 8

8.1 République du Sénégal—Ministère de la Santé Publique et Affaires Sociales. *Statistiques sanitaires et dèmographiques du Sénégal, Année 1973*, Juillet 1974.

8.2 Pierre Cantrelle, Mortalité: facteurs, *L'institut National de la Statistique et des Etudes Economiques*, Afrique Noire, Madagascar, Comores: Demographie comparée. Tome II, Paris, 1967.

8.3 Pascal J. Imperato, Health care systems in the Sahel, chapter 13 of "The Politics of Natural Disaster", edited by Michael H. Glantz, Praeger, 1976.

8.4 République du Niger, Ministère de la Santé Publique et des Affaires Sociales. Direction de la Santé Publique. *Rapport sur l'activité des Services de Santé*, Année 1972.

8.5 République du Tchad. Sous direction de la Statistique. *Annuaire du Tchad*, Volume I, Chapitre IV, La Santé, 1974.

8.6 H. Sheets and R. Morris, Disaster in the Desert, Chapter 2 of *"The Politics of Natural Disaster"* edited by Michael H. Glantz, Praeger, 1976.

8.7 Keesing's Contemporary Archives, November 12–18, 1973 (26192).

8.8 Proposals for a programme to control the repercussions on Public Health of the Drought in the Sudano–Sahelian regions of Africa, *WHO COR*/79.1 Rev. 1, Geneva, 1974.

8.9 World Health Organization Publication AFR/NUT/68.

8.10 "Problèmes de Nutrition dans la Sahel-Situation en mi-1974", *OMS*, AFR/NUT/72, 15 Octobre, 1974.

8.11 *Policy of Imperial Ethiopian Government on Agricultural Land Tenure*, August 1972 (Draft Memo).

8.12 Rents are a fixed share of the total crop. The Civil Code laid down that in absence of stipulated conditions rents shall be 50 percent but the maximum should not exceed 75 percent. *Land Policy Project in Tenancy Reform in Ethiopia* (1964EC/1972GC).

8.13 The land reform has improved the lots of the peasants. Tenants no longer have the crushing burden of turning over one-half of their crop as rent to the landlord. The landless labourers and small-holders benefitted as they are also entitled to up to 10 hectares of land.

8.14 See for example: (a) Underemployment in underdeveloped countries by Alfredo Navarett and Iflijemia M. de Navarette (1953) in the *Economics of Underdevelopment*, edited by A. N. Agarwala and S. P. Singh, London: Oxford University Press, 1970, pp. 341–347. (b) The factor-proportions problem in Underdeveloped areas by R. C. Eckaus (1955), *Ibid*, pp. 348–381.

8.15 The size of the labour force in 1973 was estimated to be about 8.7 million people. From this 81 percent were engaged in agriculture while 7.8 percent were in the industrial sector and about 8.1 percent in the service sector (Table 1).

8.16 *Unemployment Problems*, CPCO, Unpublished, 1973.

8.17 Joan Robinson (1536) quoted in Gunnar Myrdal, *Asian Drama* (New York: Pantheon), Vol. II, p. 965.

8.18 The reasons for this phenomenon are explained elsewhere. What we will be interested in in this section is the magnitude of the problem as an indicator of the standard of living.

8.19 The word disguised unemployment stems back to Joan Robinson who noted its possible relevance in underdeveloped countries, although her first concern was with the wasted skills during depression in developed economies. Joan Robinson, Disguised unemployment, in the *Economic Journal*, Vol. XLVI, No. 182, June, 1936, pp. 225–237.

8.20 The method of estimation is known as the "income approach" whereby unemployment was defined as those earning less than 200 birr per annum. Source: *Unemployment Problems*, CPCO, unpublished materials (1973).

8.21 *Economics of underdevelopment, Ibid.,* p. 345.

8.22 Population structure like health conditions is the function of the socio-economic set of a country. With high infant mortality and high general mortality Ethiopia has a young age distribution. Resulting from this, the dependency rate is high. In 1975 every 100 working persons of age 15 to 54 supported over 86 children under 15.

In contrast in Sweden, for instance, every 100 persons of working age had to support only 32 children under 15 (Source: R. McNamara, *Address to the Massachusetts Institute of Technology*, April 28, 1977).

Note that the productive age in Ethiopia is believed to start from about the age of 15 while for Sweden it is at a much later age. If the productive age of about 20–54 is applied in Ethiopia, every 100 persons of working age supports over 96 children. Thus, the unproductive age group over-whelms the existing productive capacity of the economy that has been produced.

8.23 *Population of Ethiopia*, CSC, Addis Ababa, January 1971, p. 15.

8.24 Solomon Ayalew, Macro-Evaluation of Health Expenditure in *Ethiopia Observer*, Vol. XVI, No. 1973, pp. 205–206.

8.25 In 1973 out of the 4.2 million people in Wollo and Tigrie it was estimated that about 2 million were victims of the drought. In 1974 the severely affected areas shifted from the highland areas to the lowland pastoral areas, Southern lowland nomadic areas of Harrarghe, Sidamo, Bale, Gemu Gofa, Wollo, Tigrie and Eritrea where animal losses are around 80 percent for cattle, 50 percent for sheep and 30 percent for camels and goats. In 1974 the number of nomadic people affected by the drought was over 1 million. Source: *Relief and Rehabilitation Commission*, September 1975, p. 7.

8.26 Ansely I. Coale, *The Growth and Structure of Human Population: A mathematical Investigation*, Princeton: Princeton Univ. Press, 1972, pp. 8–9.

8.27 Goeran Sterky, Degree of preventiveness in infant mortality, in *Action for children: Towards an Optimum Child Care Package in Africa*, Uppsala: The Dag Hammarskjoeld Foundation, 1975, pp. 140–151. A similar observation may be made from an interesting characteristic of a general mortality statistic. For discussion of this, see for example, Solomon Ayalew, *Ibid.*, pp. 204–205.

8.28 *Ethiopia Nutrition Survey*, A Report by the Interdepartmental Committee of National Defence, September 1959.

8.29 The hungry season is one or two months when the previous year's stocks of grain have been exhausted and the next harvest is not yet ready. There are two annual harvests in most parts of Ethiopia, associated with the main rains (occurring between July and September) and the short rains (occurring between February and April). The harvest from the main rains gathered in October to December, and part of the harvest from the small rains provides all the food for the following year. The small rains are also important in providing seed for sowing later on in the year.

8.30 Ruth Selinus, Abeba Gobezie, K. E. Knutsson and B. Vahquist, Dietary Studies in Ethiopia: dietary pattern among the Rift Valley Arsi Galla, in *the American Journal of Clinical, Nutrition 24:* March 1971, pp. 365–377.

8.31 Mehari Gebre Medhin and Abeba Gobezie, Dietary intake in the third trimester of pregnancy and birth weight of offspring among non-privileged and privileged women, in the *American Journal of Clinical Nutrition 28:* November 1975.

8.32 The study covered Zun (in Arusi province), Marimita (Tigrie), Kossoye (Gonder), Haro (Keffa), Ijaji, Addis Ababa, Woloncomi (shoa), Itang (Illubabor) and Shakalla (Wellega). The study was con-ducted by ENI (1975) but the results are not yet published.

8.33 Gunnar Arhammar, Some observation on protein calorie malnutrition at the Swedish pediatric clinic in the *Ethiopian Medical Journal*, Addis Ababa: November 1966, p. 15.

8.34 The food item of nomadic populations include grain obtained from an exchange in local markets.

8.35 Unlike the rest of the population, the weight–height chart of the well-to-do families in Ethiopia was found to be similar to that in the developed economies of the West. Source: Ethiopian Nutrition Institute.

8.36 Solomon Ayalew, *op. cit.* p. 22.

8.37 Education and Training, *Economic Growth Prospects in Ethiopia*, Volume IV, September 22, 1970, Annex 7.

8.38 Unemployment problems, *ibid.*

8.39 The reasons for this are clear. Students and teachers showed a consistent antifeudal stand for over a decade. In 1974 the agitation against the aristocracy was started by students and teachers:

1. On 18 February 1974, Ethiopian teachers went on a strike in opposition to the proposed Education Sector Review—which literally excludes the poor from higher education.

2. On 20 February 1974 students and workers staged peaceful demonstrations in Addis Ababa against the government and made political demands.

CHAPTER 9

Counterpoint One: India and China

Introduction

OBSERVERS of the contemporary scene have made it a habit to compare the experiences of India and China: neighbours, the world's two most populated countries, with an extended history of extended human suffering, and which underwent significant political changes at roughly the same time: independence from Great Britain in 1947 and complete takeover by a Communist regime in 1949. The comparison is not quite fair: although the baseline level of poverty was about the same (perhaps China's was worse than India's), the former had been a unified Empire for over 3000 years compared with the latter's fragmentation, and in it a combination of weaker traditional religious bonds, a common ideographic written language and a small number of spoken languages made it *a priori* into a better starting point than India.

Yet, comparisons are still being made, and what arises strikingly from them is that—despite the similarities in both countries as regards few resources and the political inacceptability of famine deaths in both of them—India has resigned itself to accepting a high level of chronic malnutrition among its population, while China has attempted to eradicate it, and the Chinese have also attempted—many will say succeeded—in doing away with the structural conditions which, so to speak, cause the effects of drought.

A 30-year observation period in both countries helps to make salient whatever differences in policies were applied in each of them, and an added element of saliency for observers is that India and China represent two different models of development, which Third World countries have been encouraged to imitate.

Banerji's paper provides a brief and vivid description of the background of poverty and malnutrition in India, against which one has to analyze the impact of a drought or any other natural disaster. It illustrates our contention, repeatedly pointed out in preceding chapters, that famines "produced" by a climatic anomaly are only found in societies already having a low level of nutrition. This is the *permanent* catastrophe referred to in the title of this book.

The lesson we can learn from this case-study goes, however, much further. Few other countries, within the developing world, have in fact, set up and implemented such a system of relief measures to alleviate the effects of natural disasters as India has done after independence. The three examples of "Patterns of Response" to famines, described by Banerji are, in this respect, very illuminating. The sharp difference between the Bengal famine of 1943, on the one hand, and the Bihar (1966–69) and the Maharashtra (1971–73) famines on the other, are quite eloquent.

The latter provide "a dramatic instance of the extent to which distress caused by drought and economic exploitation of such conditions can be avoided by prompt launching of large-scale relief measures". It is doubtful that other countries could be more effective under similar conditions. And yet, the examples also provide "a dramatic instance" of the strict limitations of the emergency aid programmes. We have referred to it, in Chapter 7, as the "Red Cross Approach" or RCA, and pointed out that however large and generous it may be, it cannot do more than it is intended to do: alleviation of suffering when calamity is present. Moreover, the effectiveness of these measures is entirely conditioned by social receptive structures which alone will determine whether the calamity is at all manageable or not. In this respect the contrast with China is very striking. It could hardly be denied that RCA is not and cannot be eliminated in China in extreme cases of natural disasters. But here the modalities of operation change, and the effectiveness of application increases as the social receptive structures are quite different. The essential point is that the difference is not—or, perhaps, not only—due to a difference in the output of the food production system. Neo-Malthusians are ready to "explain" Indian poverty and the recurrent famines on the basis of overpopulation and "uncontrolled" demographic growth. We have disposed of this argument in Chapter 6 by showing that India is and has always been, a net exporter of food.

In case there remains any doubt about the fact that the problem of India, as far as food is concerned, is *not* the race between production growth and population, the following remark contained in a U.N. study may serve to dissipate it. The U.N. "Supplement to World Economic Survey, 1976" referring to the 1976 Indian agricultural production says the following (page 122):

> "Though the food-grain crop was nearly 10 percent below the 1975 record of over 120 million tons, it left the country with a reserve of over 200 million tons, twice as much as its silos were capable of storing. As 1977 brought another copious monsoon, much of the stock—about 5 million tons—stored in jute bages under polyethylene sheets was vulnerable to moisture damage. Thus, the prospects of another good harvest was modified somewhat by the incidence of reserve deterioration."

This statement alone is shocking, but it is not all. There is a footnote which requires no comment: "Much of the grain exposed to undue moisture was assigned for use as foodstuff."

There is another point of sharp contrast between the agricultural situation in India and in China. We have already referred (Chapter 6) to the failures of the Green Revolution in India. The marvels of high-yield varieties were not so for vast sectors of the rural population in these areas where high-level agricultural technology was implanted to save them from starvation. And we have said in this connection, advanced technology *per-se* is not the answer. The detailed description provided by Stavis of technological improvements in Chinese agriculture, and of their role in the eradication of malnutrition and hunger, proves our point. The Chinese carried out their own "Green Revolution", but they did not start with it. The starting point was a profound and dramatic change in the structure of the productive system and, in particular, of the system of food circulation. This aspect of the problem is developed by Stavis in the second part of his contribution included in Chapter 10.

The thesis—which cannot be overemphasized—that what matters is the accessibility of the food to people, much more than the actual output of the food productive system, could hardly find any better confirmatory evidence than in the "counterpoint" contained in this chapter.

The conclusions are not a set of technical statements but rather a formulation of a political challenge. As Stavis clearly states, "major political changes were needed ... to assure that food would be shared reasonably equally over time, space, within the village, and within the family.... Whether or not violent revolution was an unavoidable pre-condition for improvements is a long-debated and unanswerable question. It is, however, clear that a set of political changes were needed."

ANNEX 1

Impact of Drought on Nutrition and Health Status of the Population of India

by *Debabar Banerji*

Drought and the Social, Political, Economic and Ecological Setting

Nutrition and health implications of a condition of severe drought are only one of many very closely related aspects of an entire complex of situations which are precipitated by it. Secondly, even with drought of the same severity, the nature and degree of the consequences will vary very widely with variations in the social, economic, political and ecological conditions prevailing in different regions. At one extreme, when the conditions prevailing are most unfavourable, consequences, including those in terms of nutrition and health, are very serious and extensive. At the other extreme, when the conditions are most favourable, the population has considerable capacity to absorb the impact of a drought and thus greatly minimize its consequences. There is also the important question that, apart from the so-called "acts of God", social, economic and political issues are of relevance in determining the degree of intensity of a drought. Impact of drought on nutrition and health status of an affected population in India will, therefore, also have to be seen against the social, economic, political and ecological setting of the country.

By far the most dominant feature of this background in India is the all-pervading poverty. The national average *per capita* consumption (at 1960–61 prices) is barely Rs. 21.47 (less than U.S. $3) per month. (9.1) The fact that the consumption of 71.53 percent of the urban and 69.25 percent of the rural population is below this average not only gives an indication of the gross maldistribution of income but also the extent and the depth of poverty prevailing in India. Due to obvious political and economic reasons, the brunt of the consequences of a drought is borne by the people in rural areas, who constitute 80 percent of the total population.

Nutrition and Health Status in Rural India under Normal Conditions

Data from a yet unpublished study conducted at the Centre of Social Medicine and Community Health of Jawaharlal Nehru University, New Delhi, covering 19 villages from 7 states (Gujarat, Haryana, Karnataka, Kerala, Rajasthan, Uttar Pradesh and West Bengal) provide a somewhat deeper insight into the poverty in rural India. A preliminary communication on this study was published in 1973. (9.2) These data were obtained as a part of an investigation of the health behaviour of rural populations. For the design of this study, the selected villages, in economic terms, had to be mostly from within the upper quadrile of the villages in the corresponding states. However, even in this selected group, responding to a question in the course of the interview of a 20 percent stratified random sample of the households (numbering 975), it was revealed that as many as half of them (49.7 percent) do not get two meals all the year round just to satisfy their hunger; they are compelled to remain hungry for varying periods during a "normal" year. 4.6 percent of them do not have two full meals for six months or more; 31.6 percent do not get two full meals from 3–6 months; 9.3 percent do not get two full meals for 3 months or less; and 3.8 percent get food irregularly. These findings tally with those from a large number of other studies (9.3–9.6) which have also revealed such high prevalence of hunger in India.

Data from anthropological field work which was also carried out in these 19 villages revealed what this prevalence of widespread hunger among the millions of sufferers means and how it is intertwined with other aspects of their lives—their domestic lives, their child-rearing practices and socialization of the children, state of health, environmental sanitation, housing, clothing, employment, indebtedness and social and political relationships. To these people life appears to be an unending chain of misery, degradation and deprivation till they finally die.

It could also be seen in the course of this study that there is, in addition, another substantial group of rural population, comprising small farmers and artisans who manage to get two full meals all the year round, but they live in almost perpetual fear of being pushed down into the "hunger classes" by a variety of natural calamities and individual catastrophes such as prolonged sickness and death of the breadwinner, old age and crushing social obligations like marriage expenses and accommodating destitute relatives. The moneylenders and exploiting upper classes prey on these individuals when they are in distress and take advantage of such distress conditions to "swallow" their lands, their livestock, their ornaments and other available assets. Broadly, therefore, the rural population in India has three major components—a vast mass of oppressed people who are caught in the vicious circle of poverty—degradation—deprivation—illness—poverty; a group comprising of small farmers and artisans who struggle hard to avoid getting caught in the vicious circle; and, a small upper class which owns substantial assets and which gets richer by exploiting the poverty and helplessness of the masses and by using its political power to usurp community-sponsored services and financial allocations mainly for its own benefit.

Diseases literally thrive under the conditions that are prevailing in Indian villages. A vast majority of the people have to fight an intense struggle against these very adverse conditions right from their birth. The mother is exposed to serious hazards which cause high mortality and morbidity rates at the time of childbirth. Their children face acute problems of nutrition and infection in the very early phase of their lives. These children are left to the "care" of whoever is left behind, very frequently their sisters or brothers who might be a few years older than them, when the mother has to go out to work to eke out a subsistence for the family. If the child survives these formidable hazards, he grows up as a weakling—falling way behind in time in reaching the principal landmarks in his growth and development. And, then, like his parents, he is launched in the same grim, if not grimmer, struggle to survive—to ward off hunger, to escape from diarrhoeas, dysenteries and other water-borne diseases and other communicable diseases such as tuberculosis, leprosy, filariasis, trachoma, tetanus and worm infestations. Millions become blind by conditions which are easily preventable.

Because of the same forces emanating from the power structure of Indian society, the masses of people have very limited access even to the very rudimentary health services that are existing in rural areas to get alleviation of the suffering due to these diseases; at the same time, the upper classes have at their disposal benefits of the health services, most of which are almost entirely set up and maintained through public funds. (9.2) The weak thus become weaker because they have limited access to health services to get at least some alleviation of their suffering due to ill-health, while the strong become stronger still by getting full advantage of the community-financed health services and they are thus able to keep the weak in a perpetual state of weakness.

Implications of State of Chronic Undernutrition and Ill-health

It is obvious that such severe forms of deprivation for such prolonged periods should have severely hampered a normal growth and development of an individual. In recent years, a section of nutritionists have gone a step further to contend that severe malnutrition during early childhood causes permanent damage to the brain so that the individual is unable to acquire normal mental facilities later in life, notwithstanding any degree of improvement in their nutritional status. (9.7) These nutritionists could raise so much alarm all over the world that the then Secretary-General of the United Nations, U Thant, called for action on a global scale to fight what was perceived as an impending disaster.

However, a closer scrutiny of the scientific evidence adduced by these scientists revealed that it was far from being conclusive. There is, in the first place, the entire range of questions whether intelligence tests actually measure mental health, more particularly in the cultural and social context of Third World countries. Secondly, evidence of biological damage to the brain which is irreversible and which is responsible for mental retardation in humans is at best fragmentary and contradictory. And, finally, no such evidence of permanent brain damage was discernible in a recent study of those who were exposed to severe conditions of malnutrition in concentration camps during World War II. Why then did a contention, which had such a fragile scientific base, get so much attention all over the world? This is evidently a case of use (or misuse?) of science to subserve political ends. The exploiting classes can possibly take advantage of such "scientific" findings to assert that the masses of hungry and dispossesed people have become mentally inferior—a "race" which is inferior to them—because of exposure to malnutrition during early childhood. This could thus provide a "medical" rather than racial or biological justification to assert supremacy of one group of human beings over another and legitimize the "right" of the superior group to dominate and exploit the inferior creatures.

A phenomenon of even more far-reaching political and social consequence relates to possible ecological effects of chronic starvation and hunger over generations. There is substantial evidence to assert that the levels of living of the lower 60 to 70 percent of the population in India has not improved to any significant extent in the past three decades or so. Similarly, as the Union Minister of Health and Family Welfare has frankly admitted recently (9.8) these people have very little access to community health services. But then there is sound demographic evidence, based on reasonably reliable census data, that the expectancy of life at birth in India has shot up from around 20 years in the forties to around 55 years at present. (9.8) There has also been a marked decline in the infant mortality rate. (9.9) Taking more specific instances, neither socio-economic factors nor the degree of development of health services can fully explain the remarkably steep fall in the mortality and morbidity rates due to syphilis and puerperal sepsis in India in the past three or four decades. There are also strong indications that there is a declining trend in the incidence of tuberculosis in India. (9.10) This declining trend also cannot be explained by socio-economic changes or by the impact of tuberculosis control programmes in the country. Grigg's hypothesis (9.11) to explain this fall in mortality of tuberculosis in terms of biologically favourable changes in the host–parasite relationship may not only be pertinent to that disease but it may also be relevant to a much wider spectrum of community health problems.

There is some evidence, though by no means conclusive, to indicate possibilities of some sort of biological adjustment within the people affected by chronic hunger and ill-health, so that they are able to survive even at a lower level of subsistence. B. K. Anand and his colleagues at the All India Institute of Medical Sciences, New Delhi, has provided very convincing scientific evidence that an accomplished practitioner of yoga can very severely cut down his metabolism as indicated by pronounced fall in his consumption of oxygen. (9.12) More recently, K. N. Sharma and his colleagues at St. John's Medical College, Bangalore (personal communication), obtained evidence which indicates that construction labourers had their basal metabolic rates below what scientists had hitherto considered as the irreducible minimum requirement for man.

Whatever be the possible mechanism, acquisition of ability of man to further lower the survival threshold in both immunological and nutritional terms has profound political and social implications. The power elites had retained their control on the population by keeping the weak in a state of weakness. In the forties the weak died in large numbers when they went below the threshold of minimum conditions for survival. But in the ecological situation in the seventies, a significant proportion of the weak, who would otherwise have died away, managed to survive in a state of weakness which is even more pronounced than what was the condition in the forties. They thus become a still easier prey to the mechanizations and manipulations by the power elites. The political significance of this ecological phenomenon lies in the fact that this adds a new dimension to the power struggle of the have-nots to wrest their rights from the haves.

Political and Social Response to Drought

Impact of a condition of drought on nutrition and health status of the population in India can only be understood against the combined effects of the social, political, economic and ecological forces. These forces create a condition of chronic malnutrition and undernutrition and extensive prevalence of preventable diseases even under "normal" conditions. In most parts of the country, a substantial proportion of the population has to suffer diseases during what are called the "lean" agricultural seasons of a "normal" year. A drought represents an extreme and a specially unfavourable climatic condition which has a catastrophic effect on the "normal" agricultural production of the affected region. Such extreme scarcity conditions precipitate three major types of issues:

—First, as the distress conditions threaten to affect the sections of the population which are politically more influential, it becomes politically expedient for the ruling classes to come to their rescue by launching relief measures.

—Second, while the high rates of morbidity and mortality due to undernutrition and malnutrition and preventable diseases among the weaker and exploited sections are tolerated under "normal" conditions, the threat of an acute exacerbation of these rates during a condition of severe drought, which would cause a large number of deaths due to frank starvation and outbreak of epidemics, becomes politically unacceptable and intolerable.

—Third, political compulsions and sheer dimensions of the catastrophe invoke sympathy and "charitable response" from the rest of the country and national and international organizations from abroad.

A cruel irony of such calamities is that they provide the richer sections of the population an opportunity to take advantage of the so-called "distress sale" and buy the assets of the less prosperous sections at bargain prices. Further, sometimes influential individuals siphon off some of the resources which are meant for relief of the afflicted to reward bosses for political support or even for their own personal benefit.

Because of these potentialities for "leakages", exaggerated accounts of drought conditions are given to milk out of the government and other relief-giving agencies as much scarcity relief as possible.

Patterns of Response to Three Different Famines in India and their Impact on Nutrition and Health Status

The actual nature of the response to the issues precipitated by a drought condition is determined by the political will of the leadership, resource mobilization and mobilization of managerial talents to contend with the challenge. At one extreme, there is the example of the Great Bengal Famine of 1943. As brought out by the Famine Inquiry Commission, which was appointed by the then British Indian Government (9.13) in this case, along with the rainfall anomalies, the governments at both provincial and central levels were not only astonishingly inept but they were downright callous in dealing with the situation and they left the field wide open for all sorts of exploiters and unscrupulous elements—hoarders, black-marketeers and profiteers—to capitalize on the distress of the people. According to the estimates of the Commission, a million and a half human beings perished "as a direct result of the famine and the epidemics that followed in its train". (9.13) (Other estimates, also quoted by the Commission (9.13), went as high as 3.5 million.) The Commission has given a graphic account of what famine meant to these people. "Many of the patients in the hospitals were picked up on the streets in a state of extreme weakness and collapse, often on the point of death. They were for the most part emaciated to such a degree that the description of "living skeletons" was justifiable. Weight was often reduced by as much as one-third of the normal; that of a man who normally weighed 120–130 pounds fell to 80–90 pounds."

Devastating epidemics of malaria, smallpox and cholera were associated with the famine. So-called famine diarrhoea, famine dropsy and anaemia also took a very heavy toll of lives. An analytical study of famines in India during 1860–65 (9.14) has given instances of several such grim tragedies, when distress due to a national calamity got compounded because anti-social elements were allowed to capitalize on the distress of the people.

The Bihar Famine of October 1966–September 1967 provides an instance where much greater efforts were made and relief was provided promptly and on a much more massive scale. It has been unprecedented in its magnitude, intensity and duration. A Report published by the Central Institute of Research and Public Co-operation, New Delhi, has pointed out some conspicuous features of this famine: (9.15)

> "It was the first officially declared famine of independent India and as such it posed a formidable challenge to our national honour and ingenuity. It stirred the conscience of entire mankind transcending boundaries of race, nation, religion and ideology. It was a 'Total' famine encompassing in its octopus-like hold not only the humans but all living creation. It was pregnant with potentials that would have wrought incalculable destruction but, which, however, could not become manifest due to relief organized on a scale and in a manner unknown before. In spite of this massive relief, the national and international support and sympathy, people of Bihar had to suffer untold miseries, indignities and degradation that shall ever hang on their consciousness like an incubus.

Out of the 587 blocks of the State, 186 were stricken with famine and 221 with scarcity. The area where the crop failure was 75 percent and over was declared famine area and where the failure was 50 percent and over scarcity area. Out of a total number of 67,665 villages in the State, 23,636 villages lay in the famine area and 23,018 in the scarcity area. Of the 53 million people of the State, 13.4 million people were faced with famine conditions and 20.9 million with scarcity conditions."

The Report also gives a vivid account of the impact of the famine. (9.15)

"Many eye-witness accounts of famine conditions were available from the respondents and were also reported in the newspapers which give a fair idea about the ravages of this famine. Perhaps the greatest damage that the famine could do was the undermining of people's health, especially of children, already undernourished due to their chronic poverty. They got emaciated, devitalized and susceptible to many deficiency diseases. Some had become too weak to walk even half a mile to the free kitchens and resignedly awaited death. The belly of the poor was criss-crossed with lines of hunger. At free kitchens men with gaunt frames and cadaverous eyes, women tattered and distraught, little boys and girls with spindly legs and bloated bellies, all rickety specimens of humanity scrabbled for food. They all wore the sullen, listless and glossless faces of despair. Protein deficiency in thousands caused anaemia, vitamin deficiency, eye diseases and water infection jaundice. The undernourishment that children had to suffer for long may result according to medical research, in permanent mental and physical retardation and lower resistance to diseases that normal children take in their stride. During the peak period of the famine, over 65 lakh (i.e. 6.5 million) persons had to be fed free. This amounted to covering one fifth of the affected population.

"Nearly 62 percent of the State's 17.6 million children up to the age-group of 10 had fallen prey to the famine. The 5 million tribal population of South Bihar was the worst sufferer. Even in normal times, they seldom consume food whose caloric value exceeded 1200. During famine, they were forced to subsist on roots, tender shoots, grass, leaves, buds of peepal trees and tubers and in some cases even on the bark of the mahua tree. According to a survey conducted by the nutrition scientists and doctors from the Nutrition Research Laboratories, Hyderabad, during the period December 1966–February 1967, only 10 percent of Bihar's population was getting an adequate diet (i.e. 2300 calories); 25 percent had a diet that yielded less than 1000 calories."

The sharp contrast of the impact of the Bengal Famine with the Bihar Famine provides a dramatic instance of the extent to which distress caused by drought and economic exploitation of such conditions can be avoided by prompt launching of large-scale relief measures. Experience with the Maharashtra drought of 1970–72 (9.16) (9.17) shows how even much better results can be obtained with better management and with some marginal increase in investment. The key factor which makes the major differences in the three experiences is the degree to which the distress of the affected people is considered politically "tolerable" by the state and national leadership and by the aid-giving countries and other external agencies.

The Maharashtra drought, persisting for three successive years, was unprecedented in its magnitude affecting about 23,000 out of 36,000 villages in 1970 and
about 15,000 villages in 1971 and 1972. Out of the 30 million people affected, 1.46
million were on relief works in September 1971, and it reached the peak of 5 million
in May 1973. These relief works cost the government Rs. 419.5 million (approx U.S.
$50 million) in 1971, Rs. 757.2 million (approx. U.S. $90 million) in 1972 and Rs.
983.1 million (approx. U.S. $20 million) in the first four months of 1973. (9.16)

Conclusion: Case Reports and Some Statistics

Case reports by Borkar and Nadkarni (9.18) of two villages in the drought-
affected Maharashtra in 1972, one severely hit and the other only moderately
affected, provide a valuable insight into the economic relations in rural India under
conditions for normal rainfall. They found that both small farmers and agricultural
labourers in the other village felt that their income was higher that year than the
wages earned during the scarcity relief works. It is possible to imagine the plight of
vast masses of the rural population of the country during the years when the
rainfall is not normal but also not abnormal enough to force the political leadership to take to relief work. The author's conclusions are very pertinent: (9.18)

> "It is a painful commentary on the state of agriculture of small and medium
> cultivators that they should find their occupation less remunerative than
> working in metalbreaking centres; and it is equally poignant that it needed
> the scarcity of this magnitude to improve their lot as also that of agricultural
> labour. This experience also reflects the effectiveness of the relief work organ-
> ized by the government."

It so happens that one of the 19 villages of the health behaviour study, the village
Rohat in the Pali district of Rajasthan, was also declared a famine area when it was
being studied in 1972. Findings from this village also confirmed the observations of
Borkar and Nadkarni that the income of landless labourers and small farmers was
more during the scarcity relief works than what they earn "normally".

It is wellknown that vital statistics available in India are very inadequate indeed.
It is possible to get some statistical data of acceptable reliability about only a few
vital events from parts of India. The situation is much worse in many other Third
World countries. This inadequacy of the vital statistics in the Third World countries is not simply a reflection of the state of management of health and other social
services: not having such statistics could also be a deliberate move on the part of
the ruling classes to cover up its failure to keep its promise to the people. It so
happens that the catastrophes of Bengal, Bihar and Maharashtra were of such
gigantic magnitude that even the very crude statistics that could somehow be
gathered was enough to expose not only the dimensions of nutritional and health
impact of the drought, but also to lay bare the degree of suffering these conditions
caused to the vast masses as a result of interplay of a complex of social, political
and international forces. It also so happens that for the state of Maharashtra, crude

birthrates are available for the years 1970–75 through a reasonably reliable (or at least comparable) system of National Registration Scheme. (9.19) (9.20)

Year		1970	1971	1972	1973	1974	1975
Crude	Rural	13.0	13.5	14.5	15.6	12.6	12.2
death rates	Urban	9.8	9.7	9.0	9.3	9.0	9.5

The crude death rates for the urban population remain almost the same through-out the 5 years but for the rural population there is a distinct rise during the drought years of 1971, 1972 and 1973. It fell again in 1974 and 1975. The death and devastation due to the Bengal Famine were so far-reaching that the Famine Inquiry Commission Report on Bengal could observe as much as 100 percent increase in the "reported deaths of those years". (9.13) Unfortunately, the Sample Registration Scheme was not in operation at the time of the Bihar Famine, but here again, the data obtained by other means were good enough to see the nature of the impact of the famine on nutrition and health status of the population in Bihar.

ANNEX 2

Ending Famines in China

by *Ben Stavis*

Introduction*

In 1926 a book was published called *China: Land of Famine*. (9.21) The title of the book was tragically accurate. In most years in China before 1949, some localities suffered from serious food shortages. In some years, natural disasters—particularly floods or droughts—triggered famine on a scale so vast as to defy comprehension. International relief programmes went on for decades and helped somewhat, but they were totally unable to change the basic situation. But now things have changed completely. Shortage or excess of rainfall—such as the drought in North China in 1972—may still bring inconvenience and suffering, but no longer produce famine and death. What policies have brought about this tremendous improve-ment?

Four major policies seem crucial:

(a) Massive programmes mobilizing and co-ordinating national and local resources have brought China's flood-prone rivers under control.

* Comments from Pierre Spitz and Michael Ellman have been most helpful in revising this paper.

(b) Agricultural production has been increased and stabilized through major investments in irrigation equipment, fertilizer, new seeds and research in agricultural sciences.

(c) An egalitarian social order has been established so that available food is spread quite evenly, and any shortfalls do not fall disproportionately on any one sector of the population.

(d) Government at the central and local levels has the financial logistic and political capacity to procure food, store it, and transport it to regions of need.

While each of these policies involves a technical component, in all cases the crucial element was the political determination to carry out these policies. Urban interests and rural elite interests had other priorities, and in China a profound revolution seemed necessary to implement these policies. Internal political processes have proved far more important than foreign assistance to tame natural disasters.

Partially because natural disasters and famine have been brought under control, and also because of improved diets, rural sanitation, and health services, the Chinese people now have greatly improved health. Life expectancy has increased dramatically. Children are taller and heavier now and this is a most sensitive indicator of improved health.

This paper is organized into four major sections. The first one reviews the types of natural disasters which used to render China a "land of famine". The second section analyzes the experience with natural disasters since 1949. The third section examines the policies used to control floods and droughts and the fourth section collects data confirming an improvement of health.

I. Natural Disasters in China before the Revolution

Geographical, environmental and human factors conspired to make China very susceptible to natural disasters in the past. Indeed, disasters were not sporadic, unusual events but were regular occurrences that everyone expected from time to time. In the 2000 years from the Han to Ch'ing Dynasties, China experienced 1392 droughts and 1621 floods. In recent centuries, as China included a larger area and could collect more information, there averaged one or two floods and an equal number of droughts each year. (9.22) Towards the end of the nineteenth century, it was not unusual for about 400 reporting units (countries) in the 12 provinces of the Yangtze and Yellow River basins (with a total of about 900 reporting units) to suffer from droughts, floods or insects (Fig. 1). In roughly 53 percent of China's countries, adults interviewed in the early 1930s had experienced three or more famines. (9.22) In 29 percent of the localities, the average food intake was below standard, defined as 2800 calories per day per adult. (For logistical reasons, this survey did not include regions with serious famine, and therefore understated the food problem.) (9.24)

Different regions of China had peculiar problems. North China was especially prone to drought. During winter months, the Siberian high-pressure region sends dry winds from central Asia across North China. Rainfall is virtually nil. Summer breezes tend to parallel North China's shore, rather than blow on-shore, so summer rainfall is irregular. The Tsingling mountains effectively keep moisture-laden air south of the Huai River. Together these factors make rainfall in North China both sparse (about 400–600 mm) and highly variable. Indeed, "in no other thickly-populated part of the world is the amount of variability of rainfall so great as in North China". (9.25)

Catastrophic drought lasting two years strikes North China every few decades. In 1878–79, perhaps 10 million people perished. About forty-two years later, in 1920–21, North China was again parched. In 1928–30, drought hit Northwest China and 3–6 million people were lost. (see Table 1) About forty-four years later, in 1972, North China again suffered drought, but for reasons to be explained later, the consequences were not severe. Droughts could not strike all of China simultaneously, as in India where a delayed monsoon affects most of the country; but China's climatic fluctuations are indeed severe.

Ironically, an equally serious problem for North China has been flooding. "Floods in China imperil the lives of a greater number of people than anywhere else on earth".(9.26) Natural and human factors interact to create the problem. The Yellow River has produced a vast, almost level delta that is the North China Plain, covering Shantung, Hopei, Honan and parts of Anhwei. Deforestation in the upper catchment area (Shensi, Kansu, Shansi) where the soil is very fine loess (blown there from the Gobi Desert) has resulted in extensive soil erosion. The runoff into the Yellow River is silt-laden, giving the Yellow River its name. When the Yellow River's flow reaches the flat plain, the water velocity is reduced and the silt settles and fills up the river bed. To prevent the river from overflowing, Chinese have for centuries built dikes on the sides of the Yellow River. As more silt settled in the bed, the dikes were built higher. Eventually, the river was thirty feet above the level of the farmland. Periodically, the dikes would break (due to excessive rainfall and/or failure to maintain and repair the dikes against the constant scouring action of the river flow) and vast areas of the North China Plain would be flooded. Devastation would be great, and often the river was allowed to take a new course. In 2000 years there were more than 1500 dike breaches and 26 major changes in the river course. (9.27) For this reason the Yellow River was known as "China's Sorrow". Other rivers in North China—the Huai (in Anhui) and the Hai (draining through Tientsin)—have similar conditions.

The Yellow River's dikes suffered major breaks in 1887, 1921, 1931, 1933, 1935 and 1938, with consequences ranging from severe to catastrophic, depending on how far up-stream the break occurred. In addition, the Huai had major floods in 1911, 1931, 1950 and 1954 (9.28) and the Hai had major floods in 1971, 1931, 1939 and 1963. (9.29)

In central China, the Yangtze River floods sometimes, especially if there is excessive rainfall over its great catchment area when snow is melting in Tibet. In July–August 1931 it flooded into densely-populated valley sections of five provinces, inundating about 10 million people. The Yangtze again flooded in 1954.

In South China, both serious droughts and floods are somewhat less of a problem. The climate is more stable, and the topography tends to confine problems to a limited area. Over the centuries the southern provinces have experienced roughly one-half the number of floods and droughts as have the northern provinces.

TABLE 1.

People Affected by Major Disasters in China, 1870–1943

Year	Region	People affected (millions)	People killed (millions)
1870[s]	Yangtze River flood		
1878[a,b]	North China Plain drought	50	10–13
1887[e,f]	Yellow River flood, Honan		1–7
1890[r]	Hai River flood	2.7	"immense loss"
1917[f]	Hai River flood, Tientsin (12,700 sq. miles)	5.6–6.2	
1920–21[c]	North China drought	20	0.5
1921[m,q]	Yellow River, Shantung	0.25	
1928–30[h,i,n]	Northwest China drought (Kansu, Shensi, Suiyuan)	10	3.6
1931[g,j,k,s]	Yangtze River flood	9	0.14
	North China floods (84,000 sq miles)	11	40–50
	Huai River floods	19	
1933[l]	Yellow River	3.6	0.02
1935[m]	Yellow River Shantung (6000 sq. miles)		
	[n]Han River, Hupei	3.7	0.08
1938[l,o]	Yellow River dikes blown up, Honan	12.5	0.89
1939[r]	Hai River flood		0.02
1942–43[p]	Honan		2

[a] New Look of Yangtze River, NCNA Peking, October 10, 1974.

[b] Archaeological Survey of the Yangtze River, *Peking Review*, No. 31 (July 29, 1977), p. 31.

[c] David Hill, trans., A Record of the Famine Relief Work in Lin Fen Hien, *Chinese Recorder*, 11:4 (July–August 1880), p. 260.

[d] J. Dudgeon, The Famine in North China, *Chinese Recorder*, 11:5 (September–October 1880), p. 349.

[e] Paul Richard Bohr, *Famine in China and the Missionary* (Cambridge: Harvard East Asian Research Center, 1972), pp. 13–26.

[f] Walter Mallory, *China: Land of Famine* (New York: American Geographical Society, 1926), pp. 2, 49–53.

[g] John R. Freeman, Flood Problems in China, *Transactions of the American Society of Civil Engineers*, 85 (1922), p. 1405.

[h] *Harm into Benefit, Taming the Haiho River* (Peking: Foriegn Languages Press, 1975), pp. 4–5.

[j] Famine Notes, *Chinese Recorder*, 43:2 (February 1912), p. 91.

[k] Andrew James Nathan, *A History of the China International Famine Relief Commission* (Cambridge: Harvard East Asian Research Center, 1965), pp. 1–10.

[l] Oliver Todd, Taming 'Flood Dragons' Along China's Huang Ho, *National Geographic*, 81:2 (February 1942), pp. 205–234.

[m] Edgar Snow, *Red Star Over China* (New York: Grove, 1968), pp. 214–218.

[n] G. Findlay Andrew, On the Trail of Death in Northwest China, *Asia* 32:1 (January 1932), pp. 42–48, 60–62.

[o] Flood Damage in China during 1931, *Chinese Economic Journal*, 10:4 (April 1932), pp. 341–52.

[p] Edmund Clubb, Floods of China, A National Disaster, *Journal of Geography*, 31:5 (May 1932), pp. 199–206.

[q] George Stroebe, The Great Central China Flood of 1931, *Chinese Recorder*, 63:11 (November 1932), pp. 557–680.

[r] Harnessing the Han River—Major Yangtze Tributary, NCNA Peking, February 5, 1976.

[s] *China Tames Her Rivers* (Peking: Foreign Languages Press, 1972), p. 5.

TABLE 2.
Floods and Droughts Throughout Chinese History (floods and droughts per thousand square kilometers per century)

	Floods	Droughts
Northern provinces	0.38	0.30
Central provinces	0.56	0.46
Southern provinces	0.22	0.18

Source: Yao Shan-yu, "The Geographical Distribution of Floods and Droughts in Chinese History, 206 B.C.–A.D. 1911", *Far Eastern Quarterly* 2:4 (August 1943), p. 363.

(Table 2) Surveys in the 1930s also show the situation in South China to be somewhat less pressing. (Table 3)

The frequency of disasters has changed over time. While this may reflect some subtle cyclical changes in climate, it also clearly reflects the political situation. When the central government was weak and unable to maintain river dikes, disasters were more common. Figure 1 shows an increase in disasters during the time of the Taiping rebellion (1846–65) and during the end of the Ch'ing Dynasty under the venal leadership of the Empress Dowager, Tzu Hsi.

Another type of disaster to which China has been vulnerable has been earthquakes. Earthquakes have caused catastrophic loss of life when they hit densely-populated regions. The Chinese stone and mud houses collapse, and if the earthquake comes at night when everyone is indoors, the toll can be staggering. Some major earthquake disasters are listed in Table 4.

Some famines were caused almost entirely by political conditions. Warlord armies sometimes extracted all the food from a locality, leaving famine behind. In some parts of China (particularly in the West) farmers were forced to plant opium in the 1920s. This both displaced food grains from good farm land and attracted armies seeking to control it. (9.30)

TABLE 3.
Disasters and Famines in North and South China, 1930s

	North	South
Percent of countries in which adults experienced three or more famines	73	39
Average number of famines per county	3.6	2.5
Average duration of famine (months)	13.3	8.8
Percent of population starving in famine	8	1
Percent of population seriously affected in famine (migrating, starving, or eating grass and bark)	60	21
Percent of localities in which average caloric intake is below standard (2800 calories per adult per day), excluding regions of severe famine	40	17

Source: John Buck, *Land Utilization in China* (New York: Paragon Reprint 1968), p. 124, 407.

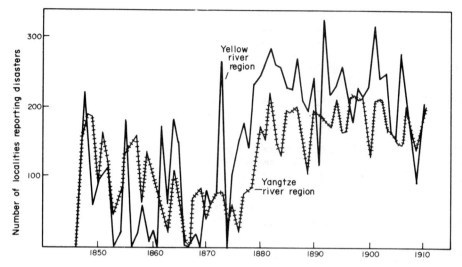

FIG. 1. Number of localities reporting disaster in twelve provinces of Yellow River and Yangtze River basins, 1846–1910

Source: Li Wen-tze, *Chung-kuo Chin-tai Nung-yeh-shih Tzu-liao* (Materials on Recent Agricultural History in China), Volume 1 (Peking: Hsin Hua, 1957), pp. 720–23, 733–35.

TABLE 4.

Major Earthquakes in China, 1303–1976

Date	Place	Death toll
September 17, 1303	Shansi	
January 23, 1556	Shansi	820,000
December 29, 1604		
July 25, 1668	Shantung	
September 2, 1679	Peking	
May 18, 1695		
January 3, 1739		
September 6, 1833		
August 22, 1902		
December 23, 1906		
June 5, 1920	Kansu	180,000
December 16, 1920		
May 23, 1927		
August 11, 1931		
August 15, 1950		
March 18, 1951		
March 8, 22, 1966	Hopei	
January 25, 1972	Yunnan	
February 1975	Liaoning	
July 28, 1976	Hopei (Tangshan)	655,000

Sources: "Earthquake Research in China", *EOS American Geophysical Union* 56 (1975), pp. 228–38; Ross Munro, "Quake Left Chinese City a Rubble Pile", *Washington Post*, June 11, 1977.

What did people do when disaster struck? What were their strategies for survival? Naturally the strategy was related to the type of disaster. With floods and earthquakes, the initial period is most destructive. With droughts, however, there is a slow but continuing aggravation of the situation until rains come and a crop can be harvested. In a serious drought, the first step a family takes is to reduce food consumption. Instead of bread, people eat thin gruel, and add weeds, grass and other greens, and almost anything else not poisonous. Part of the family go off as refugees. If the remaining food will not suffice until the next expected crop, people begin to sell their few possessions—first livestock and farm utensils, then windows of a house, then the roof. Farm land and the remaining skeleton of the house are sold. (9.31) Next, daughters and wives may be sold off as servants, slaves or wives. In Sian in 1929 during a great drought, the market price for females was one Mexican dollar* for each year of age. When demand for females was filled, children were simply abandoned. (9.32) The remainder of the family could only turn to begging. Sometimes families committed suicide rather than beg. When famine gets this serious, human flesh is eaten—usually from famished corpses; but sometimes from murdered kin, kidnapped children, or defeated bandits. (9.33) At this stage of a famine, banditry becomes widespread and disease spreads rapidly, especially typhus fever. The toll of famine is difficult to specify because many people have migrated away. However, in some districts in 1878 it was estimated that 10–20 percent of the population died of starvation, and 5–10 percent fell to typhus. Perhaps 30 percent migrated away. The population of many localities was cut in half. (9.34) Peasants in North China in the early 1930s estimated that when there was famine, 14 percent emigrated, 8 percent starved and 38 percent survived by eating grass and bark. Altogether, 60 percent of the population was affected. (9.35)

Generally speaking, famine relief was not available. In theory, the local magistrate was supposed to maintain grain reserves in an "ever-normal granary" and supervize "community" granaries. In some places, where the local gentry or officials were public-minded, the system worked. Usually, however, especially towards the end of a dynasty, the granaries were rarely full, people in need could not travel to the granary, and transportation and administrative bottlenecks created numerous opportunities for graft. The people who needed help most could not get it. The main famine relief local government could provide was tax reduction—which hardly fed anyone. (9.36) Bringing in food from other regions could be done only on a very limited scale. There was little grain to be purchased near famine areas; few carts or vehicles to transport grain; few draft animals, as they had starved or been eaten; inadequate roads to permit access to famine-stricken regions. In the years before the famine of 1876–79, the government had used its resources to suppress rebellions, and had not been maintaining transportation infrastructure and granaries. (9.37)

Missionaries in China during the great famine of 1876–79 generated international participation in famine relief. (9.38) By the early 1900s international famine relief commissions were working in China, trying both to give relief and to prevent famines. By the time of the famine of 1920–21, relief efforts may have helped as many as 20 million people, and contributed to keeping the death toll down to half a million. (9.39) Relief agencies and Chinese Governments improved and built trans-

* A common currency in China.

portation and water control infrastructure in the 1920s, helped encourage credit co-operatives and distributed some food. By the 1930s relief operations could begin to tide over flood victims near major cities. (9.40)

It must be noted that disasters did not affect people equally. Landless and tenant families suffered earliest and most because they generally lacked resources (especially land) to sell for food. Families owning a house and some land might be reduced to destitution, but might survive. In contrast, wealthy families which had managed to accumulate substantial grain reserves might benefit from a disaster, because they could buy land at low prices. Indeed, perhaps some of the wealthy obstructed long-term water control projects because they anticipated that disasters and famines would offer excellent opportunities for acquiring more assets and keeping the poor in a state of dependency.

Within the family, the impact of famine was also unequal. Unborn would suffer first, through spontaneous abortion and infanticide, particularly of females. The children and elderly—those not able to migrate—might die next. Young women who were sold off as servants might get food but at the sacrifice of a future normal family life. Adult women, burdened with caring for others, probably managed only little better than others. Adult males, able to migrate and steal, perhaps survived the best.

The tragedies of periodic famine in China seems impossible to comprehend in human terms. Facts and figures permit superficial description, but how can they capture the suffering of tens of millions of people, repeated every few decades?

II. Natural Disasters After the Revolution

The success of the communist revolution in 1949 was not able to change the natural environment of China overnight. Rainfall remained variable; silt-laden rivers were still precariously retained by frail dikes. Chinese officials claimed that extensive floods and droughts in many years—and especially in 1954, 1956, 1958–61 and 1972—have hindered economic development and strained government resources. At the same time, the Chinese leaders claim that the disasters were overcome with minimal hardship because available food was shared equitably. The next section will examine food distribution and other policies to prevent natural disaster and famine. This section will examine some of the policies in the 1950s that may have aggravated the food situation in some localities. Important new policies were adopted after the critical disasters of 1958–61 to correct many of these problems.

Table 5 summarizes some Chinese data on the extent of natural disasters after the revolution. While the post-1949 period has not suffered the extreme famines associated with the droughts of 1878 or 1928, or the catastrophic flooding of 1931, or serious breaches of the Yellow River dikes, the disasters reported through 1961 were very large. It is probable that to some extent this is a statistical artifact; the situation was probably not as bad as reported. Three factors conspire to encourage local Chinese leaders to over-report natural disasters in their reports to the central government. First, by overestimating the impact of unfavourable natural conditions, they may have hoped to get more state aid, and to reduce taxes and

TABLE 5.

Partial List of Floods and Droughts in China after 1949

Year	Region	People affected (millions)	Area affected (sq. miles)
1949[a]		45	
1950[a,b]	Huai River flood	34	
1951[a]	Shantung flood, Hopei hail	30	23,000 affected 9000 "serious"
1952[a]		28	
1953[a,c]		17	23,000
1954[a,c,d]	Yangtze, Huai River floods	63	41,000
1955[a,c]		24	28,000
1956[a,c]		70	59,000
1957[a,c]		70	57,000
1958[a,e]	Drought, North China		103,000
1959[e]	Drought, floods, typhoons		154,000
1960[e]	Drought, North China; typhoons, Northeast and South		250,000 affected 77–103,000 "serious"
1961[a]			141,000
1962			
1963[f]	Hai River flood		
1964			
1965			
1966			
1967			
1968[g]	Huai flood, Anhwei, Honan		
1969[g]	Anhwei, Honan problems		
1970[g]	Anhwei, Honan problems		
1971			
1972[g]	Huai, Yangtze, Han floods; Hupei, Kiangsu; drought North China		
1973[g]	Anhwei drought; Kwangsi flood		
1974			
1975[g]	Floods, Honan, Anhwei, Shantung, Kiangsu		

[a] Michael Freeberne, Natural Calamities in China, 1949–61, *Pacific Viewpoint*, 3:2 (September 1962), pp. 33–72.

[b] Yeh Tseng-ke, The Huai River Battle, *People's China*, 4:4 (August 16, 1951), p. 21.

[c] Kang Chao, *Agricultural Production in Communist China, 1949–1965* (Madison: University of Wisconsin Press, 1970), p. 240.

[d] Hsieh Chueh-tsai, Report to the National People's Congress, September 26, 1954, NCNA Peking, September 29, 1954.

[e] D. J. Dwyer, China's Natural Calamities and Their Consequences, *Geography*, 47:216 (July 1962), pp. 301–305.

[f] Ho Chin, *Harm Into Benefit, Taming the Haiho River* (Peking: Foreign Languages Press, 1975), p. 10.

[g] Miriam London and Ivan London, The Other China, Hunger Part II: The Case of the Missing Beggars, *Worldview*, 19:6 (1976), pp. 43–44.

obligations to sell grain to the state. Secondly, reference to natural calamity can be a graceful way of covering up a wide range of politically embarrassing factors that may have reduced yield—such as unsuitable price incentives, poor field management, inappropriate technology, etc. Thirdly, local officials might claim there is a natural disaster to mobilize peasants into joining collective farms, to contribute labour to soil and water conservation projects, or to increase investments. (9.41)

Given these problems in data reporting, the precise extent and severity of natural disasters in the 1950s cannot be specified.

Some of the problems were clearly triggered by nature. The Yangtze River flood in 1954 was obviously caused by excessive rainfall. Figure 3 shows that the rainfall in Shanghai and Nanking combined for 1954 was roughly comparable to that during 1931, when the Yangtze flooded. The combined June–July rainfall for the two cities in 1954 was more (1264 mm) than in 1931 (1247 mm). (9.42) In 1959, during July and August, Peking had a total of 1086 mm of rain. This is 230 percent of the average for these two months, and could easily lead to flooding. Figures 2 and 3 show that 1959–61 was dry in the Nanking area and 1960 was dry in North China but in neither case was the drought unprecedented. However, in July and August of 1962, Tsinan had a total of 835 mm of rain, more than in 1921 when the Yellow River flooded.

The Hai River flood of Augst 1963 can be easily related to the fact that in that month, Peking experienced 422 mm of rainfall, 172 percent of the average, and exceeded (in the period after 1949) only by the rainfall in August 1959. (9.43)

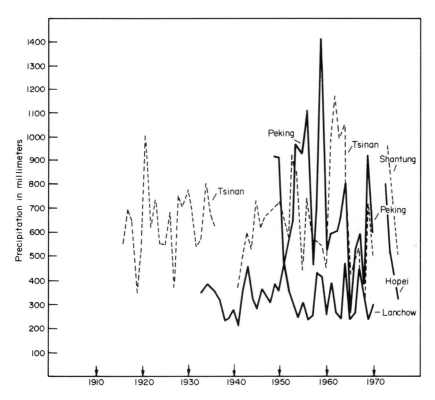

FIG. 2. Precipitation in Northern China cities, 1916–75.

Sources: 1916–50: U.S. Department of Commerce, Environmental Data Service, *World Weather Records, 1951–60*, Volume 4, *Asia* (Washington D.C.: Government Printing Office, 1967), pp. 71, 85.

1949–75: Supplied by U.S. Department of Commerce, Center for Climatic and Environmental Assessment, Columbia, Missouri.

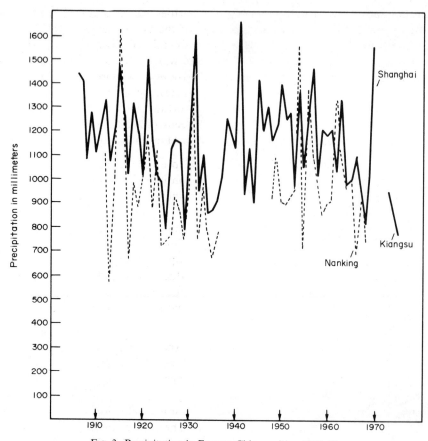

FIG. 3. Precipitation in Eastern Chinese cities, 1906–75

Sources: 1906–50: U.S. Department of Commerce, Environmental Data Service, *World Weather Records, 1951–60,* Volume 4, *Asia* (Washington D.C.: Government Printing Office, 1967), p. 75, 78.
    1949–75: Supplied by U.S. Department of Commerce, Center for Climatic and Environmental Assessment, Columbia, Missouri.

Flooding reported in Kiangsu in 1969 could be caused by excessive rainfall; in July of that year Nanking experienced 608 mm of rain, 335 percent of normal and exceeded since 1911 only once—in 1931, when disastrous floods resulted.

    While climatic stresses have been present, certain political and economic policies of the 1950s may have aggravated the natural disasters, particularly in 1959–61, when there were widespread food shortages and perhaps some regional famines. (9.44) One set of problems, particularly during the 1958–61 period, was the extremely rapid expansion of gravity irrigation systems during 1956–58. In many cases the new projects were not designed or constructed properly, and they resulted in weakening existing dikes, or uncontrolled flooding and resultant raising of the water table and salinization of the soil. (9.45) These ill-conceived projects may have made China more vulnerable to climatic fluctuations and turned normal climatic variations into serious natural disasters.

Another set of problems came from peculiarities of the statistical system and planning process. In the political enthusiasm of the Great Leap Forward of 1958, lower and middle level cadres reported grossly-inflated production figures. The State Statistical Bureau had been weakened and was unable to correct these errors. Higher levels naively accepted these inflated production figures and in turn made inflated demands for grain procurement and taxes. To protect their bureaucratic careers, local officials met these demands. Unfortunately, however, in some cases there was not enough food left to satisfy the needs of the locality. (9.46) A similar error, on a smaller scale, had occurred in 1954. Mao admitted:

> "In 1954 floods caused a decrease in production in some parts of our country, and yet we purchased 7000 million more catties (3.5 million tons) of grain. A decrease in production and an increase in purchasing—this made grain the topic on almost everyone's lips in many places last spring, and nearly every household talked about the state marketing of grain. The peasants were disgruntled, and there were a lot of complaints both inside and outside the Party. Although quite a few people indulged in deliberate exaggeration and exploited the opportunity to attack us, it cannot be said that we had no shortcoming. Inadequate investigation and failure to size up the situation resulted in the purchase of 7000 million more catties; that was a shortcoming". (9.47)

Furthermore, in 1958–59 many localities experimented with free, communal preparation and supply of food. Management was weak and controls were lax; much wastage occurred and food stocks disappeared too rapidly. Before the next harvest, there were food shortages. (9.48)

Several other factors further harmed agricultural production during this period. Co-operatives were organized into large communes, which lacked rational systems of labour organization and incentives. To some extent China's peasants expressed dissatisfaction by going on sit-down strikes. Moreover, in many places inappropriate agricultural techniques—seeds, field management practices (close planting and deep ploughing), cropping patterns—were popularized without adequate local testing. In addition, a frenzied campaign to manufacture iron in countless backyard furnaces created a labour shortage. An equally frenzied tool reform campaign was unable to save the equivalent labour. Additional problems were caused by the sudden removal of Soviet technicians in 1960, which interrupted many economic activities.

It is impossible to specify exactly how serious the food problem was in 1959–61. Edgar Snow reported:

> "... I saw no starving people in China, nothing that looked like old-time famine ... Isolated instances of starvation due to neglect or failure of the rationing system were possible. Considerable malnutrition undoubtedly existed. Mass starvation? No." (9.49)

On the other hand, L. La Dany has ventured an estimate that 50 million people died during this period, but this number is meaningless; it implies that about 16.6 million people died in each of three years, 1960–62, or 12.5 million in each of four years; (9.50) one would expect over 13 million people to die each year. (9.51) The

Londons offer reports from refugees—at least some of whom can be presumed reliable—that in widely-scattered localities, famine-related deaths were fairly common, ranging from a handful to thousands. However, they do not indicate what percentage of the population these famine deaths represent, so there is no way to use them to extrapolate to a national basis. (9.52)

Leo Orleans has guessed that the death rate in China went up from 19 per thousand in 1958 to 20 in 1959, 21 in 1960–61, back to 20 in 1962, and back to 19 in 1963. These figures imply that roughly 4 million people died prematurely in these four years. (9.53)

It is also impossible to specify the precise cause of the food shortages in 1959–61. There clearly was a complex interaction of bad weather which was seriously compounded by various types of mismanagement. Liu Shao-ch'i, then chairman of the government, charged that the crisis was 70 percent man-made and only 30 percent attributable to natural calamities. (9.54)

Whatever the precise extent of food shortages in 1959–61 and whatever the precise cause, the Chinese leadership made a series of important policy changes in 1961–62 to make sure that such widespread food problems would not occur again. These policies are reviewed in the next section.

III. Policies to Control Flood, Drought and Famine

Although many of the policies to control floods and droughts had origins in earlier years, the crisis of 1959–61 forced a reassessment of economic strategy in general and a new rural policy emerged. (9.55) No single one of these policies in isolation can be considered crucial. Rather, the effective integration of the set of policies is the distinctive, effective aspect of China's policy.

A. RIVER CONTROL PROJECTS

One of the first steps of the Communist government was to rejuvenate the Yellow River Authority and to establish regional authorities to co-ordinate long-term planning for other river basins, such as the Hai and Huai. (In the latter case, there seems to have been some reluctance of the provinces and localities involved to surrender authority to the river authority.) (9.56) These river basin authorities were under the national Ministry of Water Conservation and Electric Power.

The magnitude of the task of controlling these rivers cannot be overestimated. The problem, of course, was not the engineering plans. Certainly by the mid-1920s complex, comprehensive plans had been drafted for the Huai and Hai Rivers. (9.57) The problem was implementation. Specialists in the 1930s warned, "To control the Yellow River now is a superhuman task. Apart from river control on a hitherto unattempted scale in the plains, it would require land reclamation throughout the immense catechment basin, inhabited by an inert, individualistic people ignorant of the magnitude of the task and indifferent to the larger issues involved.... There is not much hope ...." (9.58)

After the revolution of 1949, Mao Tse-tung showed personal interest in river control work. In May 1951 (a few months after it flooded) he said, "The Huai River must be harnessed." In 1952 he said, "Work on the Yellow River must be done well"; and in November 1963, after the Hai River flooded, Mao said, "The Hai River must be brought under permanent control."

Generally speaking, the long-term river control programmes have utilized reasonably conventional techniques. On the upper reaches of the Yellow River, at least three major dams have been built—the Sanmen, Ching-tung and Liuchiahsia dams. Roughly 1000 large, medium and small-sized reservoirs and power stations have been built on its tributaries. (9.59) Naturally, erosion has been a serious problem, and silt has been filling up the reservoirs behind the dams. To control erosion in the watershed regions of the river, much land has been afforested and hillsides have been terraced. (9.60) However, much work remains to be done. On the lower reaches, careful maintenance of dikes (1800 km) and dredging keeps water under control. The Yellow River has not flooded since it was pushed back into its pre-war course in 1949.

For the other rivers, the approach is basically the same. On the Huai River, more than 30 large reservoirs and 2000 medium and small ones hold water in the upper and middle reaches. Likewise, for the Hai River, 85 large and medium reservoirs and 1500 small ones were built. To facilitate drainage of water out of the flat North China Plain, 13 major water courses were dug to connect the Huai and Yangtze to the sea; and by the Hai River, 29 main watercourses have increased the capacity for taking flood water to the sea by 500 percent. (9.61) On the tributaries of the Yangtze River, hundreds of large and medium reservoirs have been built, including 20 major flood diversion and detention works. Major canals have been dug to provide rapid drainage for the river in regions which previously had been bottle-necks. Raising and reinforcing the 3100 km of dikes along the Yangtze is important, too. (9.62)

Throughout China, 130,000 km of dikes have been repaired, reinforced, or built. Nearly 100 big drainage canals have been dug. Over 2000 large and medium-sized reservoirs have been built. In addition, there are many small projects. (9.63)

Controlling these major rivers has been a long-term project. Work on the Huai and Yellow Rivers began in the early 1950s, and took twenty years. Although small reservoirs had been built in the 1950s, large-scale work did not begin on the Hai River until after the flood of 1963 and proceeded until 1972.

In the actual construction of these projects China has developed effective local participation and contribution of resources. The river basin authority first collects hydrologic data, often by consulting with old peasants who remember previous floods. Then its professional engineering staff plans an integrated water control programme. The construction plans are phased to be done each winter, when labour is available and water levels low. The labour itself comes from the region to be benefitted. The river basin authority asks each county to provide a labour brigade and the county, in turn, asks each work team (there could be several thousand in the county) to send two or three members to the work site. In this way, over a million labourers can be mobilized within one province. (9.64) For principal projects on the Hai River, the average annual labour input over eight years was 45 million man-days. (9.65) Labourers on these projects receive work points (i.e. a share of the profit) of their own production team, just as they would for farm labour at home. (9.66) Since this diminishes the value of the work point, it means that everyone in the team is making an investment in the project.

The state does provide tractors, rollers, dredgers, derricks and trucks for moving earth and stone, and also allocates steel, cement, bricks and timber for construction purposes. The state may also transport the labourers and provides some money for living expenses on work sites. Peasants may bring carts and wheel-barrows with them. "Small" projects (i.e. 1 to 10 million cubic meter storage capacity) are constructed by communes without state aid.

It must be noted that this vast organization and mobilization of labour takes place within a particular political-economic context. People are willing to contribute labour not only because they are paid, but also because they will get benefits of the project in the future, as the productivity increases. Moreover, these projects are accompanied with much ideological mobilization, including reminders about past devastations caused by flood and drought. Political and military leaders join in the labour to maintain morale.

These giant projects appear to be working. The Yellow River has not flooded since the revolution. The Hai River has not flooded since 1963. The Huai has not, apparently, been tamed yet; it reportedly flooded in 1968. The Yangtze last flooded in 1954. Food production in North China has been stabilized and increased to the point that food is no longer brought north from South China on a regular basis.

This system seems to work less well with regard to afforestation work, where much of the benefits will come to future generations in downstream regions of the country. In these cases, a greater role for the state has proven beneficial.

Controlling China's rivers and protecting North China from flood has been a massive task, which has used tremendous material, human and organizational resources for decades. Success in this sort of work does not come quickly and easily.

B. INCREASING AND STABILIZING FOOD PRODUCTION

To prevent famine, a continuous increase in food production at least as rapid as population growth is obviously essential. China has succeeded in this. Over the entire period of 1950–1976, grain production has grown at the average annual rate of 2.5 percent, a bit more than population. (9.67) Production of other food commodities has probably gone up more rapidly; statistics are unavailable for vegetables, fruit, fish, poultry, etc. but sugar production is thought to have increased by 5.2 percent from 1957 to 1974, and hog production is estimated to have been growing at 3.9 percent. (9.68) The actual levels of food production are still modest compared to a Western diet, but are reasonably high by Asian standards—perhaps 40 percent more grain *per capita* than in India (depending on what population estimate is used for China and what year is used for India) and roughly double the animal protein *per capita*. (9.69) Since China actually has less total cultivated land than India does and has 50 percent more people, China must have more multiple cropping and higher yields for each crop. Taking both factors into account, an acre of farmland produces about 250 percent more food than an acre in India. (9.70)

Getting these high levels of productivity and growth has required extensive modernization of China's agriculture. Especially after the agricultural collapse of 1960–61, China has invested tremendous resources in agricultural modernization.

The Chinese do not think of modern agriculture in narrow terms, such as new seeds, fertilizer, or tractors. Rather they see modernization of agriculture as involving a comprehensive set of changes in eight areas: (1) soil conservation, (2) water conservation, (3) fertilizer, (4) seeds, (5) crop protection, (6) distance of planting, (7) field management, and (8) tool improvement and mechanization.

During the early 1960s the most rapid regions of growth in agriculture were the fertile river valleys and lake basins of South and Central China. Rural electrification and low-lift pumps in these regions permitted more precise control of water that was essential for the spread of high-yielding varieties and for more multiple cropping.

In the early 1970s, the massive river control projects of dry North China were complemented by the installation of mechanical tubewells thereby permitting an intensification of cultivation over more than 7 million hectares by 1974. (9.71) By 1975 China had a total capacity of power pumps roughly 2.9 million cu. sec., roughly double India's capacity. (9.72)

Altogether, the Chinese government considers that roughly 33 million hectares (roughly 27 percent of cultivated area) will have an assured harvest, despite drought or flood. (9.73) About 24 million hectares of this land are in roughly a dozen regions that have historically been centres of China's agricultural production. These projects are listed in Table 6. Another 9–10 million hectares have been improved in small projects undertaken by most communes, brigades and teams. The Chinese have announced a goal of developing by about 1980 one mou (a fifteenth of a hectare) of land per rural resident, that will give high and stable yields, irrespective of drought and waterlogging. (This would total roughly 50 million Ha.) (9.74)

Part of China's success stems from a decision made in the late 1950s to rapidly expand the chemical fertilizer industry. Since the early 1960s, production has been growing at roughly 20 percent annually. In 1963 Chinese engineers designed a type of factory that could use coal and water to produce ammonium bicarbonate. Although the operating costs of this process were fairly high and the product was not the best, most-concentrated fertilizer, the capital costs were low and start-up

TABLE 6.

Regions of Highly Productive Agriculture, with Mechanized or Secure Irrigation, 1974

	Million hectares
North China Plain	10.3
Upper Yellow River	0.8
Northeast	0.2
Middle and Lower Yangtze Valley	10.0
Pearl River Delta	0.5
Hunan, Tungting Lake Region	0.7
Fukien	0.6
Other, South China (Hainan, Kwangsi)	0.5
Total	23.6

Source: Ben Stavis, A Preliminary Model for Grain Production in China, 1974, *China Quarterly*, 65 (March 1976), p. 87.

time short. A programme was begun to install one such factory in most of China's 2200 counties.

In 1972, however, China changed its fertilizer policy somewhat. Because expansion of the petroleum and natural gas industry made new feedstocks available, because a more concentrated fertilizer was desired to reduce transportation costs, and because new industrial processes had been developed in the West that could greatly reduce the cost of making ammonia, China embarked on a remarkable programme of purchasing twenty-eight of the largest, most modern ammonia and urea factories in the world. Americans, Japanese, Dutch, Danish and the French supplied the factories for a cost of at least U.S. $442 million. (9.75) By the mid-1970s, China possessed the world's third largest fertilizer industry, surpassed only by those of the U.S. and U.S.S.R. China has been, at the same time, one of the world's largest importers of chemical fertilizers.

Despite the magnitude of China's chemical fertilizer production and imports, the amounts available per hectare are still modest because of China's large crop land. Thus, to obtain adequate crop nutrients, China continues to utilize huge amounts of organic materials for compost. Pig manure and nightsoil, combined with vegetable leaves, straw, mud and other materials are carefully composted and provide roughly half of the crop nutrients.

Production of farm machinery such as tractors, pumps and stationary threshers has also grown rapidly, particularly after 1968. Machinery is needed to save time and enable rapid harvesting, cultivating and planting of a field in multiple cropping systems.

It might be noted that before China could develop its chemical and farm-machinery industries, China had to go through a period of ten to fifteen years of creating a heavy industry base. Steel and machine tools were needed to make machines. A petroleum industry was needed to provide fuel. A transportation infrastructure was required. In short, a policy to support agriculture could not be implemented until the economy had developed somewhat.

Another indication of state support for agriculture is in the area of science, technology, and manpower training. By 1963, roughly 100,000 people had been trained at the college level in some field of agriculture. (9.76) They were able to staff a large research and extension system, as well as government and financial offices. China developed a large and effective agricultural science research programme.

During the late 1950s and early 1960s, considerable success was achieved in rice-breeding work. Chinese plant breeders did the same thing that other plant breeders did to rice—they developed dwarf varieties that could utilize large amounts of fertilizer without falling over (lodging). (The dwarfing gene came from a variety from Kwangsi province.)

A distinctive characteristic of the Chinese dwarf varieties, however, is that they mature ten to fifteen days earlier and are tolerant to the cold weather near the end of a long season. These innovations permitted not only high yields but also saved time for multiple cropping. Not until the early 1970s were Chinese breeders successful in doing the same thing with wheat, namely developing short, high-yielding, early-maturing varieties. Chinese breeders have also been doing considerable work with cotton, maize, sorghum; less work seems to have been done on vegetables. (9.77) Although the Chinese plant breeders have access to the improved varieties of seeds from the international research centres through friendly countries such as Pakistan, the Chinese breeding programme has been essentially self-reliant. The Chinese found that the rice varieties from the International Rice Research Institute required too much time for their compressed growing seasons.

Since 1970, Chinese plant breeders have made a major breakthrough in developing and applying tissue culture techniques for practical purposes. Anther or pollen culture has been developed for ten species, including wheat and rice. (9.78) Tissue culture techniques had been developed in many countries for tobacco, and Japanese scientists first published descriptions of a technique for rice in 1968. China is one of the first countries (perhaps the first) in which anther culture of wheat has been achieved. China is doing much to improve the workability of tissue culture techniques, including development of new medium for growing tissues and similar work.

Tissue culture offers a way of isolating in a single step all the potential genetic combinations which can be realized from a cross of two varieties. Unlike normal crossing, in which the genetic makeup of crosses is unstable and subject to change in subsequent generations, the genetic combinations resulting from anther culture are stable and can be multiplied and popularized rapidly. Careful screening and field testing are essential to identify superior progeny generated by tissue culture, just as they are for more traditional varietal crossing programmes. For many countries, the field testing is a bottleneck in seed improvement programmes and tissue culture would not be particularly helpful, but the extensive research network in China, with production team research groups able to test new varieties, can help do the field testing work. (An additional aid for testing varieties under specific conditions is an artificial climate laboratory at the Shanghai Institute of Plant Physiology with 360 square metres in twenty-five rooms.)

The potential saving of time with tissue culture is dramatic. The time needed to develop new, pure strains of crops can be reduced from ten to thirty years to two to three years. For three crops, the potential saving is even greater, and it is not surprising that some laboratories are working on tissue culture of trees in China (as in the U.S.).

In addition to its speed in developing new varieties, tissue culture offers other advantages. It is relatively inexpensive technology, not requiring elaborate equipment. It does, however, use much labour to do the tedious work of extracting pollen and screening thousands of progeny. It requires the careful organization that China can provide. Because of its inherent simplicity and inexpensiveness, tissue culture can be done in a highly decentralized system, with provinces and counties doing effective breeding work. By 1976, over two hundred units in China were studying tissue culture.

Another distinctive dimension of agricultural research in China has been extensive work on microbiological processes in the hope that reliance on chemicals can be reduced. (9.79) Leaves and stalks are ground up and partially digested by enzymes so that they can be fed to pigs.

Microbiological fertilizers are being developed. Plant growth regulating hormones are used to speed up the maturation of crops. Micro-organisms are used to attack insects and to cure plant diseases. Manures and refuse are fermented anaerobically to generate methane. (In China, the "Gobar" gas plants are smaller and far simpler than in India. They lack an expansion chamber and must be managed carefully to prevent excessive pressure build-up. This permits a very inexpensive design suitable for use by a small household. These pits are widespread in some regions.) To date, these types of research have had only limited practical application, and China remains dependent on chemicals for fertilizer and plant protection. However, it is likely over the years that these biological processes will be used more.

In the last few years, China has been emphasizing practical education in agriculture. Agricultural colleges have redesigned their curricula to reduce abstract theoretical studies and to stress practical problems. Students are drawn increasingly from the rural communities, and are, in fact, screened by local political officials to assure their commitment to correct social values. After graduation they are expected to go back to the countryside and work in agricultural management or development.

Some observers believe that such an education lacks the theoretical foundation necessary for long-term scientific development. This criticism is probably true, but fails to recognize that China trained thousands of scientists before the Cultural Revolution of 1966, so that by the late 1960s a more pressing need was to train people with skills that could be used in the actual implementation of agricultural modernization. Continuation of the education policies of the 1950s and early 1960s would have trained people who were not really enthusiastic about working at the commune and brigade level. There is, of course, a danger that overemphasis on practical education will eventually undercut the theoretical studies on which science is based, and many people in China are sensitive to this fact. The "gang of four" purged in autumn 1976 has been charged with undermining the development of scientific theoretical education and studies. (9.80)

Agricultural modernization in China may have a distinctive feature. In most countries, it appears that an inescapable consequence of agricultural modernization is that agricultural production becomes more variable. Techniques (including seed varieties) that are highly productive under normal climatic conditions may do poorly under conditions of climatic stress—drought, excess moisture, or high or low temperature. (9.81) This presents a special problem as it appears climate is becoming increasingly variable. Detailed data on yields of each crop and microclimatic data are not available to do a definitive analysis, but yield data on crops from six localities (presented in Fig. 4) suggest reasonable stability of grain production. These localities are not totally immune from the effects of bad weather—the impact of drought in North China in 1972 is particularly clear in the Hsipu, Tachai, and Sungchuang grain yields. However, the drought and other climatic variations usually cannot reduce yields by more than about 10 percent. Stability in yields probably stems from close attention to irrigation and from mobilization of labour to carry water in buckets to the plants under conditions of moisture stress. (The localities included in Figure 4 are not perfectly representative of China—their growth rates are somewhat above the national average; but it is likely that they do reflect a process which is going on in most places, albeit slower.)

Sensible incentive policies are needed so that peasants will adopt modern agriculture. Price, tax and procurement policy have all been adjusted, in ways described later, so that it is profitable to adopt improved techniques. Moreover, the Chinese have been sensitive to the need to produce light industrial consumer goods, so that

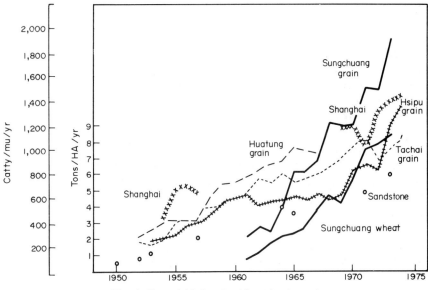

FIG. 4. Crop yields in selected production units

Sources:

Sungchuang: Chu Li and Tien Chieh-yun, *Inside a People's Commune* (Peking: Foreign Languages Press, 1974), p. 143.

Tachai: Paul Steidlmayer, *The Dazhai Model in Chinese Agriculture, 1964–74* (Stanford: Food Research Institute Dissertation, 1975), Table II-7. "How Tachai Improved its Soil," *China Reconstructs*, June 1976, p. 19.

Hsipu: "*Ch'iung-pang Tzu*" *Ching-sheng Fang-Kuang Mang* (The Spirit of a Pauper's Model Illuminates the Way) (Peking: People's Publishers, 1975), p. 168.

Huatung: Ward Morehouse, "Notes on Hua-tung Commune," *China Quarterly* 67 (September 1976), p. 586.

Sandstone: Tang Feng-chang, *Sandstone Hollow* (Peking: Foreign Languages Press, 1975), pp. 3, 5, 13, 28, 61.

Shanghai: Robert Ash, "Economic Progress in the Suburbs of Shanghai, 1949–74," unpublished paper, 1977.

farmers have things to purchase with increased incomes. In addition, a wide range of ideological incentives are used. Political meetings are common, and group social pressure is used to encourage participation.

The policies of increasing and stabilizing agricultural production have had their controversial aspects. A major shift in economic strategy was required away from the Soviet model of economic development, with an emphasis on building up heavy industry and to a new strategy, with emphasis on agriculture. This shift was symbolized in the slogan "Agriculture is the base of the economy", which gained currency around 1961. However, the switch in emphasis from industry to agriculture was balanced, as agriculture still needed steel, chemicals, cement, and power from industry; hence the slogan "Industry is the leading factor in agriculture", which was also used in 1961–62.

It has also been necessary to combat romantic, ultra-leftist visions that material incentives are irrelevant, that large-scale production units are feasible, that perfect egalitarianism is acceptable by peasants, and that science and expertise are useless.

TABLE 7.
Crude Vital Statistics for China

Year	Crude death rate per 1000			Infant mortality per 1000			Life expectancy at birth		
	Average	Urban	Rural	Average	Urban	Rural	Average	Urban	Rural
1930s, 1940s	25–30[a,b] 50 in epidemics[g]	14[g]		125–200[a,b,g]	117[g]–150[i]	125–200[a,b,g]	35[h]		
1955	20–21[c]	7–11							
1957	17–19[c]	7[g]			30–50[f]	74[g]			
1960	21–25[c]								
1965	17[c]								
1970	16[c]						53[c]	73[f] [Shanghai 1972]	
1975	12–13[c]		6[f]	20–30[d]	13[f]–19[i]		56[e]		

Sources: [a] League of Nations, Health Organisation, *Intergovernmental Conference of Far-Eastern Countries on Rural Hygiene: Preparatory Papers, Report of China* (Geneva: League of Nations Publications C.H. 1235 (f), 1973), p. 12.
[b] Victor Sidel, "Health Services in the People's Republic of China," in John Z. Bowers and Elizabeth Purcell, eds., *Medicine and Society in China* (New York: Josiah Macy Jr. Foundation, 1974), p. 104.
[c] Leo Orleans, "China's Population, Can the Contradiction be Resolved?" *China: A Reassessment of the Economy* (Washington D.C.: Joint Economic Committee, 1975), pp. 75–77.
[d] Norman Myers, "Of All Things People are Most Precious", *New Scientist* (January 9, 1975), p. 57.
[e] Leo Orleans, personal communication, based on *Some Projections on the Population of PRC* (Chicago: Community and Family Study Center, 1974).
[f] Victor Sidel and Ruth Sidel, *Serve the People* (New York: Josiah Macy Jr. Foundation, 1973), p. 265.
[g] Janet Salaff, "Mortality Decline in the People's Republic of China and the United States," *Population Studies* 27:3 (November 1973), pp. 552, 556.
[h] John Buck, *Land Utilization in China* (New York: Paragon Reprint, 1964), p. 391.
[i] Judith Banister, "Mortality, Fertility and Contraceptive Use in Shanghai," *China Quarterly* No. 70 (June 1977), pp. 287–294.

IV. Improvement in Health

Coincident with a period of agricultural growth and improved distribution of food has been a steady improvement of the health of China's population. Table 7 reveals dramatic improvements: the crude death rate has dropped from 25–30 to 12–13 per thousand; infant mortality has dropped from up to 200 to 20–30 per thousand; and life expectancy is up from 35 to 55 years.

Of course the improvements in health cannot be attributed entirely or exclusively to changes in agricultural production or food distribution. A wide range of policies was relevant, including peace and order, sanitation control and general control of disease-spreading vectors (especially snails that carry snail fever), innoculation campaigns, continued use of breast feeding, and improving access to doctors and other medical personnel. (9.82) While improved nutrition was an essential element of this improvement, it should be noted that significant improvements in health were already achieved by 1955 by establishing order and by some redistribution.

The data in Table 7 indicate that there have been substantial differences in urban and rural health. These differences existed in the 1930s and have continued to the present. Crude death rates and infant mortality rates are roughly double in rural areas as in urban. The life expectancy in the major cities appears to be fifteen to twenty years more than in rural areas. In rough terms, rural health in the 1970s approximates urban health of the 1950s.

Chinese public health officials have conducted numerous surveys in which children (usually urban) have been weighed and measured. These anthropometric measurements reinforce the conclusion of improved health over the years but also hint at some urban–rural differences.

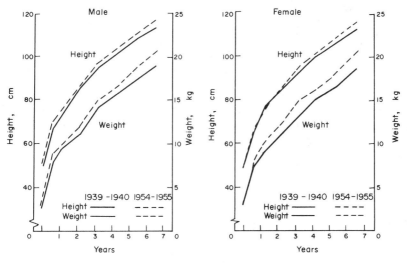

FIG. 5. Comparison of height and weight increases of pre-school age children 1939–40, 1954–55, males and females

Source: "Physical Measurements of Children Under Seven Years in Peking After Liberation," *Chinese Journal of Paediatrics*, No. 5 (1956), pp. 343–344, cited in Janet Salaff, "Mortality Decline in the People's Republic of China and the United States," *Population Studies* 27:3 (November 1973), p. 574.

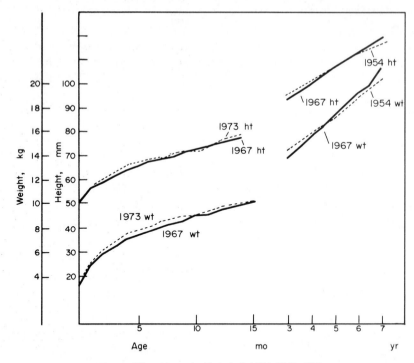

FIG. 6. Size of boys in Shanghai, 1954, 1967, 1973

Sources: 1954—Chao Lin, "Anthropometric Measurements of Shanghai Students and Preschool Children in 1954, A Preliminary Study," *Chinese Medical Journal* 75 (December 1957), pp. 1021–22.

1967—Joe Wray, "Child Health in China," 1975, mimeo.

1973—Shanghai Child Health Care Coordinating Group, "Growth and Development of Shanghai Infants Under 20 Months of Age," *Chinese Medical Journal* No. 20 (October 1976), pp. 605–606.

In Peking, the average birth weight of children went up about 3 percent from 1953 to 1963 and another 3.6 percent in the next decade. (9.83) Children aged 0–7 in Peking were both taller and heavier in 1954–55 than in 1939–40 (Figure 5).

In Shanghai, surveys in 1954 disclosed that children aged 8–15 years were substantially larger than they were in 1944, during wartime stress, and somewhat larger than they were in 1930–31. (9.84) However, in 1967 they were roughly the same size that they had been in 1954. Shanghai infants (under 20 months) were somewhat larger in 1965 than they had been in 1956, and were not noticeably larger in 1973 (see Figure 6). Health for all age groups in Shanghai is outstanding. In 1972, age-specific death rates were lower than those of the white population of New York City in 1970, and were approaching those of Sweden. (9.85)

Only one survey of size and weight of *rural* children has been located—for children in rural regions of Peking municipality in 1974. The results of this survey are charted on Figure 7 and are compared with surveys in a Peking suburban commune in 1959 and Shanghai in 1954. The Figures show that the Peking rural boys in 1974 were larger than Peking suburban boys fifteen years earlier. However,

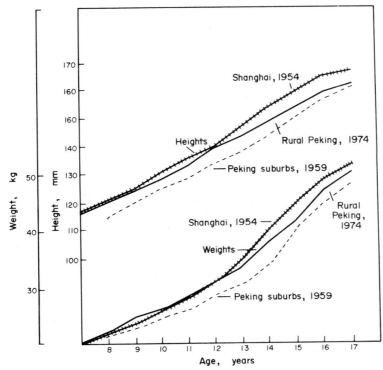

FIG. 7. Size of boys in rural Peking, 1974 and urban Shanghai and Peking, 1954 and 1959

Sources: Peking, 1959 and 1974—"A Survey of Physical Development of Elementary and Secondary School Students in the Rural Villages of Ch'ang-p'ing-hsien and Mi-yun-hsien," *Chung-hua I-hsüeh Tsa-chih* (Chinese Medical Journal) No. 1 (1976), pp. 26–27.

Shanghai—Chao Lin, "Anthropometric Measurements of Shanghai Students and Pre-school Children in 1954, A Preliminary Study," *Chinese Medical Journal* 75 (December 1957), pp. 1021–22.

the Peking rural boys were still not as large as the Shanghai city boys had been twenty years earlier. Given the lack of data, it is not possible to disentagle the effects of regional differences and urban–rural differences. Nor is there assurance that definitions of age, measurement procedures, and sampling procedures are uniform in the different surveys which have been compared. Nevertheless, these data on child size seem to agree with the general vital statistics in Table 7, that rural health is lagging perhaps two decades behind urban health. The combined effects of intestinal parasites (which are difficult to control completely, even though night soil is generally composted), hard work, and accidents keep rural health below urban health. (9.86)

V. Conclusion

China has transformed itself from a land of famine to a modestly comfortable country. By no means is China a rich country: diets are mostly grain; clothing and shelter are simple. But recurrent famines have been ended. The contrast with the past is tremendous.

These improvements have not come easily. Tremendous physical work and financial outlays have been needed. Major political changes were needed to give the central government resources for development, to assure they would be spent on rural development, and to assure that food would be shared reasonably equally over time and space, both within the village, and within the family. In China, violent revolution was an integral step in establishing a political order with these capabilities and interests, and revolution involved its own set of costs. Whether or not violent revolution was an unavoidable precondition for improvements is a long-debated and unanswerable question. It is, however, clear that a set of political changes was needed.

Ending famines in China has taken about twenty-five years. This much time was needed to build an industrial base that could support modern agriculture; to create an institutional system that could achieve both growth and equity; to build massive water works that could harness the floods and tame the droughts; and to generate new techniques to solve the complex problems of very intensive agriculture. It is difficult for most political systems to think in such long-run terms. There is a great temptation (to which China has sometimes succumbed) to have short-term crash programmes, and to seek short-term benefits. In a sense China was fortunate that its government has had so much political strength and legitimacy that it has been able to take a long-term point of view. It is not plagued by major ethnic or cultural cleavages which would place additional pressures on the political system. A strong, reasonably well unified polity for thousands of years, China has not had to build a nation, simultaneously with developing its economy.

For regions of the world still plagued by famines, the implications of China's experience are clear. Famines can be ended—but long, hard work is needed.

Notes to Chapter 9

9.1 M. L. Dantwala (1973), *Poverty in India: Then and Now: 1870–1970*, Delhi, Macmillan, (Dadabhai Naoroji Memorial Fellowship Prize, Lecture 1971), pp. 20–21.

9.2 D. Banerji (1973), Health Behaviour of Rural Populations: Impact of Rural Health Services, *Economic and Political Weekly*, VIII, 2261–68.

9.3 V. M. Dandekar & Nilakantha Rath (1971), *Poverty in India*, Bombay, Indian School of Political Economy.

9.4 P. K. Bardhan (1974), On the Incidence of Poverty in Rural India in the Sixties, *Sankhya, Series C*, 36, 2 & 4, 264–280.

9.5 A. J. Fonseca *Ed.* (1971), *Challenge of Poverty in India*, Delhi, Vikas.

9.6 National Institute of Nutrition (1976), *Annual Report 1976*, New Delhi, Indian Council of Medical Research, Section 11.2, pp. 121–128.

9.7 Glaxo Symposium on Nutrition, Growth and Develoment (1971), Session IV. Nutrition and Mental Development, *Indian Journal of Medical Research*, 59, 6, Suppl.; 177–220.

9.8 Raj Narain (1977), New Health Services in Rural Areas, *Centre Calling*, 12, 4–5; 10–15.

9.9 Central Bureau of Health Intelligence (1976), *Pocket Book of Health Statistics*, New Delhi, Govt. of India.

9.10 National Tuberculosis Institute, Bangalore (1974), Tuberculosis in a Rural Population of South India: A Five Year Epidemiological Study, *Bulletin of World Health Organisation*, 51: 473–488.

9.11 E. R. N. Grigg (1958), Arcana of Tuberculosis, *American Review of Research Diseases*, 78: 151–172; 78: 426–53; 78: 583–603.

9.12 B. K. Anand, G. S. Chhina & Baldev Singh (1961), Studies on Shri Ramanand Yogi during his stay in an Air-tight Box, *Indian Journal of Medical Research*, 49, 1; 82–9.

9.13 India, Famine Inquiry Commission, (Chairman: John Woodhead) (1945), *Report on Bengal*, Govt. of India, pp. 104–110.
9.14 B. M. Bhatia (1967), *Famines in India: A Study in Some Aspects of the Economic History of India (1860–1865)*, Bombay, Asia.
9.15 Central Institute of Research and Training in Public Co-operation, New Delhi, *Famine Relief in Bihar: A Study*, New Delhi, CIRTPC, p. 17, p. 21.
9.16 Mathur, Kuldeep and Bhattacharya, Mohit (1975), *Administrative Response to Emergency*, Delhi, Concept.
9.17 Maharashtra (1973), *Drought in Maharashtra*, Bombay, Govt. of Maharashtra.
9.18 V. V. Borkar & M. V. Nadkarni (1975), *Impact of Drought on Rural Life*, Bombay, Popular Prakashan.
9.19 *Sample Registration Bulletin*, 9, 4; 1975.
9.20 *Sample Registration Bulletin*, 10, 3–4; 1976.
9.21 Walter Mallory, *China: Land of Famine* (New York: American Geographical Society, 1926).
9.22 Yao Shan-yu, "The Chronological and Seasonal Distribution of Floods and Droughts in Chinese History, 206 B.C.–A.D. 1911", *Harvard Journal of Asiatic Studies* 6: 3/4 (February 1942), pp. 273–312. This article is an update of Cho-Ching Chu, "Climatic Pulsations During Historic Time in China", *Geographical Review* 16.2 (April 1926), pp. 274–282.
9.23 John Buck, *Land Utilization in China* (New York: Paragon Reprint, 1968), p. 124.
9.24 *Ibid.*, p. 407.
9.25 Coching Chu, The Aridity of North China, *Pacific Affairs*, 8:4 (1935), pp. 207–217.
9.26 John Freeman, Flood Problems in China, *Transactions of the American Society of Civil Engineers*, 85 (1922), p. 1405.
9.27 *China Tames Her Rivers* (Peking: Foreign Languages Press, 1972), p. 4.
9.28 Inspired by the 1911 Huai River flood, one American engineer observed, "Probably no place in the world more urgently needs improvement by works on a large scale". John Freeman, *op. cit.*, p. 1450.
9.29 *Harm Into Benefit: Taming the Haiho River* (Peking: Foreign Languages Press, 1975), p. 3–7.
9.30 John Palmer Gavit, *Opium* (New York: Bretanos, pp. 27), pp. 127–131.
9.31 Wm. F. Junkin, Famine Conditions in North Anhui and North Kiang-su, *Chinese Recorder*, 43:2 (February 1912), pp. 75–81.
9.32 G. Findlay Andrew, On the Trial of Death in Northwest China, *Asia*, 32:1 (January 1932), p. 43.
9.33 For 1878 drought, see David Hill, trans., A Record of the Famine Relief Work in Lin Fen Hien, *Chinese Recorder*, 11:4 (July–August 1880), p. 202 and Paul Richard Bohr, *Famine in China and the Missionary*, (Cambridge: Harvard East Asian Research Centre, 1972), pp. 13–26. For the 1928–29 drought, see G. Findlay Andrew, *op. cit.*, p. 45.
9.34 J. Dudgeon, The Famine in North China, *Chinese Recorder*, 11:5 (September–October 1880), pp. 349–57.
9.35 John Buck, *Land Utilization in China* (New York: Paragon Reprint, 1968), p. 124.
9.36 T'ung-tsu Ch'u, *Local Government in China under the Ch'ing*, (Stanford: Stanford University Press, 1969), pp. 156–61; Kung-chuan Hsiao, *Rural China, Imperial Control in the Nineteenth Century*, (Seattle: University of Washington Press, 1960), pp. 144–183.
9.37 For a detailed account of the Ching government's serious but inadequate efforts at famine relief in 1876–79, see Bohr, *op. cit.*, pp. 27–82.
9.38 *Ibid.*
9.39 Andrew James Nathan, *A History of the China International Famine Relief Commission* (Cambridge: Harvard East Asian Research Centre, 1965) p. 5.
9.40 Edmund Clubb, Floods of China, A National Disaster, *Journal of Geography*, 31:5 (May 1932), pp. 199–206.
9.41 Michael Freeberne, Natural Calamities in China, 1949–61, *Pacific Viewpoint*, 3:2 (September 1962), pp. 38–41 hints at these types of considerations.
9.42 Based on monthly data available in sources for Figures 2 and 3.
9.43 A detailed report on the natural stresses leading to this flood is in *Harm Into Benefit, Taming the Haiho River*, (Peking: Foreign Languages Press, 1975), p. 10.
9.44 Mirian London and Ivan London, The Other China, Hunger: Part I, The Three Red Flags of Death, *Worldview*, 19:5 (May 1976), pp. 4–11.
9.45 By 1962 Chinese writers were suggesting that irrigation in North China be suspended to save soil from salinization and alkalinization. Hsiung I, The Prevention and Cure of Salinization and Alkalinization of the Soil in the North China Plain, *Jen-min Jih-pao*, December 18, 1962; Chang Tzu-lin and Huang Jung-han, The Problem of Improving the Alkaline and Saline Land and the Prevention of Salinization and Alkalinization in North China, *Hung Ch'i*, 15–16, August 1, 1962; cited in Wen-shun Chi, Water Conservancy in Communist China, *China Quarterly*, No. 23 (July–September 1965), p. 51. See also Kang Chao, *Agricultural Production in Communist China, 1965–1970*

(Madison: University of Wisconsin Press, 1970), pp. 129–35; and Thomas Wiens, The Evolution of Agricultural Technology in the People's Republic of China, 1957–76, (Bethesda: Mathtech, unpublished mimeo, 1976), p. 15. This problem is common in many countries, see Erik Eckholm, Salting the Earth, *Environment*, 17:7 (October 1975), pp. 9–15.

9.46 London and London, The Other China, Hunger: Part I, The Three Red Flags of Death, Worldview, 19:5 (May 1976), p. 6.

9.47 Mao Tse-tung, On the Ten Major Relationships, April 25, 1956. Available in *Peking Review*, No. 1 (January 1, 1977), p. 15.

9.48 London and London, The Other China, Hunger: Part I, The Three Red Rlags of Death, Worldview, 19:5 (May 1976), p. 6.

9.49 Edgar Snow, *Red China Today* (New York: Random House, 1971), p. 585. Snow notes that in Kwangsi in 1956, about 550 (out of 14,700) starved when the government was slow in transporting them out of their drought-stricken region. *Ibid.*, pp. 717–18.

9.50 Collapse or Recovery, *China News Analysis*, 432, August 10, 1962, p. 6.

9.51 Based on a death rate of 20 per thousand and a population of 660 million. Leo Orleans, China's Population: Can the Contradictions be Resolved? *China: A Reassessment of the Economy* (Washington D.C.: U.S. Congress Joint Economic Committee, 1975), p. 77.

9.52 London and London, The Other China, Hunger: Part I, The Three Red Flags of Death, Worldview, 19:5 (May 1976), pp. 7–10.

9.53 Leo Orleans, China's Population, Can the Contradictions be Resolved? *China: A Reassessment of the Economy* (Washington D.C.: U.S. Congress Joint Economic Committee, 1975) p. 77. It might be noted that just a few years earlier, the death rate was higher than 21 per thousand.

9.54 Liu's views were cited by a red guard group during the Cultural Revolution. *Down with Liu Shao-ch'i—Life of Counterrevolutionary Liu Shao-ch'i* (Peking: Chingkangshan Fighting Corps, May 1967). Also *Kuang-ming Jih-pao*, August 9, 1967. See *Current Background* 834, p. 20 and Kang Chao, *op. cit.*, p. 31.

9.55 The Tenth Plenary Session of the Eighth Central Committee of the Chinese Communist Party formalized this decision. See Ben Stavis, *Making Green Revolution: The Politics of Agricultural Development in China* (Ithaca: Cornell Rural Development Committee, 1975), pp. 95–108.

9.56 Chung Wen, Three Provinces Unite to Control the Huai, *China Tames Her Rivers* (Peking: Foreign Languages Press, 1972), p. 24.

9.57 For sketches, see Walter Mallory, *op. cit.*, pp. 154–55, 159.

9.58 G. V. Jacks and R. O. Whyte, *Vanishing Lands* (New York: Doubleday, 1939), p. 81.

9.59 Man's Will, Not Heaven Decides—Progress in Flood Control Work, *China Reconstructs*, January 1973, p. 11.

9.60 Kan Chang, Checking Erosion on the Loess Land, *China Reconstructs*, April 1974, pp. 22–24, describes erosion control in Kansu.

9.61 Man's Will, Not Heaven Decides—Progress in Flood Control Work, *China Reconstructs*, January 1973, pp. 11–12. See also Harnessing the Haiho River, Great Power of the Mass Line, *Peking Review*, No. 39, September 27, 1974, pp. 11–12.

9.62 New Look of Yangtze River, NCNA Peking, October 10, 1974.

9.63 Harnessing China's Rivers, *Peking Review*, December 6, 1974, p. 18.

9.64 Tung Yi-lin, Harnessing the Haiho River—Great Power of the Mass Line, *Peking Review*, No. 39, September 27, 1974, p. 12.

9.65 Curtis Ullerich, China's GNP Revisited, *Journal of Contemporary Asia*, 3:1 (1973), p. 51.

9.66 For a description of the normal wage system, see Ben Stavis, *People's Communes and Rural Development in China* (Ithaca: Cornell Rural Development Committee, 1974), pp. 67–70.

9.67 Ben Stavis, Agricultural Performance and Policy: Contrasts with India, *Social Scientist*, 5:10/11 (May/June 1977), p. 62.

9.68 Tom Wiens, Agricultural Statistics in the PRC, in Alexander Eckstein (ed.), forthcoming. Additional figures for growth rates of subsidiary agricultural products are in Vaclav Smil, Food Availability in Communist China: 1957 and 1974, *Issues and Studies*, 13:5 (May 1977), pp. 56–57; and *China: Economic Indicators* (Washington: National Foreign Assessment Center, October 1977), p. 11.

9.69 Ben Stavis, Agricultural Performance and Policy: Contrasts with India, *Social Scientist*, 5:10/11 (May/June 1977), pp. 59–60.

9.70 *Ibid.*, p. 63.

9.71 How Chinese People Control Rivers (III), NCNA Peking, November 1, 1974.

9.72 Ben Stavis Agricultural Performance and Policy: Contrasts with India, *Social Scientist*. 5:10/11 (May/June 1977), pp. 64.

9.73 Sharp Rise of Farm Machinery, *Peking Review*, 6 (February 7, 1975), p. 23.

9.74 Chen Yung-kuei, Report at the Second National Conference on Learning from Tachai in Agriculture, *Peking Review*, 2 (January 7, 1977), p. 14.

9.75 Detailed information on these plants is available in Hans Heymann, Jr., Acquisition and Diffusion of Technology in China, *China: A Reassessment of the Economy* (Washington D.C.: U.S. Congress Joint Economic Committee, 1975), pp. 726–27; Jon Sigurdson, Rural Industrialization in China, in the same volume.

9.76 Computed from Cheng Chu-yuan, *Scientific and Engineering Manpower in Communist China, 1949–63* (Washington D.C.: Government Printing Office, 1965), pp. 57, 78, 223, 236; and Leo Orleans, *Professional Manpower and Education in Communist China* (Washington D.C.: Government Printing Office, 1961), pp. 128–29.

9.77 *Plant Sciences in the People's Republic of China* (Washington D.C.: National Academy of Sciences, 1975). See also Benedict Stavis, *Making Green Revolution*, pp. 26–40.

9.78 Science for the People, China, *Science Walks on Two Legs* (New York: Avon, 1974), pp. 127–28.

9.79 These types of research are reviewed in detail in a forthcoming article I am doing on the agricultural research and extension system in China.

9.80 Ministry of Education Article on 'Gang of Four' Sabotage of Basic Theoretical Research in Natural Sciences, NCNA Peking, January 30, 1977.

9.81 Patrick Michaels and Victor Scherer, *A Predictive Model for Wheat Production in Sonora, Mexico*, and *An Aggregated National Model for Wheat Yield in India* (Madison: University of Wisconsin Institute for Environmental Studies, 1977).

9.82 Janet Salaff, Mortality Decline in the People's Republic of China and the United States, *Population Studies*, 27:3 (November 1973), pp. 551–76. Victor Sidel and Ruth Sidel, *Serve the People* (New York: Josiah Macy Jr. Foundation, 1973). Joaquin Cravioto, The State of Nutrition of Children in China, *Eastern Horizon*, 15:6 (1976), pp. 51–55.

9.83 Society of Pediatrics of the Chinese Medical Association, Child Health in New China, *Chinese Medical Journal*, No. 10 (October 1974), p. 598.

9.84 Chao Lin, Anthropometric Measurement of Shanghai Students and Preschool Children in 1954, A Preliminary Study, *Chinese Medical Journal*, 75 (December 1957), pp. 1021–22.

9.85 Sidel and Sidel, *Serve the People*, p. 261.

9.86 Leo Orleans, *Every Fifth Child: The Population of China* (Stanford: Stanford University Press, 1972), p. 54.

CHAPTER 10

Counterpoint Two: Food Distribution Policies in China and The United Kingdom

Introduction

A SENSIBLE way of doing away with human malnutrition would be through a system of food rationing. If foodstuffs are abundant, as is almost always the case, this would ensure an adequate diet for everyone; even if foodstuffs were insufficient, rationing would spread out the risk of malnutrition in an equitable way, minimizing its overall effects; and could provide a means of selectively protecting those human groups which are especially vulnerable: children and pregnant or lactating mothers.* The transferral of the basic human staple of food from the realm of profit to the realm of need is however a drastic step, possible only in cases of great national stress (as the United Kingdom during World War II) or as an effect of a drastic egalitarian restructuring of society (as in the case of China after the Communist revolution).

Rationing is by no means the only way to produce an egalitarian distribution of food. Every procedure which redistributes national income in a positive way, i.e. that increases the purchasing power of the poor automatically putting more food in their bellies (that *more* food could eventually mean *worse* food is something to be reckoned with, as is seen by some mechanisms explained in Section 3 of Chapter 2, but is not yet a problem for the majority of mankind which is now starving). The general trend in Market Economy countries since the late sixties, both developed and developing, seems to be towards a more negative distribution of income i.e. a more inegalitarian one. This could mean that time is working against this mechanism having an effect.

There is something disagreeable about the word rationing which has connotations of compulsion, of an undemocratic imposition by bureaucrats (or worse, by an isolated elite) against masses of people. This may be true, and rationing, which was adopted everywhere in Europe, even in neutral countries, during World War II was discarded also everywhere as soon as a more normal condition prevailed. Yet, dichotomic considerations of democratic/autodemocratic as criterion to judge the validity of certain procedures has to be weighed against the fact that the former ones could in many cases implicitly mean the deaths of thousands or millions of

---

* Rationing acts basically by allocating foodstuffs on an egalitarian and nutritionally adequate (as far as possible) basis, through a double system of direct State intervention and of assuring indirectly that the purchase of food adequate for human needs can be attained by everyone.

human beings, which would otherwise be spared had more of the latter proceedings been used.

There are however some important distinctions to be made within the context of the above remarks. In the first place the similarity of measures taken by the U.K. and China, as reported in the following paper, is only superficial. Although "rationing" is the basic policy adopted in both cases, the Chinese rationing is a structural measure, whereas the U.K. rationing is not. In the former case, the egalitarian access to cheap food becomes an integral part of the income of the workers; in the latter it is a distribution measure concerning a commodity which is temporarily scarce, and having only mild, indirect and reversible effects on the economic structure of the society.

In the second place, the fact that China has a Communist régime should not be taken as a *sine-qua-non* condition for the application of a rationing-based food distribution method ingrained in the structure of the socio-economic system. One can hardly think of any real solution of the nutrition problems in the developing countries without a certain type of socialization of the available food. But the fact that foods should be taken out of the circle of "commodities" subject to the rules of maximizing profit, characteristic of the Market Economy, does not necessarily mean that the socio-political system must be a certain brand of "Communism".

Those who would disagree with this statement, i.e. who would maintain that the withdrawal of food from being a commodity is incompatible with the maintenance of a Market Economy (with the enormous human suffering it entails) would be implying that market economies are incompatible with a humanitarian organization of society.

ANNEX 1

Food Rationing in the United Kingdom During World War II

by *José Carlos Escudero*

Introduction

The United Kingdom during World War II provides an interesting case study of a successfully carried out national nutritional policy in the face of the severe challenge provided by the War. A country that was very heavily reliant on food imports in 1939 was able to improve the nutrition of its population in spite of the German blockade, of the stresses on an economy which was geared to the war effort and of a manpower mobilization which depleted the countryside of manpower. Furthermore, it is generally agreed that the nutritional status of the U.K.'s population actually improved during the War. This effect, opposite to what could be expected, shows that, to a large extent, nutritional levels are not a function of the availability of current resources—considered as an unmodifiable "given"—but of national policy decisions, whose margins of action can be much larger than suspected.

The Food Supply Situation in the U.K. Prewar

Before World War II, the United Kingdom's food supplies were heavily dependent on purchase abroad. One quarter of all world trade was in food and feeding-stuffs, (10.1) of this the U.K. took in no less than 40 percent. The result of this was that the British was "an exceptionally varied and attractive diet—in which not much more than a third of the total energy value was obtained from bulky, starchy foods such as cereals and potatoes. It was only in the United States, Australia, New Zealand and Denmark, that the diet showed a lower proportionate consumption of these less attractive foods, and then but very slightly less". In terms of caloric demands of the population the United Kingdom bought abroad about two-thirds of them, and imports accounted for 96% of the consumption of butter, 88 percent of wheat and flour, 87 percent of fats and oil, 76 percent of cheese and 74 percent of fruit. On the other hand, the country was virtually self-sufficient in milk and only had to import about half of its consumption of eggs and meat.

To a large extent, this dependence on imports was caused by the variety of Britain's eating habits and by its reliance on animal protein in the form of meat. For example, four million tons of maize, barley and oats were imported each year, maize being largely used to feed cattle and barley for the brewing industry. Any diet that relies on such "end-links" of the nutrition chain as animal protein has to pay a price—in money terms, in decreased efficiency calorie-wise, in underutilization of land and labour—for this choice.

The Impact of the War and Measures Taken

Prior to the War, preparations had been made for the subsequent emergency. A number of preventive purchases of food in the international market to build up national stocks were carried out—the purchase of most of the world's stock of whale oil, for instance—and planning was carried out for the rationing of meat, fats, bacon and sugar. Ration books were printed and stored throughout the country, so that they could be posted to citizens at short notice. (10.2) At the outbreak of War, the Ministry of Food was set up "with wide executive powers for the distribution and rationing of food and over the purchase of food from abroad on a vast scale". (10.3) The "invisible hand of the Market" which largely governed the U.K.'s procurement and distribution of food pre War was being replaced by a coherent national policy. The essentials of the food policy were "first, to minimize calls on shipping ... secondly, to arrange for the equitable distribution of such food as was available in quantities sufficient to ensure an adequate diet for all persons, whatever their income may be; and thirdly, to pay special attention to those on whom the future of the nation depended." Concrete measures taken under this policy were the introduction of rationing, so that food became equally available to everyone at controlled prices, the banning of importation of non-essential food (mostly fruit), an increase of home production of food, and the creation and distribution of special diets for vulnerable segments of the population. (10.4) The effects of the War were felt not through a shortage of the world supply of food, or through lack of currencies to buy them, but through lack of shipping availabilities. War requirements increased shipping demands; it was through attacks on ships that the German blockade mostly acted, and the closing of the Mediterranean to merchant ships flying British or Allied flags forced costly diversions in routes, and further reduced availabilities. As far as the measures mentioned above are concerned for the expansion of national food production it was found out that little additional waste land could be put to use. What was done was to increase the production of human food from existing farmlands. This was done by ploughing grasslands, and thus increasing their food yield by growth of wheat and potatoes (whose production had doubled by 1943); oats (up to 60 percent); other grains (more than doubled); fodder crops (up by one-third) and sugar beet (up by 40 percent). Livestock decreased greatly, through the fact that most farm crops were used for direct human consumption, that grasslands were ploughed and that the importation of animal feedstuffs was greatly reduced. The pig population during the War was cut by 50 percent; that of poultry by 20 percent. As pigs and poultry compete with humans for cereals, and as fodder crops were being used to produce milk, which was considered essential, these were felt to be necessary prices to pay for the success of the overall policy. On the other hand, the dairy cattle population went up between 1939 and 1945 from 3.9 m to 4.3 m and cattle as a whole from 8.9 m to 9.4 m. In overall terms, home food production supplied pre War 31 percent of total national caloric demands and 44 percent of total protein demands. In 1943 the figures had changed to 44 percent and 50 percent respectively.

Results in Terms of Human Nutrition

In general terms, in the United Kingdom during the War there was food available for all, except during a period in 1940 and 1941. The régime was of a spartan nature, in which attractive foods were rationed or had disappeared. In general, there was less protein, more vegetables and more liquid milk. "The trend was towards an increase in the consumption of those foods which had been declining in popularity in the years preceding the War, when improvements in the standard of living were leading to greater variety and attractiveness in the diet of the ordinary person". (10.5) The War produced two changes in the pattern of the nation's food consumption. One was that "despite all the difficulties in the food supply situation, actual improvements were affected in the diet of the country". The other was "a greater degree of equality among all classes. The extension of rationing together with price controls meant that the consumption of the available foods became less and less unequal. Backed by high wages, full employment and food subsidies, it became possible for families in the lowest income groups to obtain many essential nutrients, the pre War consumption of which among the poorer families was low. On the other hand, the consumption of certain foods by those better-off was reduced, compared with pre War standards, and there was less room for the exercise of choice in so far as family sharing mitigated the rigidity of the distribution". (10.6)

Human malnutrition had been experienced in the United Kingdom pre War. Surveys undertaken then had shown that in poorer families, or in families with several children, the intake of protective nutrients was extremely deficient, and that also "the intake of calories was insufficient—that is, those families did not have enought to eat. For example, families with incomes of under 8/- per head weekly were receiving only about 30 percent of their calcium needs and 80–90 percent of their caloric needs, and families with five or more children about one-third of their calcium needs and 94 percent of their caloric needs". (10.7) During the War, the nutritional status of the population was monitored through Dietary and Clinical Surveys, which found little evidence of undernourishment or malnutrition which could not be attributed to the pre War crisis. There was probably less anaemia and children showed a steady improvement in growth rates. No undernourishment signs were noticed. The National Food Survey found that "people could and did get enough calories during the war years", that "the average consumptions of calories and proteins were adequate" and that "since 1939 the diet of the Nation has, on the average, deteriorated in variety and palatability, but that supplies of calories have been well-maintained, and those of most nutrients have increased". (10.8)

The United Kingdom had made provisions for a much more precarious national food situation than the one actually experienced, and it was shown that the margins for additional action were significant. A wartime study which experimented in a human test population a much more limited diet—but one which the United Kingdom could largely produce self-sufficiently—showed that "young adults, at least, could have maintained a high standard of health under dietetic conditions much more austere than those actually experienced in the War". (10.9)

Comments

It can be stated that the previously described national experience was unique—after all, the United Kingdom was the world's largest imperial power in 1939 and it had resources almost unequalled elsewhere at hand to solve its World War II food crisis: it had for example few financial limitations on purchasing abroad the food it needed. What this example shows for much poorer countries than the United Kingdom is the enormous leeway that a coherent national policy has whose aims are to improve the nutritional status of its population. Technological know-how is not a constraint, nor would current resources be an absolute one, although this point has to be proved elsewhere than in this case study. It could have been said in the U.K. in 1939 that "the malnourished would always be with us" as it was said of famines in China prior to 1941. Yet they were not in both cases, and as the next case study will show—the margins for action to combat malnutrition in a country conventionally described as "underdeveloped" are enormous—provided national energies are channelled in that direction, which constitutes ultimately a political decision. "Development", as is usually known, would not be the answer to human malnutrition, either observed or pervasive. "Malnutrition is unlikely to disappear in the normal course of development: that is in the course of normal *per capita* income growth, even with greater emphasis or expansion of food production—

barring, of course, unusual technological breakthroughs. On the contrary the situation may worsen if present higher energy cost, leading to higher cost of food production, is not fully compensated by higher agricultural productivity. Only policies deliberately designed to reallocate food or income can eliminate malnutrition". (10.10) In World War II, the United Kingdom did the first explicitly, and war circumstances forced it to do the second.

ANNEX 2

The Distribution of Food in Present Day China

by *Ben Stavis*

China has a socialist, planned economy. Allocation and distribution of most important resources, including food, are done through conscious decisions, subject to political values. Decisions are not allowed to be made in the free market place. The political–administrative process makes crucial decisions concerning urban–rural balances and distribution in both cities and countryside.

Beginning in 1955, food grains have been rationed in China. Urban residents are allotted a specific quantity of food grain each month, according to their requirements and the overall availability of food. They are given ration books which must be presented at specific grain stores, and in which all purchases are recorded. (10.11) Other commodities (such as cooking oil, sugar, meat, cigarettes and cotton cloth) may be rationed as well if demand at the set prices exceeds supply in the locality. The main purpose of the ration system is to assure that food does reach everyone in China, and to guarantee that no one starves. An important side-effect is that the ration system contributes to control of population movement. Rural people cannot freely migrate to cities and look for jobs; they first must apply for permission and receive a ration book usable in the relevant city. The planned level of the rations for urban residents in 1955–57 is shown in Table 1.

The levels indicated in Table 1 were the planned levels, but if food supplies were insufficient, the ration would be lower. In Canton in October 1956, rations were cut. They were reduced most for the men doing heavy labour (to 71 percent of normal) while children below six years got more than normal. (Of course, this could not determine precise distribution of food within the household, but it does indicate the attempts of the government to shield vulnerable children from the effects of food shortages.) A similar policy was followed in Anshan in the first half of 1958. (10.12) In reports of average *per capita* rations for 1955–59, there is some variation over time and place, perhaps influenced by different age structures in different cities. The range is from 10.2 to 15 kg per month, but 65 percent are within the 11.5 to 13.5 kg per month range. (10.13)

TABLE 1.

Food Rationing Schedule, 1955–57
(kilograms of processed grain per month)

	Rice regions	Other regions
Workers, exceptionally heavy labour	25	27.5
heavy labour	20	22
light labour	16	17.5
office workers	14	15.5
Students, university and middle school	16	17.5
General residents, children	12.5	14
Children, age 6–10	10	11
age 3–6	6.5	7
under 3	3.5	4

Source: Ta-chung Liu and K. C. Yeh, *The Economy of the Chinese Mainland* (Princeton: Princeton University Press, 1965), p. 48.

During the bad years of 1960–62, urban rations fell substantially, and there were reports that adult rations were only 7.5 kg per month in some cities. By 1963, rations were higher, and in 1965, a Chinese Vice Minister of Agriculture reported ration levels near or above the mid-1950s level—20 to 25 kg per month for workers, 18 kg per month for students, 16 kg per month for cadres. (10.14)

The basic amount of food available for distribution in a village is worked out by negotiation between the production team and higher levels when yearly production plans are made. The production plans include specific plans for delivery of grain as taxes and for sale of "surplus" grain to the state for cash. Obviously, the amount of grain left over for local food is inversely related to the amount of grain delivered to the state. The way this programme works will be described later, in the analysis of the state procurement system.

As a general target, the goal for rural rations has been 1 catty/person/day of unprocessed food. (10.15) This equals roughly 12 kg/capita/month of processed grain—roughly the same as the average urban ration. In practice rural rations dropped to almost half this figure in some localities during the bad years.

A. Sharing in the Village

How the production team distributes its food to its members is decided by the team itself, to some degree. Generally the production team will develop a list showing the maximum amount of food grains each person may have. This maximum takes into account the age, sex and level of physical activity of each person. Then each person is automatically given a certain proportion of the maximum, somewhere between 50 and 80 percent. (Actually, this food is not "given", but it is charged to a family's account.) The person receives this food, which is enough for the maintenance of life, regardless of what he does. The remainder of the food is distributed in proportion to one's labour days. Thus a person who works the required number of days in collective labour will receive the full, maximum amount of grain; a person who does not contribute fully to collective labour (perhaps he works on his private plot) will get something between the automatic distribution and the maximum. The production team decides for itself what portion to distribute automatically and what portion to relate to labour input. (10.16)

Rations are supposed to be distributed to team members at the time of harvest. Each family stores its own grain for the year.

In distributing cash and food, the production team is expected to make special provisions for families which lack adequate labour power to assure reasonable incomes. Regulations specify that up to 2 or 3 percent of the total distributable income should be used for a welfare fund to assist the elderly, weak, orphaned, widowed and disabled. Family members of martyrs, soldiers and disabled soldiers with difficulties also receive assistance. In addition, families with many children or old people and few people of labouring age can get help.

This egalitarian system of distribution of food and income in rural China means that whenever there are shortfalls in agricultural production, the shortfall is shared equally. Everyone suffers a little, but no small group suffers excessively.

The egalitarian distribution of food is a reflection of the distribution of economic and political power. In some countries, even though there is a high level of agricultural productivity, the ownership of assets is very concentrated. The few landlords and rich peasants obtain most of the benefits: the landless labourer and small tenant farmer remain impoverished. In China, however, collective ownership of land has been established, so that everyone has a roughly equal claim to rural resources. There is no division into landlords, cultivators, tenants and labourers.

Of course the system does not provide for complete equality. The units of collective ownership are village and sub-village groupings of twenty to thirty familes (called production teams). Teams vary in their amount and quality of farmland. Moreover, some teams have invested heavily in the past in improving their land, so now they may enjoy higher income. Likewise, some teams may, for historical or political reasons, have a higher proportion of profitable cash crops which give a higher income. For these reasons, neighbouring teams can have a difference in wage rates of a factor of three and differences between regions can be even greater.

Within a production team, there are also some inequalities. Wages are paid according to a "work point" system, in which the value of the work point is determined by the profitability of the team and the number of work points each person receives depends on how hard he works. Family income, then, depends on how many workers a family has and how hard they work. A family with several workers and a few dependants will have a comfortable income. In contrast a family with few workers and many children or elderly people will be relatively poor. The collective unit will assure adequate food (subsidized by welfare allotments, if necessary) but such a family may have little cash for purchases of consumer goods.

Another factor accounts for some inequality in the village. Roughly 5 to 7 percent of the farmland is set aside and assigned to families as private gardens. Although the land cannot be bought or sold, its produce is owned by the families. Vegetables, tobacco and, most important, food for pigs are grown in the private plots. Families with more labour power or more skills and energy can pay more attention to their gardens and pigs and earn substantially more money. It is likely, but by no means certain, that this source of inequality counteracts the inequalities that result from differences in family structure, because the families with a large number of dependants may be able to raise many pigs.

Another source of inequality is the fact that some of the rural jobs have higher wage rates. These include jobs in administration or in rural factories. These wage rates may be as high as 50 percent above normal farm labour, although still somewhat less than wage rates in regular urban factories. (10.17)

China is not trying to have complete equality, at least for the foreseeable future. Some differences in wage rates are needed to assure incentives. Moreover, there are some differences in wage rates which have a long historical standing (for different types of work and for different regions of the country) and these cannot be obliterated in a few years or even a few decades without serious political opposition. The general policy for egalitarianism is to "level up", and not "level down", that is, increase the incomes of the poorer people, but not to reduce the incomes of the wealthier. Sometimes this is difficult, however, because the richer regions and units have a greater surplus for investment, which generates greater wealth in the future.

The current agricultural programme appears to be sensitive to the problems of inequalities of the backward regions, and subsidies are available for productive investments and health and education services. However, a suggestion to reduce inequalities between production teams by merging them and making the brigade the main accounting unit appears to have been rejected.

Despite these various types of inequalities, China appears to have a much more egalitarian pattern of income distribution than in other regions of Asia (Table 2). There are, of course, serious methodological problems in international comparisons of inequality, so the data in Table 2 is, at best, merely suggestive. Probably rural China is more egalitarian than implied by the figures because the prices for consumer goods are kept low to assure adequate access to essentials for low-income people, while luxury goods include high taxes. In other countries, some of the poorest may migrate to urban areas or become migrant labourers, and may not be included in these rural surveys. China's pattern of income distribution now is probably more equal than in the past, but most of the income and consumption data for the 1930s collected by Buck have been averaged on the basis of the village, thereby obscuring differences between classes within the village. For one village for which data are available for 1939–40, the richest 20 percent had income twenty times that of the poorest 20 percent. However this village probably is not representative of China as a whole, as families with little land did not have off-farm income sources. (10.18) The clearest indication that some people were more vulnerable to famine than others is the data presented in Chapter 9, Table 3, showing that in time of famine 21 percent of the rural population in South China and 60 percent in North China were seriously affected. These undoubtedly were the labourers, tenants and small farmers.

To protect people from the effects of seasonal fluctuations in production, the Chinese leaders have energetically urged local units to maintain reserves of grain. Production teams and brigades are encouraged to build granaries and accumulate food reserves during good years. Reserves should be adequate for about a year. (10.19) This is in addition to reserves held by the families and by the state at higher levels. (10.20)

TABLE 2.

Indicators of Rural Income Distribution

		Ratio of top 20% to bottom 20%
China		
Within villages		
Three villages, 1955–56[a]		2.3–3.5
One village, 1962[a,b]		2.8–5.2
Two villages, 1974[a]		2.1
Nationwide sample, 1952[c]		3.1
For 36 communes, 1960s[b]		4.3
For 24 communes, 1970s[d]		3.6
Egypt	Personal, 1966–67	2.3
Sri Lanka	Household, 1969–70	4.8
Korea (South)	Household, 1971	4.7
Taiwan Province	Household, 1964	5.1
Japan	Household, 1963	5.2
Punjab State	Household, 1969–70 (excluding landless)	5.4
Bangladash	Household, 1963–64	5.4
Yugoslavia	Household, 1968	5.6
Pakistan	Household, 1968	6.3
India	Household, 1964–65, 1967–68	8.3
Indonesia	Household consumption, 1964–65	5.6
Philippines	Household, 1971	12.3
Malaysia	Household, 1970	12.9
Thailand	Household, 1968–69, 1970	14.0
Turkey	Household, 1963, 1968	16.2

Sources: China—[a] Marc Blecher, Income Distribution in Small Rural Chinese Communities, *China Quarterly 68* (December 1976), pp. 797–816; [b] A. R. Khan, The Distribution of Income in Rural China (Geneva: International Labour Office, World Employment Programme Research Working Papers, October, 1976), p. 29; [c] Charles Roll, *Incentives and Motivations in China: The "Reality" of Rural Inequality* (Santa Monica: Rand, 1976), p. 26; [d] G. B. Ng, Rural Inequalities in China (Geneva: International Labour Office, World Employment Programme Research Working Papers, October 1976), p. 9.

Other Countries—Norman Uphoff and Milton Esman, *Local Organization for Rural Development in Asia* (Ithaca: Cornell Center for International Studies, 1974), p. 147.

Notes: Data for Taiwan and Japan are national, not rural, surveys and thus include urban families. For India, some recent studies suggest that the ratio of the top and bottom quintile is not much different from that in China—4.1 to 5.3. Uma Datta Roy Choudhury, Changes in Distribution of Household Income, Consumption and Wealth in Rural Areas, *Economic and Political Weekly*, October 1, 1977, pp. 1709–1712.

Effectively organizing a system of village food reserves has several difficulties. There are a wide range of technical problems concerning the design and maintenance of granaries and the protection of food against rodents, insects and fungus. Careful drying of grain is of critical importance.

There is also a wide range of political problems. To permit teams or brigades to maintain food reserves, peasants need to have confidence that the reserves will be administered properly. They have to be assured of several factors: that the central government will not seize the reserves; that local administrators will not be corrupt and will not permit someone to steal the reserves; and that the administration of the reserves will be technically proficient so that storage losses will be minimal. If peasants are not confident about the technical capabilities of the managers and the political environment, they will be reluctant to allow reserves to be maintained at team or brigade level.

B. Keeping Benefits in the Countryside

China has followed a policy of assuring that the benefits of modernization stay in rural areas and will not be extracted for the benefit of urban dwellers and urban-centred industrial development. Tax and price policies have consciously been used to benefit the rural sector. Agricultural taxes have basically remained at a fixed amount (and therefore declining rate). The price the government pays for agricultural products has roughly doubled in the past twenty years, while the prices of industrially-produced means of production have been declining and prices of consumer goods have remained stable. Of course, state control over grain marketing was necessary to use the price mechanisms to regulate urban–rural exchanges.

Another policy assures that much of the benefits of modernization stay in the rural sector. Small-scale rural industry, such as brick factories, cereal-processing plants and farm-tool repair shops are owned directly by communities or brigades. The profits of these enterprises become part of the local budgets and are used to subsidize health, education and welfare services.

There is one other very important policy instrument supplementing investment, tax and price policies for regulating urban–rural relations, namely, manpower planning. In China trained manpower—including doctors, engineers, agronomists, and teachers—are assigned jobs by the central or state labour departments, in a manner analogous to the way it plans the allocation of capital for investment (or the way an army assigns its specialists). After 1965, increasing numbers of medical personnel were assigned to rural areas. After 1967, more agricultural researchers and teachers were sent to the communes. Moreover, large numbers of high-school graduates have been assigned to rural areas, where most become ordinary farmers although a few become technicians or accountants. Needless to say, such a policy involves many restrictions on the freedom of individuals. People who have grown up in cultures that emphasize individualism might consider these restrictions intolerable and even many people in China consider them onerous.

These various policies have resulted in an approximate doubling of rural real income over the past twenty years. (10.21) Diets have improved; security of livelihood is far better; health, access to health, education and entertainment services are much improved; rural electrification is widespread (probably around 50 percent of the villages); many new houses have been built and simple consumer goods are available. Rural China is still poor, but no longer perched on the brink of survival.

The rural bias in China's development policies undoubtedly is controversial. Many people in China, including urban dwellers, industrial managers, teachers and bureaucrats, might have preferred to focus development on the urban–industrial sector. They might have wanted to extract the benefits of agricultural modernization for urban consumption or to encourage production of agricultural speciality products for export, which would generate foreign exchange for consumer goods or industrial equipment. They may have wanted to increase the wages of urban factory workers, maintain health services for the urban population and to orient education and culture to urban tastes. This appears to have been the pattern implicit in the Soviet model, which the Chinese emulated in the early 1950s. Sporadic outbreaks of urban protest imply some dissatisfaction with a stagnant urban standard of living. Factory wages were raised somewhat for autumn 1977.

Similarly, many of China's military leaders may have preferred to use more of the fruits of industrialization to modernize China's army, aircraft and navy. According to one estimate, 22 percent of industrial output consists of military goods. (10.22) Nevertheless, China's "modern" weapons basically reflect Soviet designs of the 1950s, and China's military would be at a severe disadvantage in war with any forces with up-to-date weapons. Military procurements actually declined after 1971, (10.23) but it is expected that China's new administration will increase military expenditures.

Constant political struggle has been required to make sure the rural sector receives priority. The personal values of Mao Tse-tung appear to have been important in maintaining these biases, and his passing may alter this political balance. However, the rural sector has other political resources as well. Political stability and economic growth in the rural sector is crucial for growth of the urban–industrial sector. This is because the agricultural surplus in China is small and easily dissipated by unsuitable policies. In addition, many top military leaders have their roots in the countryside and remain concerned with rural welfare. Nevertheless, it is unlikely that China's new administration will continue to give the same priority to the rural sector that it has enjoyed in the past.

C. Government Transfers of Food

The main food policy in China is self-reliance. Each locality should feed itself. Of course this is not always possible. Cities cannot feed themselves; nor can the army; nor can agricultural regions that specialize in non-food grain crops; nor can localities that suffer from natural disaster and crop failure. Hence an important element in national food policy is the procurement and distribution of food by the State.

The State obtains food in several ways. First, the State collects a tax in grain from agricultural production units, as mentioned previously.

Second, as described before, the State "purchases" grain from agricultural production units. In reality this "purchase" is worked out in a negotiation in which the State has strong leverage. County and commune cadres want to please the State and sometimes may be willing to sacrifice local interests. Moreover, the State can link input supplies to procurement. In order to get electric wires or a pump, a commune may have to sell more grain to the State. During the 1950s, when economic strategy emphasized urban–industrial development, procurement rates were very high. In one production unit, virtually all increments (and declines) in grain production were absorbed in State procurement from 1955 to 1964 (Fig. 1). In Huli Brigade (Fukien) in 1962, the state bought about 85 percent of the increments of production (Fig. 2). Grain procurement in the 1950s under these conditions rose to about 50 million tons each year (Table 3). Indeed, procurement during this period may have worked too well. The State was able to buy so much food at such a relatively low price that peasants saw little incentive to produce more. This contributed to the agricultural crisis of 1959–61.

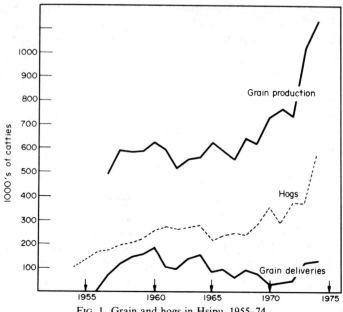

FIG. 1. Grain and hogs in Hsipu, 1955–74

Note: Sales probably includes taxes.
Source: "*Ch'iung-pang Tzu*" *Ching-sheng Fang-kuang Mang* (The Spirit of a Pauper's Model Illuminates the Way) (Peking: People's Publishers, 1976), pp. 168, 169.

Moreover, when the central government tried to procure grain and ship it from one province to another, it apparently encountered strong objections from powerful party leaders of the surplus regions. Li Ching-chuan, party leader in Szechwan, was said to have refused a central order to ship grain to other provinces in 1962. He supposedly falsified provincial statistical reports to show reduced production and therefore reduced capacity to export grain to other provinces. (10.24)

In around 1964 a new procurement policy was implemented. The data for Hsipu show clearly that in that year, procurement dropped, even though production went up. In the following years, grain sales stayed low, compared to the 1950s. The additional production not sold to the State presumably went into improved local diets for the first few years. After 1968, it seems likely that some of the increment in grain production was used to finish hogs, primarily for cash sales. Similarly, data for scattered locations in various years after 1965 (Fig. 2, points a–j) suggests much lower rates of procurement than in 1962 in Huli Brigade and suggests implementation of the 1950s plan to leave at least one catty/capita/day for rural consumption.

Current practice is to fix the quota for sales to the State for a three-to-five year period. During this period, sales over the quota receive a bonus of 30 percent over the regular price. Naturally this is strong incentive to increase sales. (This system is in striking contrast to normal market systems, where overproduction may lead to a drop in price.)

With procurement at somewhat reduced levels now, the State also obtains grain in two other ways. One is by importing. Since 1961, China has had net imports averaging 4.0–4.2 million tons of grain (mostly wheat) annually. (10.25) Importing

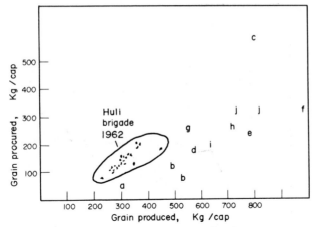

FIG. 2. State procurement of grain

Sources: 1962—Huli Brigade—C. S. Chen and Charles Price Ridley, *Rural People's Communes in Lienchiang* (Stanford: Hoover Institution Press, 1969), pp. 60, 63, 74.

After 1965

[a] Jan Myrdal, *Report from a Chinese Village* (New York: Pantheon, 1965), p. 198.

[b] Stavis Diary, April 28, May 2, May 4, 1972.

[c] Stavis interview L.

[d] Notes from Ward Morehouse.

[e] Ian Davies, "The Chinese Communes, an Australian Student's View," *Eastern Horizon* 8:1 (1969), p. 37.

[f] Jack Chen, *A Year in Upper Felicity* (New York: Macmillan, 1973), p. 380.

[g] Leo Goodstadt, "Poverty a Frequent Theme," *Far Eastern Economic Review* (May 21, 1973), p. 49.

[h] Team in Huatung, H. V. Henle, Personal Communication, 1974, p. 198.

[i] Chin Chi-chu, "New Picture on a Blank Sheet of Paper," *Peking Review* No. 31 (July 29, 1977), pp. 20–24.

[j] Kuo Feng-lien, "The Tachai Road," *Peking Review* No. 40 (October 4, 1974), p. 23. Data are for 1965 and 1973.

grain has been facilitated financially by exporting high-priced rice, and using the receipts for lower-priced wheat. This has not paid for all of the grain imports, but has reduced the burden. (10.26)

Another source of procurement comes from State farms. How important this is remains unknown. In 1958 State farms were in Northern and Western regions,

TABLE 3.
Grain Procurement, 1953–58 (Million metric tons)

Year	Grain production	Tax	Sales	Total procurement	Procurement as percent of production
1953	157	20	23	43	27
1954	160	22	32	54	34
1955	175	22	29	51	29
1956	183			49	27
1957	185	20		nearly 50	27
1958				53	25

Source: Audrey Donnithorne, *China's Economic System* (New York: Praeger, 1967), p. 357.

where yields are low, so their gross production could not have been very high—perhaps a total of 2–2.5 million tons of grain. The extent to which this might have expanded in recent years is not known.

A corollary of the policy of keeping procurement relatively low is keeping a lid on urban population growth. In cities, family planning campaigns are intense, and birth rates have dropped drastically. In urban Shanghai, the birthrate is near 6.2 per thousand, and other cities are near 10; in urban Peking, it is still near 15. (10.27) Moreover, over 12 million urban youths have left the cities and settled in the countryside. (10.28) This alone has reduced procurement needs by about 3.5 million tons.

Another policy to reduce the need to procure grain was to provide tube-well irrigation on the North China Plain, so that this traditionally grain-deficient region could increase production. It no longer needs food imports on a regular basis now.

Over the years the State used grain to meet needs of disaster-stricken areas as well as chronically deficient regions. Between 1953 and 1957, the State supplied deficit areas with 15 million tons, and in the twenty years of 1952–72, grain-deficient Hopei received over 10 million tons. (10.29) For one locality in Hopei, the State supplied about 150 catties *per capita* per year from 1950 to 1957; self-sufficiency was declared when local production reached the generous level of about 556 catties *per capita* per year, or about 23 kg per month. (10.30) Little is known about the precise terms under which the State will supply food to a disaster-stricken area. How serious must the disaster be? Does the locality have to pay for either chronic and/or famine relief? These questions need further research.

Even with reduced government procurement after the mid-1960s, the state is not without resources. In 1970 the state commanded grain reserves of 40 million tons. (10.31)

It might be noted that one element in the ability of the state to procure and transfer food to regions of special need is the improved logistical system. The transportation infrastructure, while still rather thin, is vastly improved compared to the 1920s and 1930s, when relief agencies had great difficulties moving grain to places of need.

Notes to Chapter 10

10.1 K. G. Fenelon, *Britain's Food Supplies*, Methuen, 1952. Unless otherwise stated, all of the following statements or quotations of figures in this section will be from this book.

10.2 R. J. Hammond, Food, Volume 1: *The Growth of Policy*, His Majesty's Stationery Office and Longmans Green, London, 1951.

10.3 Chapter: Nutrition—contributed by the Medical Dept. of the Ministry of Health—in A. S. McNalty (editor) "*The Civilian Health and Medical Services*", Volume 1, His Majesty's Stationery Office, 1953.

10.4 McNalty, *op. cit.*

10.5 McNalty, *op. cit.*

10.6 McNalty, *op. cit.*

10.7 *Report of the Committee on Nutrition*, The British Medical Association, London, 1950.

10.8 *Report of the Committee on Nutrition, op. cit.*

10.9 R. A. McCance and E. M. Widdowson, *An experimental study of rationing*, Medical Research Council, Special Report Series No. 254, His Majesty's Stationery Office, 1946.

10.10 Shlomo Reutinger and Marcelo Selowski, *Malnutrition and Poverty*, World Bank Staff, Occasional Papers Number Twenty Three, The Johns Hopkins University Press, 1976.

10.11 Ralph Huenemann, Urban rationing in communist China, *China Quarterly*, No. 26 (April–June 1966), pp. 44–57.

10.12 Chen Ting-chung, Food production on mainland China as estimated from its food consumption, unpublished paper, Taipei, Institute of International Relations, 1970, p. 4.

10.13 *Ibid.*, pp. 30–31.

10.14 K. S. Karol, *China: The Other Communism*, New York: Hill and Wang, 1967, p. 195.

10.15 Chen Yun, Some questions regarding the problem of unified food purchase and food distribution, *Jen-min Jih-Pao*, July 22, 1955. Cited in Chen Ting-chung, *op. cit.*, p. 7.

10.16 In Tachai, the national agricultural model, a system was used as described above, in which grain rations were determined both according to need and according to labour. At one point, there was a provincial regulation specifying that grain should be allocated on a *per capita* basis, but the people in Tachai simply refused to implement such a system. They argued that it was phony equalitarianism, not in conformity with the principles of socialism or with Mao Tse-tung thought, and could only hamper production. Later Tachai switched to a system in which people declared their needs for grain at a public meeting. See Gerald Tannebaum, The Real Spirit of Tachai, *Eastern Horizon*, 10:2 (1971), p. 29.

10.17 Dwight Perkins, ed., *Rural Small-Scale Industry in the People's Republic of China*, Berkeley: University of California Press, 1977, p. 36.

10.18 Marc Blecher, Income distribution in small rural Chinese communities, *China Quarterly* 68, December 1976, p. 800.

10.19 At the time of the drought in North China in 1972, a particularly vigorous campaign was undertaken to get teams and brigades to store grain. *Jen-min Jih-pao* October 24, 1972; November 14, 1972. SCMP 5249–53, pp. 109–112; SCMP 5263, pp. 112–116.

10.20 The policy of encouraging team and brigade reserves is, of course, similar to the traditional idea (only occasionally implemented) of having community reserves.

10.21 Benedict Stavis, *Making Green Revolution*, pp. 54–60.

10.22 Robert Dernberger, The economic consequences of defense expenditure choices in China, *China: A Reassessment of the Economy*, Washington, D.C.: Joint Economic Committee, 1975, p. 474.

10.23 Sidney Jammes, The Chinese Defense Burden, 1965–74, *Ibid.*, p. 462.

10.24 *News from Chinese Provincial Radio Stations*, September 5–11, 1967, No. 224, p. Q6.

10.25 China: Net foodgrain imports calculated on the basis of data obtained from gross imports in *People's Republic of China: Handbook of Economic Indicators* (Washington D.C.: Central Intelligence Agency, August 1976), p. 33. Exports: *Agricultural Trade of the People's Republic of China 1935–69* (Washington D.C.: U.S. Department of Agriculture, Foreign Agricultural Economic Report No. 83, 1972), p. 33; *The Agricultural Situation in the People's Republic of China, 1975* (Washington D.C.: USDA, Foreign Agricultural Economic Report no. 124, 1976), p. 40. Alternative figures come from Alva Lewis Erisman, China: Agriculture in the 1970s, *A Reassessment of the Economy* (Washington D.C.: Joint Economic Committee, 1975), pp. 343–345.

10.26 Ma Feng-hwa, Why China imports wheat, *China Quarterly*, 45, January–March, 1971.

10.27 Pi-chao Chen, *The "Planned Birth" Program of the People's Republic of China, with a Brief Analysis of its Transferability* (New York: Asia Society, 1974), p. 17; Harland Cleveland, *China Diary* (Washington D.C.: Georgetown University Center for Strategic and International Studies, 1976); Han Suyin, Population growth and birth control in China, *Eastern Horizon* 12:5 (1973), p. 15; Norman Myers, Of all things people are most precious, *New Scientist* (January 9, 1975), p. 58.

10.28 Twelve Million School Graduates Settle in the Countryside, *Peking Review*, No. 2, January 9, 1976, pp. 11–13.

10.29 Rational Distribution of Food Grain, *Peking Review*, No. 1, January 3, 1975, p. 13.

10.30 Tang Feng-chang, *Sandstone Hollow*, Peking: Foreign Languages Press, 1975, p. 3.

10.31 Edgar Snow, Talks with Chou En-lai, The Open Door, *New Republic*, 164:13, March 27, 1971, p. 20.

CHAPTER 11

A General Panorama of Malnutrition in Latin America

Introduction

LATIN AMERICA would be another case in point to exemplify the general arguments put forward in Chapters 3 and 4. A vast, depopulated continent, where Malthusian arguments do not apply; composed of countries which are generally exporters of food, some massively so; with a coverage of Vital and Health Statistics which is far better than that of Africa or Asia (so that its biases become much more salient); it is also a continent where malnutrition is rampant.

Mortality from malnutrition, as recorded through the official health statistics system and as published in the relevant official publications, gives a serious picture of the prevalence of malnutrition in the continent, but it still greatly underestimates its real impact, as the limitations of this type of data expressed in Chapter 4 operate here in full force.

Mortality from Malnutrition as Reflected in Vital Statistics

Even "officially" recorded malnutrition represents a serious mortality problem in Latin America, as witnessed by Table 1, which shows a total of 38,687 annual deaths from malnutrition recorded in 17 countries for various years during the early 1970s. From another source it can be gathered that deaths due to malnutrition in Argentina during 1970 were 2439 of which 1655 corresponded to children of under one year of age. (11.3) As those countries for which information is unavailable are generally also those where nutritional levels are among the lowest, it can be assumed, for example, that deaths from malnutrition in Bolivia, Brazil and Haiti are as high as in all the rest of Latin America. As we shall see, the rural magnitude of mortality from malnutrition in Latin America is several times higher than that recorded in Table 1.

UNDER-REGISTRATION OF DEATHS IN LATIN AMERICA

The Puffer–Serrano study, referred to in Chapter 4 carried out an exhaustive study on the under-registration of deaths in its Latin American study areas, as shown in Table 2. Again, the 35,000 deaths of five-year-olds that were studied were likely to have a better registration standard than the average: the study areas were largely urban or suburban and thus more within reach of registration officials. The

TABLE 1.

Annual Deaths Recorded as due to Malnutrition (as "basic cause of death") in some Latin American Countries, Various Years[a]

Country	Year	No. of recorded deaths for all ages, all causes	Deaths caused by malnutrition			Subtotal of deaths from malnutrition in children under 5	
			Total[b]	Avitaminosis and other nutritional deficiencies	Anaemias	No.	% of all deaths from malnutrition
Chile	1973	82,988	1245 (1.5)	1006	239	632	51
Colombia	1972	160,380	10,242 (6.4)	7142	3100	6417	63
Costa Rica	1973	9702	165 (1.7)	96	69	88	53
Dominican Republic	1973	24,429	771 (2.9)	547	224	521	68
Ecuador	1972	67,837	2576 (3.8)	1048	1528	1406	55
El Salvador	1973	31,905	1221 (3.8)	625	596	503	41
Guatemala	1971	75,223	3508 (4.6)	1682	1826	1164	34
Honduras	1973	20,932	681 (3.2)	304	377	311	46
Mexico	1973	458,915	11,781 (2.6)	6498	5283	5066	43
Nicaragua	1973	11,729	157 (1.3)	50	107	68	43
Panama	1973	9173	224 (2.4)	98	126	83	37
Paraguay	1973	12,354	420 (3.4)	235	185	205	48
Peru	1972	92,568	3259 (3.5)	2331	928	2014	62
Puerto Rico	1973	19,257	183 (0.9)	88	95	22	12
Trinidad and Tobago	1973	7517	192 (2.5)	114	78	82	43
Uruguay	1973	28,436	495 (1.7)	418	77	314	63
Venezuela	1973	76,506	1567 (2.0)	1178	389	1081	69
Total		1,191,851	38,687 (3.2)	23,460	15,227	19,917	51

[a] Data for all countries except Guatemala were modified from material in reference (11.1). Guatemala data are from reference (11.2).
[b] Numbers in parentheses signify percentage of all deaths that are caused by malnutrition.

TABLE 2.

Under-registration in Deaths of Children under 5 years of Age Studied by the
Inter-American Investigation of Mortality in Childhood (1970–72)[a]

Study area	No. of deaths studied	No. registered by vital statistics system	Percent registered	Percent not registered
Chaco, Argentina	1701	1616	95.0	5.0
San Juan, Argentina	2156	1934	89.7	10.3
La Paz-Viacha, Bolivia	4276	3778	88.4	11.6
Recife, Brazil	3635	3534	97.2	2.8
Ribeirão, Prêto, Brazil	1126	1122	99.6	0.4
São Paulo, Brazil	4312	4286	99.4	0.6
Santiago, Chile	2714	2370	87.3	12.7
Cali, Colombia	1627	1567	96.3	3.7
Cartagena, Colombia	1255	1002	79.8	20.2
Medellín, Colombia	1348	1297	96.2	3.8
San Salvador, El Salvador	3820	3494	91.5	8.5
Kingston–St. Andrew, Jamaica	1903	1687	88.6	11.4
Monterrey, Mexico	3953	3765	95.2	4.8

[a] Source, modified from reference (11.4).

high percentage of deaths which had not been registered came as a surprise to Public Health Statisticians, and incidentally cast a doubt on official infant mortality rates: this under-registration of deaths which is much higher than the under-registration of births (for reasons of legal convenience, almost all births end up by being registered) tends to diminish the numerator of the quotient between deaths and births out of which the infant mortality rate is constructed, and thus to artificially diminish the actual rate.

A LOW MEDICAL CERTIFICATION OF REGISTERED DEATHS

Latin America stresses quite clearly the points raised in Chapter 4 on the shortage of physicians: on the one hand, local oligarchies control access to medical schools, in order to assure the earning power of physicians who are already in practice, on the other hand, medical emigration towards the central capitalist countries (especially the U.S.) further denude the continent from a resource which is in short supply to begin with. Table 3 gives an idea of this phenomenon.

It is sobering to realize that, out of one hundred physicians in El Salvador, the Dominican Republic and Haiti, there were in 1972 respectively 13, 33 and 95 in the U.S.A., and that, at current graduating rates, eight Latin American countries would take over two years (the Dominican Republic 5.7 and Haiti 8.5 years) to replace their physicians who have emigrated to the U.S.

In all of the Latin American countries where it is the "market", i.e. purchasing power that predominantly allocated resources, physicians will be spatially distributed according to the criteria described in Chapter 4: they will drift to the cities,

TABLE 3.

Latin American Physicians in the United States, from each of the Latin American Countries, and Annual Number of Graduating Physicians, Circa 1972

Countries	Number of physicians in the U.S. in 1972 (1)	Number of physicians in each country (2)	Percentage of physicians in the U.S. over number of physicians in country (3)	Annual number of graduating physicians (4)	Years for replacement of physicians in the U.S. (5)
Argentina	1536	49,950 (1970)	3	2972 (1970)	0.5
Bolivia	188	2143 (1970)	9	290 (1970)	0.6
Brazil	497	46,051 (1970)	1	3171 (1970)	0.2
Colombia	1161	10,317 (1972)	11	407 (1970)	2.9
Costa Rica	26	1067 (1970)	2	50 (1970)	0.5
Chile	257	4462 (1971)	6	327 (1970)	0.8
Dominican Republic	722	2220 (1972)	33	127 (1971)	5.7
Ecuador	183	2080 (1970)	9	189 (1970)	1.0
El Salvador	128	952 (1972)	13	86 (1970)	1.5
Guatemala	135	1208 (1972)	11	62 (1970)	2.2
Haití	391	412 (1972)	95	46 (1970)	8.5
Honduras	65	780 (1972)	8	24 (1970)	2.7
México	2107	38,000 (1972)	6	2240 (1970)	0.9
Nicaragua	96	1385 (1972)	7	36 (1970)	2.7
Panama	29	1070 (1972)	3	46 (1970)	0.6
Paraguay	105	1071 (1972)	10	45 (1970)	2.3
Perú	754	8023 (1972)	9	258 (1970)	2.9
Uruguay	66	3250 (1972)	2	228 (1970)	0.3
Venezuela	222	11,222 (1972)	2	690 (1969)	0.2

Sources: Column 1 (11.5); Column 2 (11.6); Column 4 (11.7).

where the clients are, and to the medical specialities which can provide clients: surgery (including cosmetic surgery), chronic diseases, rare illnesses, etc.

As a result of this, a high percentage of deaths in Latin America are not registered by physicians (Table 4).

The physicians in Latin America are recruited from a social class, which is of course not representative of the whole population of the countries: it has been remarked that the expansion in secondary and university in Latin America has been a consequence of pressures by the urban middle classes for education for their offspring, as it offers them an opportunity for social advancement. (11.9) A study undertaken in six medical schools in Latin America (11.9) showed that, of a total of 2326 students, the upper, upper-middle and middle classes supplied 70 percent, with the lower-middle and lower classes providing the remaining 30 percent. The ideological conditioning that these physicians receive during their medical training reinforces the tendency, analyzed in Chapter 4, of underestimating malnutrition: let us stress again that malnutrition affects population groups with which physicians are likely not to be in contact (as these cannot generate "economic demand" which is by far the most important factor in receiving or not receiving medical care in Latin America), whose treatment does not need to use the products of medical technology which physicians are trained to handle, whose study would give them little credit, as it is not a "frontier of knowledge" subject which produces Nobel

TABLE 4.

Percentages of Medically Certified Deaths and Deaths Not Certified in some Latin American Countries, Various Years[a]

Country	Year	Medically certified deaths %	Deaths not certified %
Barbados	1971	81.1	18.9
Colombia	1970	67.1	32.9
Costa Rica	1972	57.2	42.8
Chile	1971	83.4	16.6
Ecuador	1970	43.8	56.2
El Salvador	1970	20.5	79.5
Guatemala	1971	21.8	78.2
Mexico	1971	75.8	27.2
Panama	1971	60.0	40.0
Péru	1970	57.0	43.0
Uruguay	1971	99.7	0.3
Venezuela	1971	79.4	20.6

[a] Source, reference (11.8).

prizes, and finally the fact that ultimately, the causes of malnutrition call for a type of analysis and types of solution which are completely beyond the scope of medicine as it is being taught now in Latin America.

Observations on Mortality from Malnutrition in Children Under Five Years of Age in Latin America: The Puffer–Serrano Study

Latin America has been fortunate in that a very thorough study on the causes of death of children under five years of age was carried out there in 1970–72. This was the Puffer–Serrano Study, mentioned in Chapter 4 and above, whose findings provide an illuminating comparison with the statistics on mortality from malnutrition just presented in Table 1.

This study was carried out in 13 different Latin American areas corresponding to eight countries. In total, approximately 35,000 deaths of children under five years of age, selected through a probabilistic method, were investigated. The allocation of causes of death was not the restrictive one used by the Eighth Version of the International Classification of Diseases, reviewed in Chapter 4, but one which attempted to locate malnutrition as one of the elements of the dialectical relationship between malnutrition and infection, on which there have been extensive writings in the last decade.

Use was made of all of the clinical information available concerning those deaths: reports from physicians, hospital records, autopsy findings. The general conclusion was that "nutritional deficiency was the gravest problem that manifested itself through the study as measured by its intervention in mortality". More specific findings, were the following.

On the mortality of children under one year of age, Puffer and Serrano concluded that:

"Nutritional deficiency..., which includes the various forms of protein caloric malnutrition, constitutes another important group of causes (of death). In the past, the observance of the principle of "basic cause" has hidden the role played by nutritional deficiency and immaturity in mortality, these two conditions being assigned as associated causes."

Tables 5 and 6 show the weight of malnutrition as a basic or associated cause of mortality of children under 1 year of age, and of one to four years of age, as revealed by Puffer and Serrano. (11.4)

TABLE 5.

Weight of Nutritional Deficiency as a Basic or Associated Cause of Death in Children of Under 1 Year of Age in Some Latin American Countries 1968–72[a]

Study area	Total no. of deaths	Deaths caused by malnutrition	% of total
Argentina			
Chaco Province			
Resistencia	747	270	36
Rural departments	663	215	32
San Juan Province			
San Juan (city)	295	55	19
Suburban departments	696	187	27
Rural departments	909	269	30
Bolivia			
La Paz	2685	746	28
Viacha	105	25	24
Brazil			
Recife	2773	1080	39
Ribeirão Prêto			
Ribeirão Preto (city)	400	116	29
Franca	364	119	33
Communities	195	64	33
Saõ Paulo	3788	1062	28
Chile			
Santiago	2207	494	22
Comunas	197	66	33
Colombia			
Cali	1153	306	26
Cartagena	856	278	32
Medellin	924	308	33
El Salvador			
San Salvador	2094	597	28
Rural *municipios*	638	198	30
Jamaica			
Kingston-St. Andrew	1589	243	15
Mexico			
Monterrey	3220	1003	31
Total	26,508	7701	29 (av.)

[a] Source, modified from reference (11.4).

TABLE 6.

Weight of Nutritional Deficiency* and Measles as a Basic or Associated Cause of Death in Children from One to Four Years of Age

Area	Total number of deaths	Number due to malnutrition	Number due to measles	Percentages Malnutrition	Measles	Malnutrition and measles
Argentina						
Chaco						
Resistencia	117	66	14	56	12	68
Rural departments	174	80	16	46	9	55
San Juan City	31	7	5	23	16	39
Suburban departments	84	20	13	24	15	39
Rural departments	141	49	35	35	25	60
Bolivia						
La Paz	1430	608	403	42	28	70
Viacha	56	21	14	37	25	62
Brazil						
Recife	862	536	267	62	31	93
Riberào Prêto City	64	37	21	58	33	91
Franca	70	36	7	51	10	61
Communities	33	15	5	45	15	60
Saõ Paulo	524	181	104	34	20	54
Chile						
Santiago	282	68	11	24	4	28
Communes	28	12	—	43	—	43
Colombia						
Cali	474	254	66	54	14	68
Cartagena	399	242	81	61	20	81
Medellín	424	228	72	54	17	71
El Salvador						
San Salvador	644	344	81	53	13	66
Rural municipalities	434	272	35	63	8	71
Jamaica						
Kingston-St. Andrews	276	78	5	28	2	30
	38	18	—	47	—	47
Mexico						
Monterrey	733	316	177	43	24	67
Total	7318	3488	1432	48	19	37

* Those deaths are excluded in which malnutrition is the consequence of other diseases.
Source: Modified from (11.4).

With regard to nutritional deficiency, the researchers state that:

"The analysis of multiple causes (of death) on the basis of data gathered from clinical studies and autopsies, and of interviews of relatives of deceased children, together with data on medical certificates of cause of death, shows that nutritional deficiency is the most important contributing factor of the excessive mortality that was observed in the 13 Latin American projects of the study."

As said before, malnutrition was evaluated using information from clinical studies, autopsies and household medical interviews, and it was found that "Autopsy results produced valuable complementary proof that malnutrition exists in areas where the magnitude of this important health problem had not previously been recognized". Its assignation as cause of death was made very cautiously. In the case of malnourished children with grade I malnutrition (e.g. children whose weight was 75 to 89 percent of the norm), nutritional deficiency was not considered a cause of death. Malnutrition was accepted as a cause of death only in grade II and grade III forms (weights, respectively, of 60 to 74 percent of the norm, and of less than 60 percent), and it was accepted as a basic cause of death only in grade III children. The overall results of the study are presented in Table 7.

General findings on mortality caused by malnutrition have shown that incidence is highest in children between the ages of 28 days and 2 years; that mortality is much higher in rural than in urban areas; that nutritional marasmus (overall nutritional deficiency) is both earlier in occurrence and more widespread than kwashiorkor (protein malnutrition); and that deaths from specific vitamin deficiencies are very rare.

Immaturity, which appears in Table 6 as a basic or associated cause in many deaths, was measured by Puffer and Serrano according to body weight at birth, and immaturity was assigned as a cause in many deaths. It is known that immaturity in a newborn child is closely related to the nutritional status of the mother.

According to Béhar (11.10), children of malnourished mothers are handicapped from birth because of their low birth weight. He goes on to show that this problem cannot be corrected by improving the nutrition of pregnant women because the low birth weight of their infants is a result not only of antenatal malnutrition but also of the small size of the mothers, which is in itself a manifestation of their own malnutrition during childhood. (11.10, p. 316)

The final conclusion of the Puffer–Serrano study regarding malnutrition and immaturity is that:

> "A sort of vicious circle gets established, in which mothers who have suffered nutritional deficiencies at an early stage in their lives, and have been subject to other unfavourable environmental influences, have children with low birth weight. Many of those children die as a result of infectious diseases due to their higher vulnerability, and those who survive continue being exposed to a higher risk from environmental factors and malnutrition than those who are born with a satisfactory weight."

To break the vicious circle will take two to three generations, which must not deter us from advocating strong efforts now to start.

The Study's findings on mortality from measles deserve special consideration. Measles is a relatively harmless disease in a well-nourished child, and it is malnutrition that turns it into a disease with a massive mortality. Historically, emphasis has been placed on measles infection as the "cause" of death in malnourished children due to the infectious disease orientation of the medical profession, which is reflected in the International Classification of Diseases and which has been analyzed in Chapter 4.

TABLE 7.

Mortality of Children Under 5 Years of Age Caused by Nutritional Deficiency as a Basic or Associated Cause of Death in Some Latin American Countries, 1968–72[a]

Study area	Total deaths	% Caused by malnutrition	% Caused by immaturity	% Caused by malnutrition and immaturity
Argentina				
Chaco Province				
Resistencia	864	40.0	22.1	62.2
Rural departments	837	37.6	13.6	51.3
San Juan Province				
San Juan (city)	326	20.2	33.1	53.4
Suburban departments	780	27.4	30.4	57.8
Rural department	1050	31.1	23.7	54.9
Bolivia				
La Paz	4115	36.0	11.5	47.6
Viacha	161	30.4	10.6	41.0
Brazil				
Recife	3635	46.2	20.2	66.4
Ribeirão Prêto				
Ribeirão Prêto (city)	464	34.5	35.3	69.8
Franca	434	36.4	27.6	64.1
Communities	228	38.2	28.5	66.7
São Paulo	4312	30.4	28.4	58.8
Chile				
Santiago	2489	23.7	31.8	55.5
Comunas	225	35.6	17.8	53.3
Colombia				
Cali	1627	36.4	19.7	56.2
Cartagena	1255	44.7	20.2	64.9
Medellín	1348	42.3	19.7	61.9
El Salvador				
San Salvador	2738	37.2	17.1	54.3
Rural *municipios*	1082	46.9	7.9	54.8
Jamaica				
Kingston-St. Andrew	1903	19.4	39.7	59.1
Mexico				
Monterrey	3953	36.1	18.3	54.5

[a] Source, modified from reference (11.4).

The investigators stated that "measles as a basic cause" accounted for 2108, or 6 percent, of the 35,095 deaths of children under 5 years of age in the study. If the neonatal period is excluded, the percentage reaches 9.4 percent. Measles accounts for 19.9 percent of all deaths in the second year of life, a proportion reaching 29.7 percent in one study area (Recife in Brazil).

The efficacy of measles vaccination under these circumstances can be questioned here. Vaccination could be an ideal technocratic solution: a drug which fights against a specific pathological condition and does not attempt to modify any underlying socio-political situation. This "solution" calls for skepticism. It is well known that the relationship between malnutrition and infection, in which the original causal base is a person weakened by malnutrition, is observed not only in measles but also in many other infectious and parasitic diseases, such as bronchopneumonia, diarrhoea and gastroenteritis. A malnourished child "produces" a mortal case of measles in the same way that it "produces" a mortal diarrhoea. During the 1972 Sahel famine in Africa, it was observed that, independently of whether measles incidence was high or low, the overall mortality rate hardly changed. When measles had a low incidence, other diseases accounted for a death rate that was equally high, but as those diseases could not be identified with any certainty, they were not as salient for the affected population. (11.11) Thus, measles immunity would channel toward other "final" causes the deaths of many malnourished children.

It can be argued that the findings of the Puffer–Serrano Study cannot be generalized to other areas of the countries where it was undertaken, or to other countries in Latin America. Generally, research of this type is undertaken in areas which are more favourable (due to their accessibility) than the average, which might mean that their health conditions are better. In the case of this study, "six of the projects (study areas) were strictly urban, while the remaining nine included urban, suburban and rural areas". According to Pan American Health Organization statistics, in 1970, 54 percent of Latin America's population was urban and 46 percent rural. (11.12) A repeatedly observed finding in the Puffer-Serrano study was that rural mortality was higher than urban mortality, e.g. mortality in the rural "municipios" in El Salvador and Viacha (Bolivia) was twice as high as that in neighbouring cities, and in suburban and rural areas in San Juan province (Argentina) mortality was almost twice as high as in its capital city of San Juan. With this in mind, the authors' conclusion that "it is likely that in many sectors of Latin America mortality rates in a rural setting are at least twice as high as those in cities" seems reasonable. Although such clear-cut findings were not observed in other areas, it can be assumed that the conditions projected by the study are representative of the nutritional situation in Latin America and its impact on mortality, and that, lacking more solid information, its findings can be extrapolated in order to quantify malnutrition-induced mortality in the Latin American countries.

Coverage of Health Services in Latin America and of the Statistics that they Generate: the Puffer–Serrano Findings

As was stated in Chapter 4, statistics on morbidity which have received care in a health facility could be, in theory, a good source of data on the incidence of malnutrition in a country. In practice, things do not happen that way in Latin America (or in the rest of the developing countries in general), due to the incomplete and biased coverage of health services in those countries, where it can be said that the density of health facilities is in an inverse ratio to the health and nutritional needs of the population. The Puffer–Serrano Study (whose universe was a *total* population) confirms this.

The data provided by the Study are an indirect indicator of the insufficient coverage of Latin America health care systems. In spite of the predominant urban

TABLE 8.

Percentage of Deceased Children who had No Prenatal Care and who were Born or Died at Home in Some Latin American Countries, 1968–1972[a]

Study area	% under 1 year of age who had no prenatal care	% under 1 year of age who were born at home	% 28 days to 4 years of age who died at home
Argentina			
Chaco Province			
Resistencia	30.2	24.7	33.2
Rural departments	53.3	48.5	36.1
San Juan Province			
San Juan (city)	11.5	6.9	18.8
Suburban depts.	17.2	13.3	19.4
Rural depts.	22.4	21.1	26.0
Bolivia			
La Paz	53.5	56.0	78.6
Viacha	83.1	84.9	92.2
Brazil			
Recife	42.6	19.4	55.9
Ribeirão Prêto			
Ribeirão Prêto (city)	18.9	4.9	19.2
Franca	29.6	14.1	32.6
Communities	25.6	12.1	21.8
São Paulo	25.2	13.1	16.8
Chile			
Santiago	17.0	4.7	38.0
Comunas	25.7	23.0	48.4
Colombia			
Cali	43.3	48.4	52.6
Cartagena	29.2	29.4	32.8
Medellín	19.6	12.5	44.6
El Salvador			
San Salvador	53.8	18.4	68.5
Rural *municipios*	66.3	66.0	88.6
Jamaica			
Kingston-St. Andrew	23.8	11.9	36.3
	18.2	60.0	55.2
Mexico			
Monterrey	34.5	13.2	29.2

Source: modified from reference (11.4).

setting of their study referred to previously, implying greater accessibility to health services on the part of the population, a high percentage of the deceased children studied had lacked prenatal care, and many of them had been born and died in their homes (Table 8).

Nutritional Surveys

Latin America has been relatively favoured with nutritional surveys of the type mentioned in Chapter 4. Children are weighed and measured, and these sources are plotted against a "normal" parameter.

The Puffer–Serrano findings are supported (and the official Vital and Health Statistics systems discredited) by evidence derived from a nutritional survey in Latin America. Although the probabilistic nature of some of the studies are likely to be suspect, Table 9 gives a sobering picture of the state of nutrition of the people of the Latin American countries, and on the uselessness of the "mean" availability of food "*per capita*" as revealed in Table 10.

TABLE 9.
A Classification of Nutritional Status among Children of Less than Five Years of Age

Country or political unit	Years	Total number examined	Normal %	I%	Malnutrition grade[b] II%	III%
Antigua[d]	1975	535	56.9	35.3	6.8	0.8
Bahamas[d]	1974	321	46.4[h]	14.6	0.6	0.9
Barbados[e]	1969	248	48.8	39.0	11.0	1.2
Belice[a]	1973	3546[c]	40.8	40.0	18.0	1.2
Bolivia[a]	1966–69	968	60.1	29.0	10.2	0.7
Brazil[a]	1968	569	31.7	48.4	17.2	2.7
Colombia[a]	1966	3378	33.4	45.6	19.3	1.7
Costa Rica[f]	1966		42.6	43.7	12.2	1.5
Chile[a]	1975	881,517	82.2	13.7	3.2	0.9
Dominica[a]	1970	117	71.8	19.7	5.1	3.4
Ecuador[a]	1965–69	9000	60.3	28.9	9.6	1.2
El Salvador[f]	1965		25.5	48.5	22.9	3.1
Guatemala[f]	1965		18.6	49.0	26.5	5.9
Guyana[e]	1971	964	39.3	43.0	16.0	1.7
Haiti[i]	1975	1542	17.8	28.9	35.6	17.4
Honduras[h]	1966		27.5	43.0	27.2	2.3
Virgin Islands					—5.0—	
Jamaica[e]	1970			39.0	9.4	1.4
Montserrat[f]	1971	372	63.1[h]	28.0	3.5	0.0
Nicaragua[h]	1966		43.2	41.8	13.2	1.8
Panama[f]	1967	632	39.3	48.8	10.8	1.1
Paraguay	1973	41,750	92.2	4.9	2.2	0.7
Peru	1965–71	83,165	56.0	32.8	10.9	0.8
Dominican Republic	1969	1100	25.0	49.0	23.0	4.0
San Cristobal, Nieves & Anguila	1974	1209	61.2	33.3	5.4	0.1
San Vincent[e]	1967	2490	37.5	47.0	14.0	1.5
Santa Lucia[e]	1974	363	56.1	33.0	9.0	1.9
Venezuela[g]	1974	23,271	51.1	35.3	12.2	1.4

[a] Quadrennial health projections 1971–75 and various sources.
[b] Grades of malnutrition according to the Gomez classification.
[c] Children of $5\frac{1}{2}$ years of age only.
[d] MCH Profiles for the Commonwealth Caribbean Area PD 75/8. WHO/PAHO 1975.
[e] National Nutrition Surveys CFNI (data for Barbados regrouped for this classification).
[f] National Nutrition Surveys INCAP/ICNND.
[g] 0–6 years of age.
[h] The difference corresponds to children with 10% over weight (Bahamas 37.4% and Montserrat 5.4%).
[i] Nutrition Bureau (Toureau S. *et al.*) 1976.
Source: (11.13).

TABLE 10.

Daily Supply of Kilocalories and Protein per Person in the Latin American Countries, and Percentage of Satisfaction of Needs[a]

Country	Daily kcal	% of needs of kcal satisfied	Grams of protein per day
Argentina	3060	115	100
Barbados	—	—	—
Bolivia	1900	79	46
Braazil	2690	110	65
Chile	2670	109	77
Colombia	2200	95	51
Costa Rica	2610	116	66
Cuba	2700	117	63
Dominican Republic	2120	94	48
Ecuador	2010	88	47
El Salvador	1930	84	52
Guatemala	2130	97	59
Guyana	2390	105	58
Haiti	1730	77	39
Honduras	2140	94	56
Jamaica	2360	105	63
Mexico	2580	111	62
Nicaragua	2450	109	71
Panama	2580	112	61
Paraguay	2740	119	73
Peru	2320	99	60
Surinam	2450	109	59
Trinidad and Tobago	2380	98	64
Uruguay	2880	108	100
Venezuela	2430	98	63

[a] Source, reference (11.14).

If arithmetical means were true, there would apparently be little problem with malnutrition in Latin America, as Table 10, on mean consumption *per capita* of calories and proteins would indicate. According to this Table, children in Argentina (115 percent of caloric needs satisfied) or Brazil (110 percent of needs satisfied) would not be dying of malnutrition.

The other papers included in this Chapter will give a different picture.

An Estimation of Mortality Caused by Malnutrition in Latin America

It is now possible to estimate the number of deaths caused by malnutrition in Latin America. The cause of death is assigned to malnutrition by use of a very simple mechanism of causality: the fact that the death would not have taken place if the person had not been malnourished. This determination has operational advantages, for if it is assumed that statistical data are useful insofar as they indicate measures to correct a given situation, it is evident that malnutrition is the weakest link and the most useful one for action in the causal-chain of malnutrition and infection. It is much cheaper, as well as more useful and simpler, to supply a population with food than to supply it with medical care when it becomes ill with parasitosis, diarrhoea, bronchopneumonia, or measles. Such an allocation of causality to malnutrition in certain processes of disease and death would be the most rational one if the goal of the societies involved were the welfare of its citizens.

Tables 11, 12 and 13 are an attempt to extrapolate some of the findings on malnutrition that have been presented in this paper. The method used is, by necessity, a simplification of reality, and it is used only because the means for a more refined approach are lacking. Thus it would be most desirable if the health statistics systems currently in use in Latin America could be improved so as to produce more accurate figures, leading to new empirical findings and more sophisticated estimations that would permit us to correct the figures presented here.

TABLE 11.

Estimate of Annual Deaths Caused by Malnutrition in Children Under 1 Year in the Latin American Countries, Various Years

Country	Year	Annual no. of deaths of dhildren under 1 year[a]	Estimated no. of annual deaths caused by malnutrition[b]	Estimated % of deaths caused by malnutrition[b]
Antigua	1965	79	23	29
Argentina	1970	32,099	9630	30
Bahamas	1973	135	39	29
Barbados	1972	182	53	29
Belice	1972	167	48	29
Bermuda	1972	23	7	29
Bolivia	1966	8258	2312	28
Brazil	—	250,000[c]	72,500	29
Chile	1971	19,296	4438	23
Colombia	1971	50,084	15,025	30
Costa Rica	1973	2394	694	29
Dominican Republic	1972	8721	2529	29
Ecuador	1971	19,119	5544	29
El Salvador	1971	8099	2349	29
Grenada	1969	110	32	29
Guatemala	1971	18,736	5433	29
Guyana	—	1000[c]	290	29
Haiti	—	17,000[c]	4930	29
Honduras	1971	4637	1345	29
Jamaica	1970	3227	645	20
Mexico	1971	141,261	43,791	31
Nicaragua	1965	3679	1067	29
Panama	1971	2064	599	29
Paraguay	1971	3072	891	29
Peru	1970	31,212	9051	29
Surinam	—	800[c]	232	29
Trinidad & Tobago	1973	660	191	29
Uruguay	1971	2661	772	29
Venezuela	1971	20,360	5904	29
Total		649,135	190,364	

[a] For most of the countries, figures as presented in the *United Nations Demographic Yearbook* and year to which they correspond. No corrections made for under-registration.

[b] For the countries included in the Inter-American Investigation of Mortality in Childhood, figures represent the observed percentages in the areas of the countries that were included in the study. For other countries, an application of the percentage observed in the study for the whole of Latin America.

[c] Estimated.

TABLE 12.

An Estimation of Annual Deaths Caused by Malnutrition and Measles in Children Aged 1 to 4 in the Latin American Countries, Various Years

Country	Year	Annual no. of deaths of children aged 1–4[a]	Estimated no. of annual deaths caused by malnutrition[b]	Estimated % of deaths caused by malnutrition[b]	Estimated measles deaths[c,d]
Antigua	1965	25	12	48	5
Argentina	1970	6236	2557	41	935
Bahamas	1973	22	11	48	4
Barbados	1972	25	12	48	5
Belice	1972	75	36	48	15
Bermuda	1972	5	2	48	1
Bolivia	1966	7880	3310	42	2206
Brazil	—	110,000[e]	42,900	39	28,600
Chile	1971	3119	811	26	94
Colombia	1971	30,541	17,103	56	4887
Costa Rica	1973	629	302	48	126
Dominican Republic	1972	4288	2058	48	858
Ecuador	1971	13,716	6584	48	2743
El Salvador	1971	4092	2332	57	450
Grenada	1969	36	17	48	7
Guatemala	1971	18,675	8964	48	3735
Guyana	—	500[e]	240	48	100
Haiti	—	6000[e]	2880	48	1200
Honduras	1971	3225	1548	48	645
Jamaica	1970	1448	449	31	29
Mexico	1971	59,047	25,390	43	14,271
Nicaragua	1965	1889	907	48	378
Panama	1971	1337	642	48	267
Paraguay	1971	1913	918	48	383
Peru	1970	22,781	10,935	48	4556
Surinam	—	400[e]	192	48	80
Trinidad and Tobago	1972	163	78	48	33
Uruguay	1971	255	122	48	51
Venezuela	1971	7114	3415	48	1423
Total		305,436	134,727		67,987

[a] For most of the countries, figures as presented in the *United Nations Demographic Yearbook* and year to which they correspond. No corrections made for under-registration.

[b] For the countries included in the Inter-American Investigation of Mortality in Childhood, figures represent the observed percentages in the areas of the countries that were included in the study. For other countries, an application of the percentage observed in the study for the whole of Latin America.

[c] For the countries included in the Inter-American Investigation of Mortality in Childhood, figures represent the observed percentages in the area of the countries that were included in the study. For other countries, an application of the percentage used in the study for the whole of Latin America. This procedure was used to determine the weight of mortality by measles due to the numerous inaccuracies that have been observed in the registration of mortality by measles in the vital statistics systems.

[d] Malnutrition has been assigned a causal role in 50 percent of deaths whose "basic cause" is measles.

[e] Estimated.

The total annual number of deaths caused by malnutrition, which has conservatively been estimated to be approximately 400,000, adds up to approximately 17 percent of deaths from all causes in the Latin American countries (estimated as 2.3 million). This magnitude of malnutrition as a cause of death in Latin America makes any comment superfluous.

TABLE 13.

An Estimation of Annual Deaths Caused by Malnutrition in Persons Over 5 in the Latin American Countries, Various Years

Country	Year	Annual no. of deaths of persons over 5[a]	Annual no. of deaths caused by malnutrition[b]
Antigua	1965	380	10
Argentina	1970	183,778	784
Bahamas	1973	1016	26
Barbados	1972	1838	47
Belice	1972	427	11
Bermuda	1972	360	9
Bolivia	1966	17,901	465
Brazil	—	400,000[c]	10,400
Chile	1971	61,041	613
Colombia	1971	126,272	3825
Costa Rica	1973	6679	77
Dominican Republic	1972	14,529	250
Ecuador	1971	31,071	1170
El Salvador	1971	16,561	718
Grenada	1969	622	16
Guatemala	1971	37,812	2344
Guyana	—	3300[c]	86
Haiti	—	30,000[c]	780
Honduras	1971	12,543	370
Jamaica	1970	9518	247
Mexico	1971	258,015	6715
Nicaragua	1965	6540	89
Panama	1971	6456	141
Paraguay	1971	9241	215
Peru	1970	58,049	1245
Surinam	—	3000[c]	78
Trinidad and Tobago	1972	6132	110
Uruguay	1971	26,235	181
Venezuela	1971	43,004	486
Total		1,372,320	31,508

[a] For most of the countries, figures as presented in the *United Nations Demographic Yearbook* and year to which they correspond. No corrections made for under-registration.

[b] For countries listed in Table 10, number of deaths caused by malnutrition as recorded in the *United Nations Demographic Yearbook*. For Argentina, see reference (11.3). For all other countries an estimation, based upon the assumption that their percentage of deaths by malnutrition in this age group is the same as in the countries for which there is information (those listed in Table 10—2.6 percent).

[c] Estimated.

ANNEX 1

Malnutrition in Argentina

by *José Carlos Escudero and collaborators*

A. The Case of Argentina

Argentina is a massive producer and exporter of foodstuffs. At the same time it is a country which reported 2439 deaths whose "basic cause" was malnutrition in 1970, 1655 of them children under one year of age. (11.3) As these are deaths whose "basic cause" was malnutrition, the actual total of malnutrition-induced deaths is much higher, as many as 13,000 according to the estimation in the preceding section.

The problems of measuring malnutrition in Argentina are the usual ones: little data, a conceptual underestimation on the role of malnutrition in causing deaths and the various other elements reviewed elsewhere. The following report has gone beyond those "official" malnutrition deaths, and attempted to get a more realistic picture of this phenomenon in a country in which neither overpopulation nor a drought, or an ungenerous Nature can be blamed for this state of affairs.

Infant Mortality and Malnutrition

Any analysis on the causal structure of infant mortality in Argentina, and thus a quantification of the impact of malnutrition on them, is perforce limited. This is, on the one hand, the result of the under-registration of deaths, a phenomenon of a differential weight in different areas in the country. On the other hand, it is in those areas where the phenomenon is more marked that socio-economic conditions are worse, and where there are fewer health resources and a higher proportion of infant deaths without medical care.

As Table 14 shows, the high proportion of infants who have died without having medical care in the provinces of Catamarca, Chaco, Chubut, Formosa, Jujuy, Neuquen, Rio Negro, San Luis and Santiago del Estero, at the same time these being provinces where infant mortality rates are highest, make an accurate knowledge of the phenomenon of ascertainment of cause of death very inaccurate. If to these percentages there are added those in which the recorder of cause of death was "other physician" i.e. not the one who followed the terminal disease of the child— and those in which it was unknown whether they had received medical care or not, it has to be concluded that the recording of cause of death in Argentina is faulty, both in integrity and in quality. (11.15)

Another basic factor, which adds to the aforementioned, is the underestimation of malnutrition as a cause of death through use of the Classification Rules of the

TABLE 14.
Deaths of Children under One Year of Age According to Medical Care Received. Argentina Republic—1970*

Province	Total Number	%	Children dead with medical care Reported by physician in attendance %	Reported by other physician %	Unspecified %	Dead without medical care %	Unknown %
TOTAL REPUBLIC	32,099	100.0	59.9	13.8	1.9	11.4	15.9
Capital Federal	3,727	100.0	63.8	30.4	1.7	1.9	2.2
Buenos Aires	7,202	100.0	54.2	13.5	1.5	4.4	26.4
Catamarca	371	100.0	68.5	4.0	—	21.3	6.2
Córdoba	2,095	100.0	62.5	18.5	1.3	7.3	10.4
Corrientes	1,261	100.0	56.0	9.8	0.5	18.8	14.9
Chaco	1,620	100.0	53.4	14.6	1.4	24.0	6.6
Chubut	449	100.0	55.5	9.2	2.7	20.0	12.5
Entre Ríos	1,048	100.0	72.9	4.9	1.0	7.0	14.2
Formosa	476	100.0	57.0	6.1	—	31.5	4.6
Jujuy	1,520	100.0	45.5	13.9	—	35.9	4.7
La Pampa	143	100.0	71.3	5.6	—	12.6	10.5
La Rioja	331	100.0	60.4	5.5	0.6	15.1	18.4
Mendoza	1,447	100.0	65.6	16.7	1.5	3.9	12.3
Misiones	1,087	100.0	46.8	17.2	0.6	18.6	16.8
Neuquén	578	100.0	54.5	11.4	0.2	29.2	4.7
Río Negro	799	100.0	52.4	15.5	—	21.2	10.9
Salta	1,897	100.0	41.1	7.0	0.7	13.5	37.7
San Juan	911	100.0	34.4	14.8	22.9	6.4	21.5
San Luis	303	100.0	56.8	11.5	0.7	20.1	10.9
Santa Cruz	112	100.0	75.9	8.0	0.9	10.7	4.5
Santa Fe	2,333	100.0	62.0	7.2	4.6	6.3	19.9
Sgo. del Estero	771	100.0	40.1	4.4	0.1	32.6	22.8
Tucumán	1,601	100.0	78.3	6.3	—	7.3	8.1
T. del Fuego Antartica and Islands Atlántico Sud.	17	100.0	64.7	35.3	—	—	—

Source: * National Programme of Health Statistics, Secretariat of Public Health, Ministry of Social Welfare, Argentina.

International Classification of Diseases (ICD). This has been explained in Chapter 4 of this book.

A measure has been developed, the Rate of Premortality–morbidity (11.16) as an indicator of the prevalence of a given pathology as a basic or associated cause of

TABLE 15.
"Rate of Premortality–Morbidity" as a Percentage of Total Deaths in the Province of Chaco, Argentina 1968–70)

Under one year	34.4
One to two years	64.5
Two to four years	52.1
Under five years	38.9

Source: (11.16).

TABLE 16.

Infant Mortality by Selected Causes—Argentina 1970

Province	Total deaths (absolute no. in brackets)	Acute respiratory (1)	Acute diarrhoeal (2)	Acute new-born (3)	Parasitical (4)	Immaturity (5)	Congenital malform (6)	Malnutrition (7)	All other special causes (8)	Ill-defined (9)
Total	(32,099) 100.0	16.4	13.3	12.7	10.9	7.2	5.8	5.0	18.6	10.1
Capital Federal	(3727) 100.0	10.7	5.3	21.6	19.5	7.7	11.5	2.6	19.5	1.6
Buenos Aires	(7202) 100.0	16.2	11.0	12.5	9.7	7.6	6.9	4.3	26.2	5.6
Catamarca	(371) 100.0	18.6	25.1	10.5	2.7	4.9	2.4	3.0	11.2	21.6
Córdoba	(2095) 100.0	15.7	17.2	17.5	8.2	9.3	8.1	3.6	15.6	4.8
Corrientes	(1261) 100.0	16.5	25.5	4.9	11.2	4.0	2.1	7.4	10.9	17.5
Chaco	(1620) 100.0	17.4	17.7	9.3	8.5	6.7	2.6	7.1	13.6	17.1
Chubut	(449) 100.0	15.8	10.0	10.5	16.0	5.4	4.9	3.8	15.6	18.0
Entre Rios	(1048) 100.0	11.1	9.4	15.6	8.5	7.4	6.1	8.1	29.4	4.4
Formosa	(476) 100.0	19.1	21.2	5.0	8.4	5.9	1.9	5.5	14.3	18.7
Jujuy	(1520) 100.0	17.8	10.1	6.5	8.9	3.3	1.6	7.0	9.1	35.7
La Pampa	(143) 100.0	16.0	14.7	18.2	6.3	11.9	4.9	3.5	16.8	7.7
La Rioja	(331) 100.0	16.9	8.8	6.1	4.8	2.7	4.2	12.4	26.3	17.8

		(1)	(2)	(3)	(4)	(5)	(6)	(7)	(8)	(9)
Misiones	(1087) 100.0	25.0	18.8	7.1	9.8	5.4	3.3	7.9	13.1	9.6
Mendoza	(1447) 100.0	26.2	17.2	16.9	5.0	5.3	7.5	9.2	11.9	0.8
Neuquén	(578) 100.0	22.3	17.0	10.2	6.9	11.1	3.1	0.7	11.1	17.6
Río Negro	(799) 100.0	20.5	22.5	8.9	9.5	11.2	5.4	5.1	11.6	5.3
Salta	(1897) 100.0	13.1	16.5	6.1	8.1	9.6	1.5	5.9	18.8	20.4
San Juan	(911) 100.0	16.0	20.3	14.8	11.5	5.9	5.0	7.3	14.9	4.3
San Luis	(303) 100.0	14.8	23.8	14.5	4.0	6.3	3.6	1.6	17.2	14.2
Santa Cruz	(112) 100.0	20.5	6.2	13.4	5.4	12.5	10.7	2.7	24.1	4.5
Santa Fe	(2333) 100.0	13.1	26.5	14.8	9.0	8.6	7.1	5.0	12.9	3.0
Sgo. del Estero	(771) 100.0	10.0	11.0	7.2	6.5	2.7	1.6	1.6	13.7	45.3
Tuenmán	(1601) 100.0	24.4	1.7	13.7	10.6	8.5	3.5	3.3	22.2	12.1
T. del Fuego	(17) 100.0	23.5	—	5.9	5.9	23.5	11.8	5.9	17.6	5.9

Source: (11.17)

(1) Corresponds to codes 460–466; 470–474; 480–486; 490 of ICD.
(2) Corresponds to code 009 of ICD.
(3) Corresponds to codes 764–768; 769–772; 774–775; 776 of ICD.
(4) Corresponds to codes 001–002; 011–012; 013–019; 032–033; 037–038; 040–043; 055; 086; 090; 136.
(5) Corresponds to codes 777 of ICD.
(6) Corresponds to codes 740–759 of ICD.
(7) Corresponds to codes 267; 268; 269 of ICD.
(8) Includes all other useful codes of ICD.
(9) Corresponds to codes 780–796 of ICD.

death. This indicator consists of a quotient in which there appears in the numerator the number of times a given diagnosis appears as a basic or associated cause of death in death certificates, the numerator being the total number of deaths from all causes. The application of this rate to the results of the Interamerican Investigation of Mortality in Childhood in the provinces of Chaco and San Juan (11.17) re-evaluates the meaning of nutritional deficiency, and presents a striking contrast with the figures derived from ICD criteria as to the relative weight of malnutrition as a cause of death. (Table 15)

As is seen, malnutrition as a basic or associated cause appears in fully one-third of the deaths of under one-year-olds, in almost two-thirds of deaths of one- to two-year-olds, and in over half of deaths of two- to four-year-olds.

As to the overall infant mortality in the country, the following structure of causes of infant deaths in Argentina is instructive. (Table 16)

The percentage distribution of infant mortality shown in Table 16—with the official ICD criterion of assignation of basic cause of death—can be analyzed further, and in this the Interamerican Investigation of Childhood Mortality (11.18) will again be helpful.

Excepting for the provinces of Jujuy, La Rioja, Salta and Santiago del Estero, where "ill-defined" causes constitute a high percentage of all deaths, and even in other provinces where this also happens (Catamarca 21.6 percent, Corrientes 17.5 percent, Chubut 18.0 percent, Formosa 18.7 percent and Neuquen 17.6 percent); the causes (1) (7), most of which are eminently preventable or curable, provoke over two-thirds of all infant deaths.

Acute respiratory diseases are the largest single cause of death overall—16.4 percent. It is either the first or the second cause in all provinces, except Capital Federal, Cordoba and Santa Fe. Diarrhoeal disease is the next highest specific cause of death overall—13.3 percent. It is among the three more important causes of death in all provinces except Chubut, Santa Cruz and Tierra del Fuego. For both respiratory diseases and diarrhoea, and especially for the latter, the Interamerican Investigation found a high coexistence of malnutrition with the more specific cause. Acute diseases of the newborn were among the three first causes in three provinces. The Investigation found that there were widely divergent rates of mortality from this grouping of causes* between the most "favoured zones": Sherbrooke (Canada) with 848.6 deaths per 100,000 newborn on one hand, and Recife (Brazil) and San Juan Province (Argentina) with 2190.8 and 2089.0 per 100,000 respectively, a comment on a cause of death which shows the large number of deaths which would not have occurred had known technologies been applied.

Immaturity is one of the five main causes of death in seventeen jurisdictions of the country. The International Investigation has shown that immaturity is the most important factor in a vulnerability to illness in the neonatal period. In the city of San Juan the neonatal death rate per 100,000 newborn was 1786.9; while in suburban and rural departments of that province it was 2904.0 and 2536.4 respectively. Nutritional deficiences were found in a much greater abundance in those departments than in the city, which would ratify the correspondence between the two phenomena that have been repeatedly pointed out in the literature. Malnutrition—

---

* The Investigation used a grouping of causes which differs slightly from that in Table 16: codes 760–763, 764–768, 770–772, 774–778 of ICD.

TABLE 17.

Total Number of Deaths Studied, and Number of Deaths Caused by Malnutrition (as a basic or associated cause), and Rates of Mortality* by Month of Age of the Deceased (Findings of the five Argentinian zones studied by the Interamerican Investigation of Mortality)

| | Chaco Province | | | | San Juan Province | | | | | |
| | Capital | | Rural | | Capital | | Suburban | | Rural | |
	No.	Rate	No.	Rate	No.	Rate	No.	Rate	No.	Rate
Total Deaths studied	864	2070.0	837	2387.3	326	1291.6	780	2194.7	1050	2403.8
Total Deaths by malnutrition	346	828.9	315	898.5	66	261.5	214	602.1	327	748.6
−1	9	91.8	5	64.1	5	85.9	15	189.4	18	187.1
1	24	244.9	14	179.5	13	232.4	19	239.9	31	322.2
2	40	408.2	29	371.8	12	206.2	32	404.0	47	488.6
3	56	571.4	28	359.0	7	121.3	25	315.7	35	363.8
4	28	285.7	31	397.4	5	85.9	22	277.8	39	405.4
5	30	306.1	20	258.4	4	68.7	21	265.2	32	332.6
6	23	234.7	19	243.6	5	85.9	15	189.4	20	207.9
7	14	142.9	14	179.5	1	17.2	12	158.5	15	155.9
8	12	122.4	19	243.6	1	17.2	12	151.5	11	114.3
9	15	153.1	10	128.2	—	—	7	88.4	6	62.4
10	10	102.0	15	192.3	2	34.4	2	25.3	6	62.4
11	9	91.8	11	141.0	—	—	5	63.1	9	93.6
12	7	78.3	12	171.4	2	39.5	3	41.9	6	68.0
13	7	78.3	12	171.4	—	—	2	27.9	6	68.0
14	7	78.3	8	114.3	—	—	2	27.9	3	34.0
15	5	55.9	5	71.4	1	19.8	4	55.9	2	22.7
16	8	89.5	4	57.1	1	19.8	1	14.0	2	22.7
17	4	44.7	6	85.7	2	39.5	1	14.0	6	68.0
18	3	33.6	4	57.1	1	19.8	1	14.0	3	34.0
19	1	11.2	6	85.7	—	—	2	27.9	1	11.3
20	2	22.4	5	71.4	1	19.8	2	27.9	2	22.7
21	4	44.7	4	57.1	—	—	—	—	1	11.3
22	3	33.6	5	71.4	—	—	1	14.0	2	22.7
23	1	11.2	4	57.1	—	—	1	14.0	1	11.3
24–29	11	139.9	14	202.0	—	—	5	69.9	6	67.9
30–35	7	89.0	2	28.9	1	19.8	1	14.0	7	79.2
36–41	1	12.7	2	28.9	—	—	—	—	4	45.2
42–47	4	50.9	3	43.3	1	19.8	1	14.0	3	33.9
48–53	—	—	1	14.4	—	—	—	—	1	11.3
54–59	1	12.7	3	43.3	1	19.8	—	—	2	22.6

* For under one year olds by 100,000 newborn, for all others by 100,000 inhabitants.

again as a "basic cause"—is the second cause of death in La Rioja and the fourth in Corrientes, Jujuy, Mendoza and Misiones.

The Interamerican Investigation of Mortality in Childhood

The advantages of studies of this type have been repeatedly stated up to now, in Chapter 4 and in the first sector of this chapter. The study investigated 1701 deaths in seven Departments of the province of Chaco and 2156 deaths in the whole of the province of San Juan, chosen on a probabilistic basis in order to ensure an accurate extrapolation of the results. The results are presented in Table 17.

Put more simply, malnutrition as a direct or indirect cause of death has provoked approximately 40 percent of deaths in the capital city of Resistencia (Chaco), 37.6 percent deaths in the rural departments of Chaco, and 20.2 percent, 27.4 percent and 31.1 percent in the capital city, suburban departments and rural departments of the province of San Juan.

Rural mortality from malnutrition is consistently higher than the urban one, the case of San Juan being particularly noticeable in this respect, with suburban and rural rates which are 50 percent higher than urban ones.

Mortality from malnutrition is highest in the first year of life, but high rates are also observed in the second year, especially in the province of Chaco. In all areas except San Juan capital, the highest rates were observed within the first six months of life. In the latter, highest rates were observed in the first three months of life.

TABLE 18.
Mortality (both basic and associated) and Rates* in the Provinces of Chaco and San Juan, Argentina, by the Type of Nutritional Deficiency

Projects and Age Groups	Total No.	Total Rate	Vitamin deficiency (ICD 260–66) No.	Vitamin deficiency (ICD 260–66) Rate	Protein mualnutrition (ICD 267) No.	Protein mualnutrition (ICD 267) Rate	Nutritional marasmus (ICD 268) No.	Nutritional marasmus (ICD 268) Rate	Other states of malnutrition (ICD 269) No.	Other states of malnutrition (ICD 269) Rate
Under 5 years										
Chaco Pcia.	661	860.7	—	—	34	44.3	96	125.0	531	691.4
San Juan Pcia.	607	581.1	1	1.0	10	9.6	177	169.4	419	401.1
Under 1 year										
Chaco Pcia.	485	2755.7	—	—	11	62.5	66	375.0	408	2318.2
San Juan Pcia.	511	2187.5	1	4.3	2	8.6	158	676.4	350	1498.3
One year										
Chaco Pcia.	127	796.7	—	—	22	138.0	21	131.7	84	527.0
San Juan Pcia.	63	299.4	—	—	4	19.0	12	57.0	47	233.4
2–4 years										
Chaco Pcia.	49	110.4	—	—	1	2.3	9	20.3	39	87.9
San Juan Pcia.	33	52.3	—	—	4	6.3	7	11.1	22	34.8

* For under one year olds by 100,000 newborn. For all others by 100,000 inhabitants.

Table 18 describes the types of nutritional deficiency found by the investigation. As can be observed, only two cases of avitaminosis were observed. Protein deficiency was lower, at times much lower, than nutritional marasmus, except in the case of children of one year of age in the province of Chaco. "Other states of malnutrition" exhibited by far the highest rates. As to the age structure, the highest rates were among children of less than one year of age.

Malnutrition is closely allied with infection, and the investigation again confirms this. Table 19 reveals the frequently found association between different types of infections and respiratory diseases and malnutrition.

These Chaco and San Juan examples highlight the relationship between malnutrition and three groups of "basic causes". In both provinces, malnutrition as an associated cause contributed more to deaths due to infectious diseases than to other groups of causes, thus emphasizing the linkage between malnutrition and infection.

TABLE 19.

Association Between Certain Causes of Death and Malnutrition (International Investigation of Mortality in Childhood)

Groups of causes	Chaco All deaths	Chaco With nutritional deficiency No.	Chaco With nutritional deficiency %	San Juan All deaths	San Juan With nutritional deficiency No.	San Juan With nutritional deficiency %
All causes	1.133*	601	53.0	1.250*	500	40.0
All infectious &						
parasitic	677	443	65.4	579	305	52.7
diarrhoeal disease	548	365	66.6	410	238	58.0
measles	53	32	60.4	96	34	35.4
other	76	46	60.5	73	33	45.2
Nutritional deficiency	48	—	—	70	—	—
Respiratory						
diseases	225	96	42.7	343	119	34.7
Other causes	183	62	33.9	258	76	29.5

* Neonatal deaths are excluded.

Other Sources on Malnutrition

The Nutrition and Endocrinology Institute of Salta carried out, between 1967 and 1969 six clinical and nutritional studies, in order to ascertain the damages that malnutrition was producing in the population and to discover the magnitude of conditioning variables. (11.19)

The surveys included the following areas (a) urban area of the city of Salta through a representative sample of families with pre-school children; (b) Department of Guemes, Salta—a rural area; (c) Department of Cachi, Salta—also rural; (d) Antofagasta de la Sierra, a rural area of the province of Catamarca; (e) Tilcara, a rural area of the province of Jujuy and (f) Mision La Paz, a rural area of Salta inhabited by Indians. In the last five zones mentioned, the study included the whole of the population.

The nutritional status was investigated both by clinical and anthropometrical methods, using the Gomez scale.

The studies showed that of the children under five years of age studied, 45 percent had some degree of malnutrition, with values that ranged from 28.3 percent in the city of Salta to 75.8 percent in Cachi.

Thirty-six percent of the population were found to be at a malnutrition level of Grade I. Grade II encompassed 9.3 percent. Of the former it was said that they were "healthy, but awaiting some affecting factor, generally an acute infection, that could either send them into Grade II or make them die through a greater susceptibility to metabolic perturbances or to a common disease". (11.20) Table 20 summarizes the clinical findings of the studies.

Conclusions

It is a factor to wonder that none of the studies consulted on malnutrition in Argentina have been undertaken later than 1972. Latest published Vital Statistics are those of 1970. This is a surprising phenomenon, in a country which reported a

TABLE 20.
*Clinical and Nutritional Findings which Appeared Most Com-
monly in Children of Under Five Years of Age (Surveys
1967–69)*

Area	Paleness 2	Prominent belly 2	Atrophied papillae 2	Change in colour & texture of hair 2
Salta	17.5	24.9	9.1	4.2
Guemes	9.3	41.8	26.8	7.5
Cachi	13.6	38.6	44.8	*
Tilcara	20.9	50.8	33.5	4.1
Antofagasta	*	14.9	*	10.6
Mision La Paz	6.9	11.1	17.7	4.2
Weighed mean	12.4	29.5	19.2	4.3

* Data not registered.
Source: (11.19).

slight increase in its infant mortality between 1960 and 1970. (11.21) To this must be added the high proportion of deaths which do not report on the type of medical care given, or the high percentages of under-registration of deaths. Thus, an analysis of the mortality structure of Argentina has to be outdated, incomplete and biased, due to the criteria of allocation of cause of death, which tends to significantly underestimate malnutrition.

Argentina is a markedly uneven country in terms of health levels and national development. There is a privileged zone, composed of the provinces of Buenos Aires, Cordoba, Santa Fé, Entre Rios, La Pampa and the city of Buenos Aires. The rest of the country has conditions which are much less favoured. Yet the first area has many inhabitants which are in very bad conditions, and the second area has privileged sectors with high consumption levels. This calls for a redirection of mortality and morbidity studies in Argentina, emphasizing the study of those differentials between different strata of the population, and on the socio-economic characteristics which condition morbidity and mortality.

ANNEX 2

Malnutrition in Brazil

by *Alicia Gillone and Jorge Gadano*

B. The Case of Brazil

The most populous country in Latin America and seventh in population in the world gives its name to the "Brazilian economic miracle", an impressive increase in the national GNP in a few years, and also to the "Brazilian Northeast": a mass of

40 million people supposedly victimized by the vagaries of an extremely irregular rainfall. What the following paper does is to link one of the consequences of the miracle—a regressive distribution of the national wealth with deteriorating purchasing power of salaries with the phenomenon of malnutrition in the country—and presents an overview of malnutrition in Brazil which, again, would bring the effect of climatic misfortunes to a much more modest level.

Introduction

The objective of this work is a grouping of as much information as possible on malnutrition in Brazil. As an initial round figure it can be stated that, of the 110 million inhabitants in the country, at least 40 million are malnourished.

Malnutrition exists fundamentally when people do not eat enough. This can be a starting thread to a massive phenomenon of hunger, which has been aggravated by the economic model established in 1964.

Some elements of this model, whose contrasts can be exemplified in a 10 percent annual increase of GNP during several years in succession (the so-called "Brazilian miracle") and figures from the municipality of Recife in the Northeast (with 80 percent of the population malnourished and 256 per thousand of infant mortality in 1976) have been analyzed, as there are interpretations—some "scientific", some metaphysical—which state that Brazilians do not eat what they need due to lack of education or due to a natural inclination towards spiritual matters.

Initially, there will appear a description of some elements of the model: a regressive distribution of income and loss of purchasing power of salaries and their "malnutrition breeding" consequences. Secondly, mention will be made of the relationship between availability of food and its consumption. Thirdly, the magnitude of the problem is going to be assessed. Accepting a significant under-registration in Vital and Health Statistics of the phenomenon of malnutrition, recourse was made here to a variety of sources (in a sort of search of searches), in order to ascertain the weight of malnutrition as a cause of death, and the state of chronic malnutrition in the country. Fourthly, and focussing especially in the Northeast, references are made of the relationship between drought and malnutrition.

I. Some Nutrition Consequences of the Economic Model

According to those who designed it, the Brazilian economic model was supposed to increase overall wealth (the "bolo") so that, through a filtering process going from top to bottom, an increased national income would also benefit popular sectors.

Roberto Campos, Minister of Planning of one of the earlier military régimes (after 1964) had assigned blame to a "salaries orgy" pre-1964 as a determining cause in the economic stagnation and the inflation that had characterized Populist governments. Delfim Netto referred again to the "bolo" theory to justify his policy of a salar freeze, and later on Roberto Simonsen, the current Economics Minister added to the theory by stating that "it is useless to distribute misery before wealth is created". What actually happened was that in those years the national GNP increased by about 10 percent per annum (that being the "Brazilian miracle") but that poverty increased also. There had taken place a suction, rather than a filtering, from top to bottom.

Jornal do Brasil of 15 July 1977 showed testimonies on the suction theory. Hans Singer explained that "Brazil is a typical example of a country in which a physical increase in output was not accompanied by an increase in the catering for the basic needs of the population".

The doctrine of "increasing first, sharing later" of which Simonsen was an advocate, was, according to Singer, very likely to fail due to the inequality in access to a GNP in expansion. In his view, the higher income classes have a privileged access and more opportunities to profit from the GNP, thus causing greater inequalities in its distribution. Finally, he showed skepticism about the fact that "once a productive structure has been established which was adapted to an unequal distribution of income, and an internal market geared to higher-income groups it could be possible, both economically and politically, to change it later in order to reorient it towards egalitarianism".

It is this condition of submergence that a proportion of the population suffers that prompted the reactions of Maria de Conceicao Tavares, when she supported her colleague. Tavares, who had worked in ECLA, had to "hold back tears" while stating her skepticism on the possibilities of convincing the thinking elites and the governments of Latin America to bring forth social justice in the continent.

In her view, an inequality in the distribution of income in Brazil, while certainly existing pre-1964 "not only was not solved, but even grew worse with the economic model that was adopted. The accumulation of capital, as it was undertaken, worsened the distribution in the rural sector and created the same inequalities in the urban one". She ended by stating that "today we are witnessing a spectacle of an awful distribution of wealth in the cities, with poverty appearing even among those who were absorbed into the urban economy, even among those who have a job".

The Brazilian model, born in 1964 and consolidated in 1968 is not original in terms of its economic substance, as it tends to strengthen privileged relationships which come from the country's history, on the basis of the association between great exporters of primary products with multinational capital, both industrial and financial.

A small percentage of the population, formed by middle-level sectors, receives enough wealth to sustain an internal market with a high consumption level, composed of about 20 to 30 million people. At the same time, it provides consensus to a politico–institutional system of a "relative democracy", under the control of the Armed Forces, who take care of the submission of the other eighty million inhabitants.

Since its inception, the model advances upon four axes, namely: (1) Use of an industrial capacity which accumulated during the previous recession (1962–67); (2) A drastic compression of workers' salaries; (3) A delivery of produced surplus to the multinational corporations, the upper-middle class and the local bourgeoisie; (4) The mobilization of surplus through stimuli to production and consumption of durable goods, to investments and to exports.

In the text that follows, we will describe how the attack on popular income has translated itself, during the last 13 years, into levels of living which are barely comparable with survival or even incompatible with it, as the Family Welfare Society states (even though it blames it on population growth), in 1976, 600,000 Brazilians died of malnutrition.

SALARIES

As has been stated, the development strategy adopted in 1964 favoured the accumulation of capital, and promoted the consumption of durables, such as automobiles. At the same time the real earning power of workers was cut down. Thus, the income of a minority was increased, and that of a majority was decreased. Between 1960 and 1970 the distribution of the "bolo" varied as shown in Figure 1.

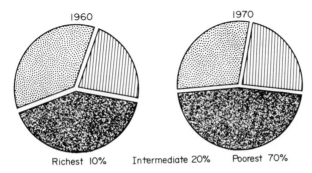

FIG. 1. The distribution of the bolo 1960–1970

The stimuli to consumption of durable goods is revealed in research carried out by Hay do Brasil S.A., undertaken in 49 industrial and 7 financial enterprises on "additional salary benefits" of their executives. Conclusions were published in July 1977. "Additional salaries" usually took the form of provision of automobiles (95 percent), sports clubs (73 percent), professional clubs (58 percent), payment of schools for children and special expenses (20 percent).

According to a Morris Morgen Study, executive salaries were increased in accordance with increases in the cost of living. In workers' salaries, however, their deteriorating purchasing power showed itself in long training working hours to pay for a given product. A DIEESE (Departamento Intersindical de Estudios y Estudios Socioeconomicos) showed the amount of hours of work, at minimum wage level, to pay for a monthly nutritionally basic diet. These hours were the following.

> December 1965: 87 hours, 20 minutes
> December 1970: 103 hours, 19 minutes
> December 1975: 154 hours.

At the same time, the structure of workers' household expenses has changed. Another DIEESE study has shown that between 1953 and 1970, while real purchasing power of salaries deteriorated by 36.5 percent, a shift in structure of working class expenditures had taken place. (Table 21)

TABLE 21.
Shifts in Household Expenditures 1953–70

Expenditures	Percentage of salaries 1953	1970
Food	64.3	51
Clothing	14.3	10.6
Health	5.7	4.7
Household cleaning	4.3	2.2
Household equipment*	4.3	8.5
Transportation	2.9	11.5
Personal hygiene	2.1	1.6
Education and culture	1.4	4.6
Recreation, tobacco	0.7	5.3

Source: Salaried families, pattern and cost of living, DIEESE, January 1974.
* 60 percent of this was composed of electric and electronic equipment.

Researchers interpreted this shift as a result of advertizing, long-term credits with accessible monthly payments, price raffles and the pressure of household salesmen.

The 1970 Population Census (the latest one carried out) showed that, out of a total of 26 million people in a productive activity, half earned less than a minimum salary, and four fifths earned less than two minimum salaries. Out of the remaining fifth, 17 percent earned between two and seven minimum salaries and 3 percent over seven minimum salaries. The overall income distribution pattern had shifted between 1960 and 1970 as shown in Table 22.

As to the minimum salary in Rio de Janeiro, its evolution was as shown in Table 23.

In 23 years between 1952 and 1975 the GNP had increased fivefold in terms of real value.

The 1976 Annual of the IBGE (Instituto Brasileiro de Geografica e Estadistica) has reported on the evolution of prices and salaries until 1975. A relationship between the minimum wage and price increase shows a deterioration of the former. (Table 24)

At this point, it is useful to know whether, even reduced to the extremes mentioned, a Brazilian worker's wages are enough to survive on without a deterioration

TABLE 22.
Wealth Distribution by Population Groups
(in %)

	Share of wealth 1960	1970	Share in the increase of wealth
50% poorest	18	14	3
30% less poor	28	23	10
10% next	15	15	13
10% richest	39	48	74
Total	100	100	100

TABLE 23.
Real Value of a Minimum Wage in Rio de Janeiro

	Nominal value	Real purchasing power
January 1952	Cr$ 1.20	100
July 1954	2.40	127
August 1956	3.80	134.5
January 1959	6.00	146
October 1960	9.60	131
October 1961	13.44	132
January 1963	21.00	122
February 1964	42.00	116
March 1965	66.00	103
June 1966	84.00	82
March 1967	105.00	81
August 1968	129.60	74
May 1969	156.00	79
May 1970	187.20	76
May 1971	225.60	77.5
May 1972	268.80	78
May 1973	312.00	80
May 1974	376.80	77
December 1974	415.20	73
May 1975	532.80	86

of his basic diet. Bertoldo Kruse Grande de Arruda, president of the National Nutrition Institute (INAN) stated in a conference (dictated at the War School, on 25 August 1976) that "the price index in the last 10 years has presented a dissociated behaviour from the curve of salary increases", a dissociation reflected in a "reduction of the minimum real wage", which in turn "this exercises an impact on family budgets and on the general health of the population, especially those sectors with a higher nutritional vulnerability". Using data from the Getulio Vargas Foundation, he presented a Table (Table 25) on food consumption and rent levels.

TABLE 24.
Relationship between Minimum Wage and Prices

	April 1972	April 1974	April 1975
Minimum wage	268.80	312.00	376.80
Prices	368.00	461.00	580.00
Wages/Prices	73	68	65

TABLE 25.
Relationship between Wages and Calorie and Protein Consumption

Wages	Calories	Proteins (grams per day)
One minimum salary	1951	43.3
2 to 2.9 one minimum salary	2317	68.3
4 to 6.4 one minimum salary	2669	83.8
10 to 19.9 one minimum salary	3360	107.3

According to FAO standards, a minimum of 2550 calories and 71 grams of protein constitute a minimum requirement, which would leave the two first categories below it.*

In Recife, a work of Sampaio and collaborators had estimated that 80 percent of the families were not in a situation to be able to purchase a minimal food ration. Grande de Arrude's comment was that "something which can imply a simple and minimal increase in the cost of living for middle and higher rent levels, certainly means, for the lower groups a penetration beyond the threshold of famine".

The Situation Today

On 1 May 1977 the minimum salary increased from 768 Cr. to 1106.40 Cr. The Labour Ministry had stated that the breakdown of a Cr. 768 wage was as follows: food 384 Cr.; lodging 192 Cr.; dress 99.84 Cr.; hygiene 49.89 Cr.; transport 46.08 Cr. A research carried out by the journal *Journal do Brasil*, showed that two train trips per day represented 60 Cr. monthly; a precarious house in a favela cost 200 Cr. monthly and minimum hygienic expenses (soap, toothpaste, toilet paper, wax, washing soap, drinkable water) amounted to 61 Cr. monthly. So far as food was concerned a research worker, a clearing clerk, spent 357 Cr. monthly on a diet which "necessarily led to malnutrition".

There is no way out. From whatever perspective the problem is tackled, a Brazilian worker's wages led him to malnutrition. The "miracle" of a GNP in a constant growth is thus shown to be a voracious machine which feeds on those who support it.

II. Nutritional Status: Availability and Consumption of Food and Biological Utilization of Nutrients

There are indications that agriculture in Brazil is being reoriented towards the foreign market, in a search for a wider margin of profit.

Table 26 shows a comparison between agricultural production geared basically to the home market, that geared basically for export, and their evolution over nine years.

During the period studied, production of rice, beans and manioc showed little change. In terms of availability "*per capita*" per year, rice decreased from 93.5 to 70.0 kg; beans from 28.2 to 21 kg and manioc from 308.5 to 239.7 kg. The influence of foreign markets makes itself felt in the case of beans and soja. The former has no international demand, and volumes fell from 2.24 million tons in 1974 to 1.84 million tons in 1976. The latter in the same years increased from 7.88 million tons to 11.22 million tons.

MORTALITY FROM MALNUTRITION

The figures on mortality and morbidity caused by malnutrition—in spite of their imperfections—show alarming levels, certainly associated with a high infant mortality. (Table 27)

* Protein standards have been revised. See Chapter 2.

TABLE 26.

*Volume of Brazilian Agricultural Production (1967–75) (Year
1967 = 100)*

Year	Products for the internal market			Products for foreign markets		
	Rice	Beans	Manioc	Soja	Sugar cane	Oranges
1967	100	100	100	100	100	100
1968	98	95	107	91	99	103
1969	94	86	110	148	98	101
1970	111	87	108	211	98	129
1971	94	97	117	310	104	134
1972	96	90	103	475	113	176
1973	105	87	97	701	119	206
1974	101	88	91	1102	125	238
1975	111	89	95	1313	118	253

Source: Modified from P.ND—Agricultural Sector—SUPLAN.

Allowing for limitations in the information, between 1941 and 1970 infant mortality was reported to have descended by 47.5 percent. Within this period, however, and from 1968–69 onwards an increase apparently started to take place. "Among the principal factors causing a deterioration in the level of health in Brazil in the last decade, economic causes come to the fore, in which an increase in rent concentration, and a deterioration in minimum wages of 20 percent resulted in a decrease in the purchasing power of salaried workers".

TABLE 27.

*Infant Mortality Rates in Capitals in
Brazil 1970, 1973, 1974*

Capital	Rate (per 1000 live births)		
	1970	1973	1974
Manaus	80.4	49.8	117.5
Belêm	60.3	68.4	64.6
São Luiz	70.0	88.4	—
Terezina	73.6	47.8	77.8
Fortaleza	152.0	136.8	140.2
Natal	166.1	140.0	104.4
João Pessoa	156.0	169.2	—
Recife	263.5	229.0	256.4
Maceió	141.0	130.4	100.4
Aracajú	32.0	40.2	—
Salvador	88.5	91.2	87.8
Belo Horizonte	107.7	124.8	96.0
Vitória	115.5	91.4	96.9
Niterói	64.0	70.2	—
Guanabara	52.9	79.5	—
São Paulo	89.8	89.8	—
Curitiba	83.9	86.4	72.8
Florianópolis	—	97.8	—
Porto Alegre	—	54.8	—
Cuiabá	—	86.0	—
Goiânia	—	98.8	—
Brasilia	—	74.9	58.8

TABLE 28.

Brazilian Mortality Structure in Brazil and in Certain Regions, by Age Groups

Ages	Brazil (1971)	South (1971)	Northeast (1975)
0–1 year	27.7	23.9	34.6
1–4 years	6.7	4.4	8.6
5–14 years	2.7	2.4	3.5
50 years	43.2	50.9	34.5
Total	100.0	100.0	100.0

Source: SUDENE (unpublished work). These data were taken by the Health Division of SUDENE in the Regional Centre for Health Statistics of the Northeast (CRESNE)—Bulletin 36, Recife, Pernambuco, 1977.

An analysis on the age structure of mortality in Brazil shows the weight that deaths of under one year olds and of one to four year olds have on the overall phenomenon. Table 28 does not account for a selective under-registration of deaths of minors, which would increase their percentages even further.

The magnitude of under-registration of births in the Brazilian Northeast can be gathered from the information in Table 29.

MORBIDITY FROM MALNUTRITION

From health statistics

Hospital-based data on malnutrition, or the pathologies which are its cause or its effect cannot really measure the problem. Firstly, only a small percentage of the population goes to hospitals. Secondly, the quality of data recording, both through an inaccurate medical diagnosis and through limitations of the International Classification of Diseases mean that many of the consultations and hospital discharges are recorded as of "ill-defined" cause. There are other sources of information which permit the discovery in Brazilian hospitals of the overwhelming evidence of malnu-

TABLE 29.

Newborn Children in Municipalities of State Capitals in the Northeast of Brazil (1975)

Regions and states	Live births Expected	Notified	%
Northeast	1,133,325	197,313	17.4
Piauí	76,500	27,772	36.3
Ceara	175,795	35,387	20.1
Río Grande do Norte	52,384	27,299	52.1
Paraiba	109,765	11,424	10.4
Pernambuco	254,021	31,437	12.4
Alagoas	63,936	23,967	37
Sergipe	31,431	18,346	58
Bahía	277,049		
Minas Gerais (zona Montes Claros)	45,924	13,044	28
Terr. Fernando de Noronha	27	31	114

trition: a monotonous finding in out-patient pediatric clinics corresponds to two diagnoses: parasitoses and gastroenteritis. When medical records of these cases are consulted, it is very usual to find that malnutritions of Grade I and II have been recorded.

Special studies

Foremost among these is the Puffer–Serrano Study, referred to in Chapter 4 and in the Introduction to this Chapter.

The Recife Study area assigned to malnutrition (as a basic or associated cause) 39 percent of deaths of under one year olds. Ribereo Preto came out with 33 percent and São Paulo with the smallest figure, 28 percent. Of all deaths of under five year olds, the corresponding weight of malnutrition would be 46.2 percent in Recife; 34.5 percent, 36.4 percent and 38.2 percent for the three Study zones in Ribereo Preto and 30.4 percent for São Paulo.

An analysis carried out by the same Study on deaths whose immediate cause had been infectious diarrhoea and measles, showed the high percentage of cases which also reported nutritional deficiencies.

This shows, again, that the "choice" of final cause of death on the part of a child who was born and lived in undernourishment is to some extent irrelevant: he will "choose" one or the other according to epidemiological circumstances.

Nutrition surveys are again useful to complement the limitations of regular health data collecting systems: In Minas Gerais, a survey undertaken by the State's Health Ministry produced a high percentage of second and third grade malnutrition in all of the regions (Table 30). The data source for the study was the weighing and measuring of all under five-year-olds who sought medical care in the valley of Jaquitinhorha, Minas Gerais and its duration was the first month of launching of the Nutrition and Health Programme, 1975, of Minas Gerais.

Other findings of the Tables which need to be highlighted are:

(a) cattle-rearing areas show a highest prevalence of malnutrition, with lower prevalences in agricultural or mixed areas (it is in cattle-rearing areas that most latifundia are situated); (Table 31)

(b) by contrast, the agricultural zone of small landholdings and of a subsistence agriculture shows lower rates.

TABLE 30.
Nutritional Deficiency as an Associated Cause in the Death of Children of Under Five Years of Age

| Area | Deaths due to infectious diarrhoea | | | Deaths due to measles | | |
| | | With nutritional deficiency | | | With nutritional deficiency | |
	Total	No.	%	Total	No.	%
Recife	1.122	766	68.3	396	294	74.2
Riberèo Prêto	278	217	78.1	46	31	67.4
São Paulo	844	529	62.7	156	74	47.4

Source: OPAS-OMS—Investigacào Interamericana de Mortalidade na Infancia—1973.

TABLE 31.

Malnutrition in Children of Under Five Years of Age, by Type of Agricultural Region of Origin and Degree of Malnutrition

Malnutrition Region	Total normal	Grade I	Grade II	Grade III	Total
Agricultural	671	753	547	85	2056
%	32.64	36.62	26.61	4.13	100
Mixed	461	520	317	57	1355
%	34.02	33.38	23.39	4.21	100
Cattle-raising	218	307	390	154	1069
%	20.39	28.72	36.43	14.41	100
Total	1350	1580	1254	296	4480
%	30.13	35.27	27.99	6.61	100

Source: PNS M6/75. Nutrition Co-ordinating Group—SES/M6

III. The Brazilian Northeast—Malnutrition and Drought

The nine States of the Brazilian Northeast: Maranhao, Piaui, Ceara, Rio Grande do Norte, Paraiba, Pernambuco, Alagoas, Sergipe and Bahia comprise over 33 million inhabitants. Forty-seven percent of the population corresponds to under 15-year-olds, and the maternal child component of the population is 70 percent. Overall mortality (when it is recorded) shows a high proportion of infant and pre-school deaths, and infant mortality (also where recorded) appears to be on the increase. (Table 32)

In the Northeast a lot of people are born, a lot of people fall ill and a lot die. Those who survive will carry with them the load of chronic malnutrition, and their life expectancy will not pass 50 years.

The lack of health facilities in the Northeast is another limitation on the gathering of a clear picture of mortality and morbidity in the area. (Table 34) Northeastern standards of density of facilities are among the lowest in the country. (Table 35)

TABLE 32.

Mortality by Age Groups in Municipia of the State Capitals of the Northeast (1970–75)

Ages	1970 No.	%	1972 No.	%	1974 No.	%
Total	50,973	100	53,663	100	55,972	100
Less than one year	18,698	36.7	18,294	35.4	18,465	33.0
One to four years	5390	10.6	5248	10.2	5142	9.2

Infant mortality appears to have risen in recorded areas. (Table 33).

TABLE 33.
Infant Mortality Rate in Municipia of the State Capitals of the Northeast

Capital	Infant mortality rates per 1000 newborn 1967–69	1970–72	1973–76
Total	99.7	102.6	111.2
São Luiz	70.2	61.0	72.4
Terezina	91.6	73.9	100.3
Fortaleza	134.9	122.0	100.4
Natal	157.9	122.6	104.2
João Pessoa	100.2	100.5	139.8
Recife	107.7	100.7	137.7
Maceió	132.2	133.1	161.6
Aracaju	30.1	33.0	37.5
Salvador	74.3	83.1	109.3
V. dos Remédios	—	80.8	55.6

Source: Statistics division of State Secretariats of Health—provisional data.

TABLE 34.

Region	Number of beds per 1000 inhabitants	Number of inhabitants per physician
São Paulo	6.4	610
Rio de Janeiro[a]	5.5	1570
South	3.8	2680
MG and Espírito Santo	3.6	2690
Centre–West	2.5	3090
North	2.4	4260
Northeast[b]	1.9	4720
Maranhao and Piauí	1.0	7000
Brazil	3.6	2040

[a] New State of Guanabara and Rio de Janeiro.
[b] Maranhao and Piauí excluded.
Source: *"Aspectos Econômicos da Saúde"* Carlos Gentille de Mello Rio de Janeiro, 1975, mimeo.

NUTRITION STATUS IN THE NORTHEAST

Malnutrition is endemic in the Northeast. According to the data gathered on apparent consumption of food (A) and to other data gathered by research undertaken by BNB, SUDENTE and the Getulio Vargas Foundation (B), the following statistics on *"per capita"* consumption have been gathered.

Hypothesis A	Vegetable origin	Animal origin	Total
Calories	1626.4	254.4	1889.8
Proteins (g)	35.1	17.1	52.2
Hypothesis B			
Calories	1695.4	327.7	2023.1
Proteins (g)	38.4	21.7	60.1

TABLE 35.
*Municipalities of Over 20,000 Inhabitants without a
Physician, by Regions, Brazil, 1973*

Region	Number of municipalities of over 20,000 inhabitants without a physician
Rio de Janeiro[a]	—
São Paulo	1
Centre–West	9
North	14
MG and Espírito Santo	15
Maranhao and Piaúi	20
South	22
Northeast[b]	57
Brazil	138

[a] New State Guanabara and Rio de Janeiro.
[b] Maranhao and Piaúi excluded.
Source: *"Aspectos Econômicos da Saúde"*, Carlos Gentille de Mello, Rio de Janeiro, 1975, mimeo.

Let us recall that, according to FAO, a minimum supply of calories *per capita* would be 2550 per day. Thus, according to data A, a "nordestino" would receive 74 percent of that figure, and according to data B, he would receive 79 percent. As to proteins, a minimum acceptable figure would be 71 grams per day.* Thus, data A would provide 73 percent of that figure and data B, 85 percent. These are averages. The concept of *"per capita"* hides a series of distortions. In the case of the Northeast, where wealth is very unevenly distributed, it is clear that a minority consumes food well above the averages mentioned above, which worsens relatively the lot of the majority who do not have this privilege.

DROUGHT AND MALNUTRITION

The States of Northeastern Brazil, plus a part of Minas Gerais, form the "Polygon of Drought". All of the information gathered until now shows that drought acts, at most, as a participant factor, added to a chronic state of malnutrition, whose basic cause lies in an economic structure whose benefits do not include the majority of the population.

A physician cannot tell his patient that he is suffering from latifundia. And yet, that is the cause of many of his illnesses. If the results of droughts and eventually of floods leave permanent marks upon humans it is because their ally is a given economic structure.

Notes to Chapter 11

11.1 *World Health Statistics Annual, 1973–76*, World Health Organization, Geneva, 1976.
11.2 *World Health Statistics Annual, 1972*, World Health Organization, Geneva, 1975.
11.3 J. C. Escudero, La Situacion Sanitaria Nacional, *Cuadernos de Contramedicina, No. 1*, Buenos Aires, 1974.

* These figures have been revised. See Chapter 2.

11.4 R. R. Puffer and C. Serrano *Caracteristicos de la Mortalidad en la niñez*, Scientific Publication No. 262, Pan American Health Organization, Washington, 1973.
11.5 S. Vahovich and P. Sherne, *Profile of Medical Practice*, The American Medical Association, Chicago, 1973.
11.6 *World Health Statistics Annual*, Volume III, World Health Organization, Geneva, 1971.
11.7 *World Directory of Medical Schools*, World Health Organization, Geneva, 1973.
11.8 *United Nations Demographic Yearbook*, 1974.
11.9 J. C. Garcia, *La Educación Médica en America Latina*, Scientific Publication No. 255, Pan American Health Organization, Washington, 1972.
11.10 M. Béhar, Nutrition and the future of mankind, *International Journal of Health Services*, 6(2): 315–320, 1976.
11.11 *Proposals for a Programme to Control the Repercussions on Public Health of the Drought in the Sudano–Somalian Regions of Africa*, COR/74.1/Rev. 1, World Health Organization, Geneva, 1974.
11.12 Discusiones Técnicos de la XXIII Reunion del Consejo Directivo de la Organización Panamericana de la Salud, *Boletin de la Organización Panamericana de la Salud*, Vol. 80, No. 6, June 1976.
11.13 Situación nutricional, alimentaria en los paises de America Latina y de Caribe, *Boletín de la Organizacion Panamericana de la Salud*, June 1976.
11.14 *The State of Food and Agriculture, 1975*, Food and Agriculture Organization of the United Nations, Rome, 1976.
11.15 F. García Scarponi, y E. Alfaro, *Mortalidad según tipo de atención y certificación médica de la causa de muerte*, República Argentina, Año 1968, Estadísticas Vitales y de Salud, Serie 1, no. 15, July, 1971.
11.16 Roberto Yabo, Premortimorbilidad: un nuevo concepto para el análisis estadístico de las defunctiónes *Revista de Atención Médica*, no. 4, Buenos Aires, 1976.
11.17 R. R. Puffer and C. Serrano, *Caracteristicos de la Mortalidad en la Niñez*, Scientific Publication No. 262, Pan American Health Organization, Washington, 1973.
11.18 *Mortalidad infantil en la Argentina*, Series 2, No. 2, Departamento de Estadísticos de Salud, Secretaria de Estado de Salud Publica, August 1974.
11.19 Instituto de Ciencias de la Nutrición del NOA, Secretaria de Estado de Salúd Publica de la Nación, Universidad Nacional de Salta, *Estado actual de la desnutrición en la Région del Nordesta Argentino*, Serie Monografías Médicas, No. 2, República Argentina, 1974.
11.20 *Instituto de Ciencias de la Nutrición del NOA, op. cit.*, p. 39.
11.21 INDEC. Serie Investigaciones Demográficas. Instituto Nacional de Estadisticas y Censos, Publicación No. 3, *Mortalidad Infantil en la Argentina, a partir de la muestra del censo de 1970*, Buenos Aires, 1975.

Sources of "Malnutrition in Brazil"

Bertoldo Kruse Grande de Arruda, A policy for food and nutrition for Brazil, INAN.
Movimento (weekly), 26.1.76, San Pablo, Brazil.
I.B.G.A. Statistic Yearbook, Brazil, 1976.
Nelson Chaves, O Nordeste do Brasil, luta contra a fome, *O Correio da Unesco*, July 1975, Year 3, No. 7.
Nutrition Institute, Federal University of Pernambuco, A Nutritional Inquest in three physiographic zones of the State of Pernambuco.
Paul Singer, *et al.*, CEBRAP, caderno No. 23, Demand of food in the Salvador area.
Joao Yunes and Vera de Carvalho Ronchezil, Evolution of General, Infant and Proportional Mortality in Brazil, Revista de Saúde Pública, Sao Paulo, August 1974.
SUDENE: Health Division, Recife, Pernambuco, 1977.
Ruth Puffer and Carlos Serrano, *Caracteristicos de la Mortalidad en la niñez*, Scientific Publication No. 262, Pan American Health Organization, 1973.
Saúde en Debate, No. 2, Review of the Brazilian Centre of Health Studies, No. 3.
SUDENE: Population Projections for Northeastern Brazil, 1975–80.
Ministry of Health, CRESNE, Health Statistics Bulletin of the Northeast, No. 20, Publication No. 43, Recife, 1973.
Carlos Gentile de Mello: *Economic Aspects of Health*, Rio de Janeiro, 1975, (mimeographed).

CHAPTER 12

Some Suggestions for Action

IN REVIEWING the situation described until now, the dominant feeling could be one of despair. It is not only that we can do nothing about the weather; the spectacle of hundreds of millions of people submerged in misery and apparently at the mercy of the elements is overwhelming in its magnitude.

This in no way implies resignation and passivity. The ways of effective action are not, however, easily found. As the so-called "effects" of drought: malnutrition, migration, disease and death are so much ingrained in society, one extreme recommendation to do away with most of these effects (technologically feasible, politically more doubtful) would be a drastic restructuring of that society, Chinese-style (although not necessarily following the Chinese model), which is likely to be violent. Extreme recommendations of an opposite type would be those of a kind which one often finds in documents of international organizations, both public and private: something that can be termed the "Showcase Project" approach to problems: through a vast infusion of resources, which cannot be generalized at large, and through encouraging an element of popular participation—which also cannot be generalized—a "Pilot Village/Project/Plan" is created. Happy peasants or whatever are photographed and interviewed against an idyllic background of intelligent use of plentiful resources. The benefits of such projects cover perhaps 1 percent of the population in need, also it is impossible to extrapolate them to the country at large, among other reasons because popular participation expressed at more than merely local level is potentially dangerous to established power-holders, who know this very well. The recommendations that accompany these projects would tend to be both obvious and unfeasible: everything would appear to be encouraged, from increased education, through enhanced consciousness to higher productivity. We shall depart from these two types of recommendations: the latter because it is, at most, innocuous, the former because it obviously goes far beyond the scope of any realistic and acceptable proposal. Possible ways of action which are suggested in what follows would attempt to be graded according to their political feasibility. This is in recognizance of the fact, which the Project has underlined everywhere, that the constraints for action are in most cases not technological or directed by a scarcity of resources, but structural (politic and economic).

I. Thus, the first order of recommendations would be those technical ones that every political system could accept without undue strain, which are not very demanding of resources and which are thus "feasible" from every possible point of view. Maximum feasibility, and a Recommendation to be acted upon at International Agency level, would be a permanent updating, in the light of the most recently gathered evidence, of the nutritional needs of humans. This is a task for joint WHO/FAO Committees, which periodically produce reports on the subject. It is likely that we already know everything that there is to be known on the subject, but recent developments (i.e. the 1973 Committee Report) seem for example to have produced guidelines on protein needs which were less demanding than previous ones, a decision of great technical significance due to the high amount of energy and resources needed everywhere to produce animal proteins.

In a rational world, this recommendation would precede all others, rationality being a path originating in human needs—the most basic of which is physical survival through nutritional—which would in turn dictate the magnitude and structure of the food that is to be grown and the mechanisms for its distribution. It is perhaps too much to ask for this type of rationality, but IFIAS can insist on having updates of those estimates of needed nutrients for humans, and then can proceed to do a thing that the WHO/FAO Committees do not do—translate this biological need at planetary level into a worldwide agricultural policy to satisfy it.

Another recommendation to be undertaken at this International Agency level concerns studies on the food system of the world. This is the structural frame behind the existence of malnutrition affecting hundreds of millions of people. IFIAS should propose a joint programme with UNRISD in order to study the linkage between the two phenomena.

Other recommendations within this order of feasibility are related to the failure of the conventional health statistics system to monitor the extent of malnutrition and of other diseases in the population, to ascertain their chronic level or the increase in them as the drought takes hold. The tremendous under-registration of vital events—births, deaths and their causes—make vital statistics very bad indicators of the health of the population, and the fact that the system as it exists is heavily biased towards recording events which occur in urban areas—which are in turn not only unrepresentative of countries that are mostly rural, but are also biased against malnutrition—make any extrapolation on their findings seem even harmful if the objective is to arrive at a nationwide determination of health problems. The statistical data that derive from Health Services activities suffer from the same biases, which can be compounded by the fact that, in many cases, what is offered to people through the Services—and which is later recorded as data which presumably measure health levels—can have little bearing on what people *need* in terms of health. Due to the scarcity of health resources everywhere in the developing countries, any kind of medical speciality is going to be crowded by patients seeking care and to immediately produce statistics showing the magnitude among the population of the problem which it is treating, whether it is straightening noses, or curing malnutrition or providing mental care. This is a case in which supply would generate its own demand, both conceivably being unrelated to health needs as measured by any objective criterion.

It would be utopian here to advocate improvements of an incremental kind for the Vital and Health Statistics systems of most of the countries reviewed in this volume. Even in the very unlikely case that they could be implemented, an 80 percent target for registration of births and deaths in, for instance the Sahel countries, Ethiopia, Sudan, Brazil and India, would be a misapplication of priorities. The resources that would be needed for this extensive effort would be channelled away from more pressing national needs. The limitations on coverage by statistics of Health Services are a function of the incomplete coverage of the Services themselves; if coverage of population by the Services were nearly complete it would be paradoxical but true to state that the health statistics of that coverage would be less needed, as the total health needs of the population would more or less be looked after. In any case, the incomplete coverage of Health Services is part of the fabric of lack of resources, which envelops these nations and one that is very difficult to change.

What would be imperative for these countries would be the setting of an alternative statistical system for health to the one evolved over the centuries by the affluent Western countries. What should be proposed would be the establishing for the countries of a basic survey frame on a sampling basis whose findings would be as representative as possible of national situations and which would become a basic statistical infrastructure for the whole Public Administration, one that should be made as inexpensive as is compatible with the deducing of correct decisions for the administration of the countries, and which could be utilized in turn by different users—sectors like education, health (by investigating such topics as causes of death, professional attendance at births, somatic and psychic growth rates in children, immunization coverage, prevalent morbidity etc.), communication, agricultural development, etc.; to draw statistical inferences of nationwide coverage and of a reasonably probablistic nature. In the case of nutritional problems, for example, a periodic nationwide sample survey of the nutritional status of the population, using simple procedures like somatic growth measures, weight/height ratios, etc., could be undertaken, and frequency of recording could be increased in the face of a natural catastrophe like the 1972 drought.

What IFIAS should propose then is a monitoring system of nutrition and health status to centralize all of the information pertaining to the nutrition of the population and to complement the Vital and Health Statistics systems currently in operation.

The monitoring system should be comprehensive in scope, covering all aspects of the society relating to nutrition and health problems, such as food production, reserves and distribution, employment, salaries and food prices, nutritional status of the population, especially children, and incidence and prevalence of nutrition-related diseases. Much of this information can be gathered from the Government agencies responsible, and the task of the monitoring system—one that can be done very cheaply—would be the collating and interpreting of the data and the putting forth of technical recommendations for their improvement; that information to be gathered directly would be collected through the survey infrastructures mentioned above, through the use of time and resource saving techniques: different types of sampling procedures and simplified instruments of demographic analysis (such as the Brass methods).

The monitoring system should be designed in a co-ordinated effort between IFIAS and ICSU, who may then elaborate a complete proposal for submission to the UN. From then onwards the steps to be taken can only be hazarded, but a possible UN co-ordinating group for this effort could be the Statistical Office of the United Nations, which could direct the establishing of an "*ad hoc*" Working Group set up from members of the statistical sections of the different international agencies: WHO and UNICEF (those most directly concerned with health and nutrition) UNESCO, UNRISD, ILO, etc.

A second recommendation closely associated with the preceding one is linked to the fact that the limitations of the statistical systems go further than the quantitative handicap mentioned above. As has been stated in Chapters 1 and 4, the under-registration of malnutrition and deaths generated by malnutrition, produces a double phenomenon: on one hand, the structural conditions of the society are ignored; on the other, when a natural catastrophe hits such a society, all the observed effects are attributed to it. Thus, by overestimating the acute emergency, the agents concerned relieve themselves of undertaking any action other than immediate measures. No one feels compelled to investigate the chronic pre-catastrophe situation and reach a more complete and useful diagnosis for the processes at play. For one thing, the International Classification of Diseases (ICD) should have its rules for selecting "basic cause of death" modified, in order to be able to reflect the real weight of malnutrition in causing a death. The ninth revision of the ICD has just come into operation virtually unchanged from the eighth revision, the shortcomings of which have been analyzed in Chapter 4. It will be the task of WHO to undertake the next revision of the ICD, and an IFIAS/ICSU proposal for modification to be effected along the lines explained by this Project could be very useful.

A recommendation within this context could be simply formulated in terms of an adequate analysis of the data once it has been collected. But this would be highly misleading and quite innocuous, if it implied a direct application of many known and tried techniques of statistical analysis. This kind of analysis, used in the traditional epidemiological methods, fail when confronted with the problems of drought and malnutrition, whose "causes" or "effects" are deeply rooted in the structure and the productive processes of society and which thus call for a thorough analysis of that society. As has been said, functionalism, which is the dominant current in epidemiology, treats these topics in a most superficial way and limits itself to statistical associations (which it calls causal associations) between this and that isolated variable.

The "Drought and Man" Projects devoted much effort to investigating the kind of basic tools required to replace the functionalist analysis. It gradually became clear that only a structural approach would be able to provide them, in as much as the decisive factors to be taken into account in diagnosing the state of a society and its vulnerability to natural disasters are of a structural type. The theoretical bases for such an approach were discussed in Chapter 5. The conceptual framework emerging from this discussion has been applied in the case studies included in Part III of Volume I, and has been guiding our thinking in various Chapters of this volume.

No set of rules could be recommended at this stage, other than a development by epidemiologists of methods of societal analysis which are in very extended use in economics (especially macroeconomics) sociology and political science.

Perhaps it would be naive to characterize recommendations such as these last ones as politically feasible, and ones that do not threaten the *status quo*. They pose a serious threat—albeit a purely intellectual one—as they challenge a basic element of the ideological superstructure of many countries and of certain economic orders of the world: namely that, historically, progress is of an incremental kind, and that more of the same things that have been happening in the last decades are of benefit

to everyone (in this case "modernized" agriculture and "mutually dependent" economies, usually meaning the diffusion of capital-intensive, low manpower production
of cash crops on one hand, and on the other hand of a great volume of trade
between developed and developing countries).

Actually, as we have shown time and time again, through this Project, "modernization" *per se*—with the word used as implied above—is a generator of social
stress and human suffering rather than its cure, and the paradigm of "mutual
dependence" is when a poor country imports food from a rich one, not to feed its
malnourished population, but to fatten animals which will end up by being
exported to the rich country or by being eaten by affluent minorities in it, with no
nutritional justification for these policies.   .

Recommendations along the line of the "Red Cross Approach" would also be
ones which can politically be accepted because they do not upset the *status quo*—
the hidden rationale behind the "Red Cross Approach" being precisely this. Food
distribution in various ways: for free, through subsidies, quotas, rationing or such
indirect means as work programmes which increase purchasing power, would be a
crucial element here.

As has been stated repeatedly, the countries which are victims of social disasters
occasioned by drought usually have been for years the victims of malnutrition of a
chronic type. What the drought does is to put the many thousands of victims of
chronic malnutrition into an acute malnutrition category, and add new population
groups to this scourge. As is also said in so many other places in this volume,
chronic malnutrition is one of the most extended diseases in the world, one whose
magnitude is coming to prominence through such phenomena as the 1972
drought, and whose dialectical relationship with infections of various kinds—each
reinforcing the other—produces millions of deaths every year as an end result. It so
happens that malnutrition is unique among diseases in possessing effective cures
which do not demand specialized skills for their application: lactation by mothers*
and provision of abundant food by whoever can do it. In "cost effective" terms
malnutrition is perhaps the disease in which most benefit can be derived from a
given cost (in macroeconomic terms). The provision of food for people who need it
has to overcome several barriers, which are of course most marked in the countries
where the problem is worst: a communication problem, lack of stocks, language or
cultural difficulties, the fact that people needing food tend to be marginal to the
dominant political, economic or ethnic groups. They tend to be functionally invisible and silent.

A monitoring of the world food situation is being efficiently carried out by
International Agencies. The final element of this monitoring would be the distribution of food to humans in times of need. As has been shown, this is the ultimate
RCA solution for food shortages. IFIAS should develop, as a continuation of this
study, a design for the setting up of reasonable food distribution policies in times of
shortage, using both an egalitarian rationing system and community control over
the actual mechanism of distribution.

---

* A problem which cannot be touched here is the diffusion of milk preparations sold commercially
(dehydrated milk, etc.) which are much more expensive and much more dangerous to handle than
human or fresh animal milk. Perhaps it could be recommended that these preparations be sold exclusively by medical prescription and never commercially to the population at large, and even that the
former should be closely supervized.

II. The next order of recommendations would work within a higher ceiling of political feasibility, or, said otherwise, a greater flexibility of the politico–economic system to accept them. Conditions as to the response of the health sector to drought and its effects would fall in this category. The underlying premise is that the behaviour of the health sector is relatively independent of the politico–economic structure—although recent developments in South America and elsewhere would indicate a different trend. The health sector has virtually no autonomy against the overall running of the economy and the political system encompassing it. As a result no possible reformist action can exist within a repressive and inegalitarian framework, and no illusions for improvement of health carried out from within the health sector. These factors are a profound obstacle to improvement of the health level of a population that is subject to increasing levels of malnutrition and unemployment.

The evident inadequacy of the health services to cope with disasters of the 1972 kind is patent. This, for the countries that suffered it, is again part of the general problem of which the famine was another example. To ask for higher rates of physicians, hospital beds, birth attendants, outpatient clinics, etc. per population is both obvious and useless. The basic philosophy has to change in order to provide these services. The ultimate task is for the countries to improve the quantity and quality of their health services taking note of the overall constraints that their society faces and out of which a particular type of Health Service has grown.

The mildest recommendation along these lines—in terms of political feasibility—would be extensive teaching of the real magnitude of malnutrition, its epidemiology and societal causes to future physicians, nurses and health attendants. This implies the rewriting or replacement of many medical textbooks in current use, and more important, the opening of medical schools to intellectural trends to which the medical teaching establishment is unsympathetic—it being usually geared to, and reproducing itself for, the affluent minorities of the country which provides its output with a clientele.

Along with better training in nutritional practices, it must be urged that the "goal" of achieving, for all people, types of diets of the European or North American kind are not only unrealistic, inefficient, and wasteful of resources, they are not conducive to the attainment of the best state of health.

More ambitious recommendations in the health sector would imply an adaptation of the health system towards serving the health needs of the population, which, according to the feasibility criteria, would place the combat against malnutrition in the first priority, and which would make maximum use of the tools of self-reliance and popular participation and organization.

An example drawn from the experience of countries which have followed this path and as a result improved spectacularly many aspects of their Health Services in a few years, would be the encouragement of popular participation in the delivery of health, using local human resources of which the "traditional birth attendant" is an example; to use labour-intensive instead of capital-intensive solutions for health problems, the ultimate and basically untapped human resource being the whole of the population of the countries; to prioritize health problems which affect large masses of the population and which have a good cost-effectiveness ratio (like malnutrition) and to give low priority for public health services (or non-priority) to diseases with low incidence/prevalence and difficult or costly treatment; to shy away from costly campaigns whose aim is to attack just one disease; and to create a health infrastructure valid for all health problems. The ultimate millstone around the neck of countries wanting to improve the health of their population is the European or U.S.-style teaching hospital, situated in the largest city of the country, which produces each year a handful of European or U.S.-style physicians, who specialize in the treatment of obscure or Western-type diseases, and who usually end up as medical migrants in some country of the First World.

III. Finally, we come to the third order of recommendations: the minimization of the social effects of drought through the organization of a society which is not geared to profit at the expense of all human values, but to the satisfaction of social needs as a first priority, and which uses mechanisms of social collaboration, of encouragement of popular participation, and of self-sufficiency in basic necessities. In agricultural terms, this type of society would encourage production of staple foodstuffs and a diversification of products; in nutritional terms it would promote an equitable distribution of food resources and a satisfaction of human nutritional requirements; in health terms, it would encourage self-sufficiency, primary health-care activities, limited use of drugs and medical technologies, a massive training of health personnel with basic skills and a popular participation in the determination and solving of health problems. No recommendation can be made at this stage, and whether this type of society, whose success in dealing with malnutrition and with drought along with other natural catastrophes is evident, is also feasible in political terms, is very much open to question; but given the current world crisis, this question will receive an unequivocal empirical answer, one way or the other in the near future. Such a type of social organization as has been outlined is—limitation of availability of resources accepted—the ultimate solution that the present times can offer the problem of malnutrition and famines in the world, whether or not drought or any other natural disaster appears to be the immediately preceding cause.

Index